Microeconomics

Economics Express

PEARSON

At Pearson, we take learning personally. Our courses and resources are available as books, online and via multi-lingual packages, helping people learn whatever, wherever and however they choose.

We work with leading authors to develop the strongest learning experiences, bringing cutting-edge thinking and best learning practice to a global market. We craft our print and digital resources to do more to help learners not only understand their content, but to see it in action and apply what they learn, whether studying or at work.

Pearson is the world's leading learning company. Our portfolio includes Penguin, Dorling Kindersley, the Financial Times and our educational business, Pearson International. We are also a leading provider of electronic learning programmes and of test development, processing and scoring services to educational institutions, corporations and professional bodies around the world.

Every day our work helps learning flourish, and wherever learning flourishes, so do people.

To learn more please visit us at: www.pearson.com/uk

Economics Express

Microeconomics

Stuart Wall

PEARSON

Harlow, England • London • New York • Boston • San Francisco • Toronto • Sydney
Auckland • Singapore • Hong Kong • Tokyo • Seoul • Taipei • New Delhi
Cape Town • São Paulo • Mexico City • Madrid • Amsterdam • Munich • Paris • Milan

PEARSON EDUCATION LIMITED
Edinburgh Gate
Harlow CM20 2JE
United Kingdom
Tel: +44 (0)1279 623623
Web: www.pearson.com/uk

First published 2013 (print)

© Pearson Education Limited 2013 (print)
© Pearson Education Limited 2013 (print and electronic)

The right(s) of Stuart Wall to be identified as author of this work has been asserted by him in accordance with the Copyright, Designs and Patents Act 1988.

The print publication is protected by copyright. Prior to any prohibited reproduction, storage in a retrieval system, distribution or transmission in any form or by any means, electronic, mechanical, recording or otherwise, permission should be obtained from the publisher or, where applicable, a licence permitting restricted copying in the United Kingdom should be obtained from the Copyright Licensing Agency Ltd, Saffron House, 6-10 Kirby Street, London EC1N 8TS.

The ePublication is protected by copyright and must not be copied, reproduced, transferred, distributed, leased, licensed or publicly performed or used in any way except as specifically permitted in writing by the publishers, as allowed under the terms and conditions under which it was purchased, or as strictly permitted by applicable copyright law. Any unauthorised distribution or use of this text may be a direct infringement of the author's and the publishers' rights and those responsible may be liable in law accordingly.

Pearson Education is not responsible for the content of third-party internet sites.

The Financial Times. With a worldwide network of highly respected journalists, *The Financial Times* provides global business news, insightful opinion and expert analysis of business, finance and politics. With over 500 journalists reporting from 50 countries worldwide, our in-depth coverage of international news is objectively reported and analysed from an independent, global perspective. To find out more, visit **www.ft.com/pearsonoffer.**

ISBN: 978-0-273-77603-1 (print)
          978-0-273-77605-5 (PDF)
          978-0-273-78559-0 (eText)

British Library Cataloguing-in-Publication Data
A catalogue record for the print edition is available from the British Library

Library of Congress Cataloging-in-Publication Data
A catalog record for the print edition is available from the Library of Congress
Wall, Stuart, 1946–
  Economics express : microeconomics/Stuart Wall. – First Edition.
    pages cm
  Includes index.
  ISBN 978-0-273-77603-1
  1. Microeconomics.   I. Title.
  HB172.W355 2013
  338.5–dc23
                              2013019285

10 9 8 7 6 5 4 3 2 1
16 15 14 13

Print edition typeset in 9.5/12.5 pt Scene std by 71
Print edition printed and bound by Henry Ling Limited,
at the Dorset Press, Dorchester DT1 1HD

Contents

Supporting Resources

→ **Understand key concepts quickly**

Printable versions of the **Topic maps** give an overview of the subject and help you plan your revision

Test yourself on key definitions with the online **Flashcards**

→ **Revise effectively**

Check your understanding and practise for exams with the **multiple choice questions**

→ **Make your answers stand out**

Evaluate sample exam answers in the **You be the marker** exercises and understand how and why an examiner awards marks

All this and more can be found at www.pearsoned.co.uk/econexpress

Introduction – Economics Express series

From the series editor, Professor Stuart Wall

Welcome to *Economics Express* – a series of short books to help you to:

- take exams with confidence
- prepare for assessments with ease
- understand quickly
- and revise effectively

There has never been a more exciting time to study economics, given the shock to so many individuals, institutions and countries in 2007/8 when long established economic certainties were suddenly brought into question. The so-called 'credit crunch' overpowered both financial and non-financial organisations. Government bail-outs of banks and businesses became the order of the day in many countries, with massive increases in government expenditures to fund these bail-outs, quickly followed by austerity budgets aimed at restoring national debts and budget deficits to pre-credit crunch levels. Looking forward, there is as much talk about 'triple-dip' recessions as there is about recovery.

As you embark on your economic journey, this series of books will be your companions. They are not intended to be a replacement for the lectures, textbooks, seminars or further reading suggested by your lecturers. Rather, as you come to an exam or an assessment, they will help you to revise and prepare effectively. Whatever form your assessment takes, each book in the series will help you build up the skills and knowledge to maximise your performance.

> You can find more detail of the features contained in this book and which will help develop your assessment skills in the *'Guided Tour'* on page ix.

Series editor's acknowledgements

I am extremely grateful to Kate Brewin and Gemma Doel at Pearson Education for their key roles in shaping this series. I would also like to thank the many lecturers and students who have so helpfully reviewed the key features of this series and whose responses have encouraged us to believe that many others will also benefit from the approaches we have adopted throughout this series.

Stuart Wall

Publisher's Acknowledgements

Figures
Figures 1.1, 1.3, 1.4, 1.5, 1.6, 2.1, 2.2, 2.3, 2.4, 2.7, 3.1, 3.2, 3.3, 3.4, 3.5, 3.6, 3.7, 4.1, 4.2, 4.3, 4.4, 4.5, 4.6, 4.8, 4.9, 5.1, 5.2, 5.3, 5.4, 5.5, 6.1, 6.2, 6.3, 6.4, 6.5, 6.6, 6.7, 6.8, 6.10, 7.1, 7.4, 7.5, 7.7, 7.8, 7.10, 8.1, 8.2, 8.3, 8.4, 8.5, 9.1, 9.2, 9.3 and 9.5 are taken from *Economics for Business and Management*, 3rd ed., (2011, Griffiths, A. and Wall, S.) Pearson Education. Reproduced with permission. Figures 7.3 and 8.6 are taken from *Applied Economics*, 12th ed., (2012, Griffiths, A. and Wall, S.) Pearson Education. Reproduced with permission. Figures 2.5, 3.8, 3.9 and 7.6 are taken from *Intermediate Microeconomics*, 2nd ed., (2000, Griffiths, A. and Wall, S.) Pearson Education. Reproduced with permission. All Rights Reserved.

The Financial Times
Examples and evidence (pp. 105–6) from 'China's Vancl trials production overseas', *Financial Times*, 09/08/2012 (Waldmeir, P.); Examples and evidence (pp. 121–2) from 'RBS outlines reward scheme to shareholders', *Financial Times*, 19/03/2010 (Goff, S. and Jones, A.), © The Financial Times Limited. All Rights Reserved.

Guided tour

→ **Understand key concepts quickly**

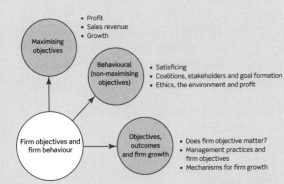

Start to plan your revision using the **Topic maps**.

Key definitions

Conditions of demand
Conditions of demand are the variables that will cause the demand curve for product X to shift, either to the right or to the left. These include the price of other products (P_o), the real income of households (Y), the tastes of households (T) and so on.

Substitutes in consumption
Substitutes in consumption are two (or more) products seen by consumers as alternatives, possessing broadly similar characteristics, e.g. gaming consoles such as Nintendo Wii, Microsoft X-boxes and Sony PlayStations

Complements in consumption
Complements in consumption are two (or more) products seen by consumers as fitting together, in the sense that purchasing one product will usually involve purchasing the other(s). Personal computers and printers are obvious examples of complements in consumption, as are tennis rackets and tennis balls.

Inferior products
Inferior products are goods or services that are cheaper but poorer quality substitutes for other goods or services. As real incomes rise the more expensive but better quality substitutes may eventually come within the purchasing power of the consumer, so that demand for the inferior product decreases (shifts to the left).

Grasp **Key definitions** quickly using this handy box. Use the flashcards online to test yourself.

→ **Revise Effectively**

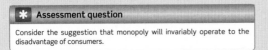

Prepare for upcoming exams and tests using the **Assessment question** at the start of each chapter.

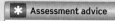

Assessment advice

The idea of consumer surplus is sometimes used when trying to put a value on the economic welfare from using resources in a particular way. It is also closely related to the idea of *producer surplus* **(Chapter 4, page 107)**.

Test yourself

Q8. Use Figure 2.6 to explain what has happened to total revenue before and after the price cut.

Q9. Can you think of other changes in the external environment which might also result in the situation shown in Figure 2.6?

Assessment advice and **Test Yourself** questions throughout each chapter to check progress.

Compare your responses with the **Answer guidelines** at the end of the chapter, with additional tips to **Make your answer stand out.**

Answer guidelines

Assessment question

Under what circumstances might you support government intervention in the economy?

Make your answer stand out

Clearly drawn and fully labelled diagrams can be presented and used to explain both the adverse effects of market failures and how government intervention can improve the resource allocation by 'correcting' for these market failures. Examples such as climate change and congestion charging can be used to show how these corrective policies work in practice.

→ **Make your answers stand out**

Examples & evidence

FAB plants and natural monopoly

Technical change has been rapid in the global semiconductor business. In recent years large integrated FAB plants costing $3bn or more have been built to incorporate new developments in chemical processes and material technologies. They can produce over three times as many chips from each wafer of silicon and indeed from lower-cost alternatives to silicon itself. As a result the average chip costs from these huge FAB plants are 40% less than for chips produced by their smaller counterparts, providing these FAB plants are used to at least 90% of capacity. Analysts see no more than 10 such giant plants being required worldwide to meet current global demand for microchips, which means that the minimum efficient size (MES) for each FAB plant is larger than the national demand for microchips of all but a few countries!

Questions

1. How does this Examples & evidence support the 'natural monopoly' argument?
2. How would international trade issues be relevant to any conclusions?

Using real-world examples can raise your marks during an exam or assessment. Read the **Examples and evidence** boxes in each chapter.

1 Markets and resource allocation

Topic map

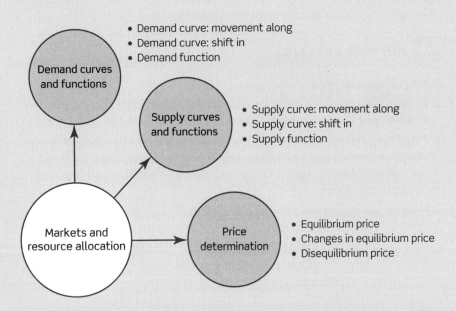

- Demand curve: movement along
- Demand curve: shift in
- Demand function

Demand curves and functions

Supply curves and functions

- Supply curve: movement along
- Supply curve: shift in
- Supply function

Markets and resource allocation

Price determination

- Equilibrium price
- Changes in equilibrium price
- Disequilibrium price

A printable version of this topic map is available from **www.pearsoned.co.uk/econexpress**

Introduction

'Gold reaches record price of almost $1,900 per ounce' was just one of the many headlines on the soaring price of gold in late 2011. In fact the gold price rose from $1,400 per ounce to a record $1,911 in just five months between April and August 2011, before falling back a little to around $1,660 per ounce in early 2013. It is vital that you are able to explain how prices are determined in a market economy and can use appropriate diagrams to support your argument, if you are to be successful in any course in microeconomics.

This chapter will help you review the workings of the market system and the role that price plays in guiding the decisions of both producers and consumers. We see that price changes can help bring about an 'equilibrium' or balance between the intentions of those who supply a product and the intentions of those who want to buy it. It is this role of prices in acting as a 'signal' to both producers and consumers which helps underpin the idea that 'consumers are sovereign' in a market economy, so that when consumer tastes change in favour of a product, the market system responds by providing the extra supply to meet this new and higher level of demand. The chapter identifies the circumstances in which the price mechanism may fail to fulfil this role and reviews alternative mechanisms for resource allocation.

 ## Revision checklist

What you need to know:
- [ ] When to use the term *movements along* the demand/supply curve and when to use the term *shifts in* the demand/supply curve.
- [ ] *Movements along* the demand/supply curve are due to changes in the price of the product itself, but *shifts in* the demand/supply curve are due to changes in other variables, which we call the *conditions of demand or supply*.
- [ ] How to use diagrams to show the impacts of changes in these conditions of demand or supply on price and output.
- [ ] How resources are allocated in situations of 'market failure' where the market is prevented from working in its usual ways.

 ## Assessment advice

Use diagrams

You can improve your analysis and gain higher marks in this topic area by using demand/supply diagrams to discuss movements to a new equilibrium price and output when the conditions of demand or supply change. When presenting a diagram, draw it clearly and label it fully, and remember to *use* your diagram by referring specifically to it as you write your answer.

Use consistent terminology

Use appropriate terms to distinguish between 'movements along' the demand/supply curves due to changes in the price of the product itself, and 'shifts in' those curves due to changes in the conditions of demand/supply! For example you could use the terms expansion/contraction for a 'movement along' a curve, but increase/decrease for a 'shift in' a curve.

Use empirical evidence

Support your market analysis with *empirical evidence,* such as facts and figures or case study examples.

 Assessment question

Can you answer this essay-type question? Guidelines on answering the question are presented at the end of this chapter.

Use market analysis to explain why the price of gold has proved so volatile in recent years.

Demand curves and functions

Demand is the amount of a product (good or service) consumers are willing and able to purchase at a given price, and is a *flow* concept, relating quantity to time (e.g. videos per month). The term 'effective demand' indicates desire supported by the means to actually purchase the product.

Demand curve: movement along

The demand curve in Figure 1.1(a) is a visual representation of how much of the product consumers are willing and able to purchase at different prices. The demand curve (D) slopes downwards from left to right, suggesting that when the price of X falls, more of product X is demanded, but when the price of X rises, less of product X is demanded. Of course, we are assuming that only the price of the product changes, sometimes called the *ceteris paribus* (other things equal) assumption. In this case changes in the price of the product will

3

result in *movements along* the demand curve, either an *expansion* (movement down and to the right) or a *contraction* (movement up and to the left).

For example, suppose in Figure 1.1(a) product X is smart phones. If the price of smart phones falls from P_1 to P_2, the demand for smart phones will expand from Q_1 to Q_2 (other things being equal) because smart phones will now be cheaper than other substitutes in consumption (e.g. non-Internet linked mobile phones etc.). We can expect some individuals to switch towards smart phones and away from these now *relatively* more expensive substitutes in consumption.

If the price of smart phones rises from P_2 to P_1 then, for the opposite reasons, we can expect the demand for smart phones to contract from Q_2 to Q_1 (other things being equal).

Demand curve: shift in

Of course, other things may not remain equal! This brings us to the **conditions of demand** which refer to the variables that cause the demand curve for product X to *shift* either to the right or to the left.

In Figure 1.1(b):

- A shift to the right from D_1 to D_2 (*increase*) means more of product X is demanded at any given price. For example, at price P_1 demand increases from Q_1 to Q_2.
- A shift to the left from D_2 to D_1 (*decrease*) means less of product X is demanded at any given price. For example, at price P_1 demand decreases from Q_2 to Q_1.

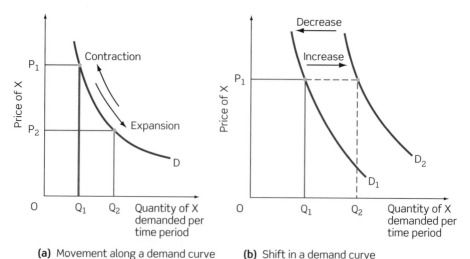

(a) Movement along a demand curve   **(b)** Shift in a demand curve

Figure 1.1 Movements along and shifts in a demand curve.

Source: Griffiths, A. and Wall, S. (2011) *Economics for Business and Management* (3rd ed.) © 2011 Pearson Education. Reproduced with permission.

Variables within the 'conditions of demand' include the price of other products (P_o), the *real income* of households (Y), the tastes of households (T), advertising expenditure (A) on product X, and so on.

To understand more about these 'conditions of demand' it will help if you are familiar with a number of terms, e.g. **substitutes in consumption, complements in consumption**, and **inferior products**.

Key definitions

Conditions of demand

Conditions of demand are the variables that will cause the demand curve for product X to shift, either to the right or to the left. These include the price of other products (P_o), the real income of households (Y), the tastes of households (T) and so on.

Substitutes in consumption

Substitutes in consumption are two (or more) products seen by consumers as alternatives, possessing broadly similar characteristics, e.g. gaming consoles such as Nintendo Wii, Microsoft X-boxes and Sony PlayStations

Complements in consumption

Complements in consumption are two (or more) products seen by consumers as fitting together, in the sense that purchasing one product will usually involve purchasing the other(s). Personal computers and printers are obvious examples of complements in consumption, as are tennis rackets and tennis balls.

Inferior products

Inferior products are goods or services that are cheaper but poorer quality substitutes for other goods or services. As real incomes rise the more expensive but better quality substitutes may eventually come within the purchasing power of the consumer, so that demand for the inferior product decreases (shifts to the left).

✴ Assessment advice

The notion of inferior products brings into play the idea of *income elasticity of demand* **(see Chapter 2, page 40)**. The 'elasticity' concept will be useful in responding to many questions involving movements along or shifts in the demand curve for a product, including price, income and cross-elasticities of demand.

Shift to right: increase in demand

Here we consider briefly the major variables that might cause an *increase in demand* for a good or service, so that the whole demand curve shifts bodily to the right from D_1 to D_2 in Figure 1.1(b):

- *A rise in the price of a substitute in consumption*
- *A fall in the price of a complement in consumption*
- *A rise in income for a normal product*
- *A change in tastes of the household in favour of the product*
- *A rise in advertising expenditure on the product.*

Shift to left: decrease in demand

See if you can identify the factors involved in a decrease in demand!

Test yourself

Q1. Write down the variables that might cause a decrease in demand for traditional laptop computers, i.e. a leftward shift in the demand curve. Try to be specific.

In the Examples & evidence box you can see how changes in the age profile of the population can shift the demand curve for various products. Providing examples, evidence or facts to support your arguments in assignments or examinations will earn you extra marks.

Examples & evidence

Age profile and demand

The average age in the UK and in many other advanced industrialised economies has increased sharply over time, with major impacts on the demand for a wide range of goods and services. Whilst a woman born in 1900 in the UK lived, on average, to an age of only 45 years, a woman born in 2013 in the UK can expect to live until 85 years and above. Indeed, in 2013 some 17% of the UK population was aged over 65 years, compared with only 11% in 1951, and some 4.5% was aged over 80 years, compared with only 1.4% in 1951. A report by the UK Department for Work and Pensions in early 2011 predicted that around 1 in 6 of the 62 million UK population would live to 100 years or more.

The increase in average life expectancy is due to two key factors: first, individuals are living longer, and second, fewer individuals are dying at younger ages than has been the case in the past. A century ago large numbers died as infants, in childhood or in their twenties or early thirties. Now most people in advanced industrial countries live to an (ever increasing) older age, as is indicated by the curve in Figure 1.2 becoming increasingly *rectangular* rather than a smooth downward-sloping curve.

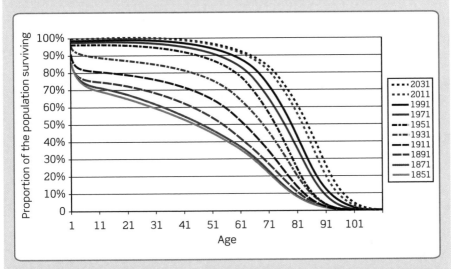

Figure 1.2 The rectangularisation of life curve, England and Wales, 1851–2031.
Source: Adapted from Government Actuary's Department.

Question

1. Explain what is shown in Figure 1.2. What impacts might these changes have on the demand for goods and services? Try to be specific.

Demand function

The *demand function* expresses the relationship between the quantity of product X demanded per unit of time (Q_x) and a number of possible variables. These include the own price of product X (P_x), and a number of other variables known collectively as the 'conditions of demand'.

The demand function is often shown as a shorthand expression:

$$Q_x = F(P_x, P_o, Y, T, A_x \ldots)$$

This can be read as meaning that the quantity demanded of product X (Q_x) *depends upon* its own price (P_x), the price of other products (P_o), real household income (Y), household tastes (T), advertising expenditure on product X (A_x) and so on.

- Any change in the product's own price P_x (other things being equal) will result in a *movement along* a demand curve.

- Any change in a variable within the 'conditions of demand' will cause a *shift* in a demand curve.

However, the demand function may also contain other variables which are often omitted from standard textbook presentations, such as technology, advertising and credit.

- *Technology (T_n):* Although new technology is more often associated with shifts in supply, it can also bring about shifts in demand (see Examples & evidence).

- *Advertising (A_x):* Advertising expenditure on product X itself (A_x), on a substitute in consumption for X (A_s) and/or on a complement in consumption for X (A_c) may all contribute to a shift in the demand curve for product X.

- *Credit availability (C_A) and credit price (C_p):* Two important but often neglected variables can exert an important influence on the demand for a product, namely the availability of credit (C_A) and the price of credit (C_p).

See if you can apply your knowledge of demand functions in the next Examples & evidence. Again it is worth remembering that using examples and evidence in your answers is likely to raise your marks.

Examples & evidence

Smart phones capture retail shoppers

Mobiles with Internet access are at the forefront of what many see as a retail revolution! Smart phones accounted for around 60% of all new handsets sold in the UK in 2012, more than doubling their 26% market share of 2010. This rapid growth in smart phone demand is proving of major benefit to high street retailers. John Lewis, Tesco, M&S, Shop Direct, Mothercare and many others have adapted their websites to make them simpler and easier to navigate by smart phone. This is hardly surprising when retail analysts such as Verdict Research have predicted that mobile Internet sales would more than double between 2011 and 2013. In fact 79% of British consumers are predicted to use their mobile phones for retail sales by 2014. Verdict Research suggest that by 2015 retail sales via smart phone mobile Internet access will overtake those via PC access.

Many major retailers are now installing systems which immediately recognise whether consumers are using a PC, laptop or smart phone to search their website. If the latter, the system automatically routes the consumer to a specially designed website which makes shopping even easier for the smart phone user. The John Lewis retail chain uses a system that recognises the products consumers have been researching online at their stores even before they visit, so that they can then direct consumers via their smart phones to the correct department and inform them of price and other advantages for purchasing these items. Tesco uses a similar 'Storenav' device which guides consumers and informs them as to the location and price of specified products via their smart phones.

An interesting and as yet unresolved question is whether the rapid growth in mobile Internet sales represents new retail sales or merely a switch from sales via the high street to sales via the Internet.

Questions

1. Examine the likely impacts of these developments for smart phones on:
   (a) the demand function for major retailers;
   (b) the demand function for smart phone producers.
2. Can you suggest any other factors that might influence these demand functions in the period to 2015?
3. This question checks your understanding of the variables in the 'conditions of demand' which can shift the demand curve to the right (increase) or to the left (decrease).

For an *increase in demand*, insert letter I.

For a *decrease in demand*, insert letter D.

Changes in variable	Letter (I or D)
Rise in real income (for a normal good)	
Fall in price of a substitute in consumption	
Fall in price of a complement in consumption	
Change of tastes in favour of the product	
Fall in real income (for a normal good)	
Rise in price of a substitute in consumption	
Rise in price of a complement in consumption	
Change of tastes against the product	

Supply curves and functions

The *supply curve* in Figure 1.3(a) is a visual representation of how much of the product sellers are willing and able to supply at different prices.

Supply curve: movement along

Changes in the price of the product will (other things being equal) result in *movements along* the supply curve, either an *expansion* (movement up and to the right) or a *contraction* (movement down and to the left).

Supply curve: shift in

Of course, other things may not remain equal! This brings us to the *conditions of supply* which refer to the factors that cause the supply curve for product X to *shift* either to the right or to the left.

In Figure 1.3(b):

- A shift to the right from S_1 to S_2 (*increase*) means more of product X is supplied at any given price. For example, at price P_1 supply *increases* from Q_1 to Q_2.
- A shift to the left from S_2 to S_1 (*decrease*) means less of product X is supplied at any given price. For example, at price P_1 supply *decreases* from Q_2 to Q_1.

Variables within the 'conditions of supply' include the price of other products (P_o), the costs of production (C), tax rates (T_x), tastes of producers (T_p) and so on.

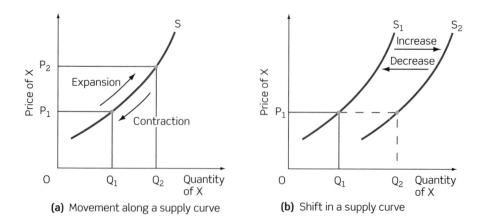

(a) Movement along a supply curve **(b)** Shift in a supply curve

Figure 1.3 Movements along and shifts in a supply curve.
Source: Griffiths, A. and Wall, S. (2011) *Economics for Business and Management* (3rd ed.) © 2011 Pearson Education. Reproduced with permission.

To understand more about these 'conditions of supply' it will help if you are familiar with the terms **substitutes in production** and **complements in production.**

Key definitions

Substitutes in production

Substitutes are used when another product (O) could have been produced with the *same resources* (land, labour, capital, raw materials, etc.) as those used for product X.

Complements in production

Complements in production are when the process of one or more production for X yields by-products. These complements in production are also known as *jointly supplied products.*

Shift to right: increase in supply

Here we consider briefly what might cause an *increase in supply* of product X, i.e. a shift in the supply curve for X from S_1 to S_2 in Figure 1.3(b).

- *A fall in the price of a substitute in production*
- *A rise in the price of a complement in production*
- *A fall in the costs of production*
- *Changes in the tastes of producers in favour of X*
- *Tax reductions*
- *Subsidy increases.*

Shift to left: decrease in supply

Test yourself

Q2. Write down the factors that might cause a *decrease* in supply of traditional laptop computers, i.e. a *leftward* shift in the supply curve.

Supply function

The supply function expresses the relationship between the quantity of product X supplied per unit of time (Q_x) and a number of possible variables. These include the own price of product X (P_x), and a number of other variables known collectively as the 'conditions of supply'.

The supply function is often shown as a shorthand expression:

$$Q_x = F(P_x, P_o, C, T_n, T_x, T_p \ldots)$$

This can be read as meaning that the quantity supplied of product X (Q_x) *depends upon* its own price (P_x), the price of other products (P_o), costs of production (C), technology (T_n), tax rates (T_x), tastes of producers (T_p) and so on.

- Any change in the product's own price P_x (other things being equal) will result in a *movement along* a supply curve.
- Any change in a variable within the 'conditions of supply' will cause a *shift* in a supply curve.

See if you can apply your knowledge of supply functions in this Examples & evidence on oil.

Examples & evidence

BP costs soar after oil spill

BP itself and other oil analysts produced a series of reports evaluating the impacts on BP of the Gulf of Mexico oil spill in 2011. BP reported that the costs of cleaning up the world's worst offshore oil spill and putting aside monies for the Deepwater Horizon Compensation Fund had reached $41.3bn, of which $17.7bn had already been paid out, with $13bn spent on cleaning up and around $4bn as compensation to businesses and individuals in the Gulf affected by the oil spill. JP Morgan estimated that the eventual bill would rise well above the $41.3bn predicted by BP, to over $69bn if BP were to be found guilty in the US courts of gross negligence, as indeed it was in 2012.

In fact oil production by BP in the US has fallen by 11% in each year since the oil spill as a result of the moratorium BP has placed on oil production in the Gulf of Mexico and 'lost production' via the extra checks and maintenance work it has conducted in other oil fields as it attempts to avoid future global oil spills.

Questions

1. Examine the likely impacts of these developments on the supply curve of oil for BP.
2. Match the *letter* of each description on the left with the *number* for its correct term on the right.

Description	Term
(a) Sometimes called a 'complement in production' with the production process for one product automatically resulting in more output of the other product (i.e. the by-product).	(1) Fall in costs of production

(b) Where the factors of production (land, labour, capital) could be used to produce either product. (c) Has the effect of shifting the supply curve upwards and to the left (decrease in supply) by a constant amount (i.e. a parallel shift). (d) Has the effect of shifting the supply curve upwards and to the left (decrease in supply) by a non-constant amount (i.e. a non-parallel shift). (e) More can now be supplied at any given price or the same quantity can now be supplied at a lower price (increase in supply).	(2) Imposing or raising a lump-sum tax (3) Substitute in production (4) Imposing or raising a percentage tax (e.g. VAT) (5) Jointly supplied product

Price determination

We shall initially assume that we have a *free market*, i.e. one in which demand and supply alone determine the price.

Equilibrium price

In Figure 1.4 we can see that at price P_1 the demand and supply curves intersect at the same quantity, Q_1. We call this price P_1 and quantity Q_1 the *equilibrium* price and quantity. Equilibrium means 'at rest', with 'no tendency to change'.

At any price other than P_1 there will clearly be a tendency for change.

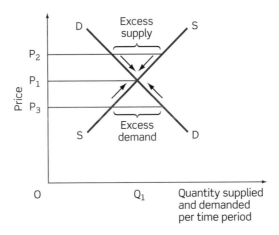

Figure 1.4 Restoring equilibrium price and quantity in a free market.
Source: Griffiths, A. and Wall, S. (2011) *Economics for Business and Management* (3rd ed.) © 2011 Pearson Education. Reproduced with permission.

Excess supply

Suppose price is higher than P_1, then supply will exceed demand. At price P_2 in Figure 1.4 there is an *excess supply*. In a free market this excess supply will cause price to fall as suppliers try to dispose of their surplus stock.

- *As price falls* consumers find the product more attractive than substitutes in consumption and some will switch away from those substitutes, so that we move rightwards along the demand curve D (expansion of demand).
- *As price falls* producers find the product less attractive than any substitutes in production and may switch resources to these alternatives, so that we move leftwards along the supply curve (contraction of supply).

Price will continue to fall until we reach price P_1, where sellers and buyers are in harmony, with all that is offered for sale being purchased, i.e. we have equilibrium in the market.

Excess demand

Suppose price is lower than P_1, then demand will exceed supply.

Test yourself

Q3. Try to explain, referring to Figure 1.4, how equilibrium is brought about in the market if the original price is P_3.

Price is acting as a *signal* to buyers and to sellers and helps direct them to take actions (expand or contract demand or supply) which bring about an equilibrium (balance) in the market.

Changes in equilibrium price

We have seen that changes in the conditions of demand or supply will *shift* the demand or supply curves. This in turn will cause changes in the equilibrium price and quantity in the market. It will be useful to consider how increases and decreases in both demand and supply will influence equilibrium price and quantity.

Increase in demand

In Figure 1.5(a) demand increases from D to D', so that the original equilibrium price–quantity P_1–Q_1 can no longer continue. At price P_1 we now have a situation of *excess demand*. In a free market, price will be bid up. As price rises, supply *expands* along S and demand *contracts* along D' until we reach the higher price P_2 at which demand and supply are again equal at Q_2. We call P_2–Q_2 the new price and quantity equilibrium.

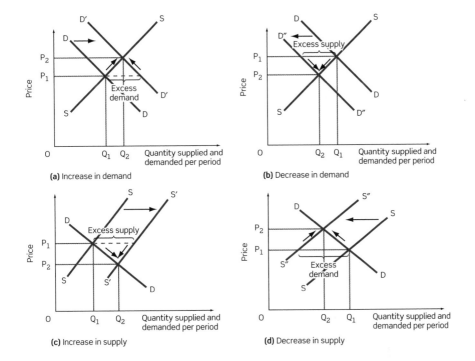

Figure 1.5 (a) Increase in demand; (b) decrease in demand; (c) increase in supply; (d) decrease in supply.

Source: Griffiths, A. and Wall, S. (2011) *Economics for Business and Management* (3rd ed.) © 2011 Pearson Education. Reproduced with permission.

- An increase in demand will raise equilibrium price and quantity.

Test yourself

Q4. Try to explain, referring to the relevant figures, how the new price and quantity equilibrium is reached in each of the following:

(a) Decrease in demand: see Figure 1.5(b)

(b) Increase in supply: see Figure 1.5(c)

(c) Decrease in supply: see Figure 1.5(d).

See if you can apply your knowledge on price determination using this Examples & evidence on cotton.

Examples & evidence

Volatile cotton prices

Some three years after a massive price jump in 2008 destabilised global cotton markets, the price of cotton was again surging. The benchmark cotton contract price soared in March 2011 to $2.15 a pound (weight), the highest level in the 140 years for which cotton has traded on an exchange. The increase revived uneasy feelings among US cotton merchants – middlemen between growers and mills – recalling the rapid rise in March 2008 to $1 a pound (weight) that had cost them hundreds of millions of dollars, forcing some old industry names out of business.

Cotton's latest surge in price in 2011 came after China, the largest producer and consumer of the plant, announced in early 2011 that its crop had fallen 14.6% to 6.4m tonnes, the fourth straight year of declining global production as farmers cut the planting of cotton due to higher costs and to the attractions of switching land previously used for cotton over to the planting of corn and soya beans. China had also reopened its doors to cotton imports after previous restrictions on imports had cut into its cotton inventories. For US textile mills, which had lost out to cheaper rival producers, the price rise for cotton, their key raw material, had a terrible effect as they had very little pricing power for their finished products and yet their raw material costs were rising rapidly. The pressure was particularly acute for underwear makers using cotton fabrics, as raw material costs account for as much as 60% of the cost of a garment.

Questions

1. Identify the demand and supply factors behind the sharp rise in cotton prices in early 2011. Use diagrams to illustrate your answer.
2. Why are US textile firms so concerned about these developments in the market for cotton?
3. Explain why the price of cotton has collapsed from $2.15 a pound (weight) in early 2011 to well below $1 a pound (weight) by 2013.

Disequilibrium price

Of course, in reality governments or regulatory bodies may intervene in markets, as for example in setting maximum or minimum prices. In these cases prices are *prevented* from acting as the signals which guide buyers and sellers to an equilibrium outcome.

Maximum price

The government or agency may seek to establish a *maximum price* in the market, i.e. a *ceiling* above which price will not be allowed to rise. Again we can use demand and supply diagrams as in Figure 1.6(a) to show what will then happen.

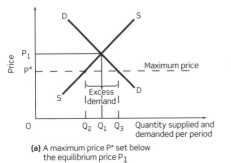
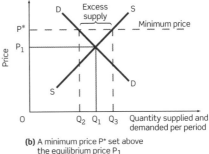

(a) A maximum price P* set below
the equilibrium price P_1

(b) A minimum price P* set above
the equilibrium price P_1

Figure 1.6 (a) A maximum price P* set below the equilibrium price P_1; (b) a minimum price P* set above the equilibrium price P_1.

Source: Griffiths, A. and Wall, S. (2011) *Economics for Business and Management* (3rd ed.) © 2011 Pearson Education. Reproduced with permission.

If the maximum price were set *above* the equilibrium price P_1, then the market would still be able to reach the equilibrium outcome of price P_1 and quantity Q_1. However, the market mechanism would not be able to reach this equilibrium outcome if the maximum price (P*) were set *below* the equilibrium price P_1. At price P* there is an excess demand and price would have risen in a free market to P_1, encouraging producers to expand supply from Q_2 to Q_1 and discouraging consumers, so that demand contracts from Q_3 to Q_1, until the equilibrium P_1–Q_1 is established. Here, however, price is prevented from providing such signals to sellers and buyers to bring their decisions into harmony, and we may be left with the *disequilibrium* outcome P* in which excess demand persists.

Test yourself

Q5. If the price mechanism is prevented from allocating resources in a situation of *excess demand*, what other (non-price) mechanisms might be used to allocate these scarce resources?

Minimum price

The government or agency may seek to establish a minimum price in the market, i.e. a *floor* below which the price will not be allowed to fall. We can use our familiar demand and supply diagrams as in Figure 1.6(b) to show what will happen in these circumstances.

Suppose now that the government imposes a minimum price, P*, below which the price will not be allowed to fall. If that minimum price is set *below* the equilibrium price P_1 then there will be no problem. The market will already have reached its equilibrium at price P_1, and there will be no reason for P_1 to change. If, however, the minimum price is set *above* the equilibrium price P_1, then price will have to rise from P_1 to the new minimum, P*. We can see from Figure 1.6(b) that there will then be an excess supply at P* of Q_3–Q_2 units.

If the market had remained free, the excess supply would have been removed by the price system. However, the important point here is that the market is not free! Price cannot fall below the minimum that has been set, P*. The excess supply will therefore remain and the price system will not be able to remove it. Sellers will be unable to dispose of their surplus stocks, which will have to be stored, destroyed or disposed of in less orthodox ways which prevent the price falling below P*.

Examples & evidence

Minimum price for alcohol

In November 2012 a minimum price of 45p per unit of alcohol was proposed for England and Wales, to be followed by a 10-week consultation period. The main aim of the minimum price is to stop the heavy discounts on cheap alcoholic drinks widely available in shops and supermarkets. Many analysts believe alcoholic drinks are often used as a 'loss leader' to attract people into the shops/supermarkets, quoting prices as low as 20 pence per can of lager and less than £2 per two-litre bottle of cider.

What is a unit of alcohol?

- Half a pint of standard strength (4%) beer, cider or lager
- A single pub measure of spirit (25 ml)
- Half a standard (175 ml) glass of wine.

The following data indicates what impact a minimum price of 45p per unit of alcohol would have on a range of drinks.

Drink	Alcoholic strength (%) and size	Minimum price (£)
Lager	7.9%, 440 ml	£1.56
Cider	8.4%, 440 ml	£1.56
Wine	12.5%, 750 ml	£4.22
Whisky	40%, 700 ml	£12.60
Vodka	37.5%, 1 litre	£15.88

Research carried out by Sheffield University on behalf of the government indicates that a minimum price of 45p per unit of alcohol would reduce the consumption of alcohol by 4.3% per year. Over a 10-year period this would result in 2,000 fewer deaths, 66,000 fewer hospital admissions, and 24,000 fewer crimes.

- When the researchers 'modelled' a lower minimum price of 40p per unit of alcohol, all the 'benefits' outlined above approximately halved in value.
- When the researchers 'modelled' a higher minimum price of 50p per unit of alcohol (the minimum price proposed for Scotland) all the 'benefits' outlined above approximately doubled in value.

Questions

1. What arguments are likely to be used by those who support a minimum price for alcohol? Can you use a diagram(s) to support the argument?
2. What arguments are likely to be used by those who oppose a minimum price for alcohol?

'Cobweb' models

Time lags, in which supply in the current time period depends on price in a previous time period, and elasticity conditions **(see Chapter 2)**, can also play a part in preventing an equilibrium outcome, as can be seen in Figure 1.7.

In this model supply in the current year (S_t) depends on price in the previous year (P_{t-1}) but demand in the current year (D_t) depends on price in the current year (P_t). This is the case for many agricultural crops. For example, when the price of wheat is high, more land is often planted for wheat production, rather than substitutes in production, such as barley, rye, rapeseed and other cereal crops. As a result *next year's* supply of wheat will tend to increase sharply as a result of a high price this year.

- *Stable cobweb*: If we start at price P_1 in Figure 1.7, next year's supply will be Q_2 but that can only be sold at a price P_2, as demand depends on the current price. This will result in next year's supply falling to Q_3, which will be sold at a price of P_3, and so on. Notice that this situation will eventually result (after several time periods) in a stable equilibrium price P_4 and quantity Q_4, hence the term 'stable cobweb'.

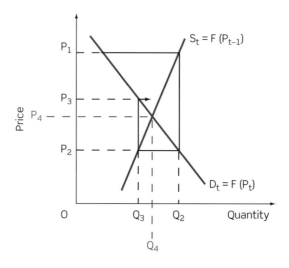

Figure 1.7 Stable 'cobweb' model.

- *Unstable cobweb:* In this case the initial disequilibrium situation simply leads to a move further and further away from any possible equilibrium solution.

Test yourself

Q6. Can you use Figure 1.7 to identify the situation in which an unstable cobweb diagram will be formed, with the situation moving further away from any possible equilibrium solution?

As we shall see **in Chapter 2 (page 30)**, the *elasticity* of the respective demand and supply curves will determine whether this cobweb model is 'stable', settling down at an equilibrium price and output, or 'unstable', diverging further and further away from an equilibrium price/quantity outcome.

The final 'Test yourself' will help to check your understanding of price determination.

Test yourself

Q7. The market for designer trainers is currently in equilibrium. Other things being equal, what will be the likely impact of each of the following events?

Event	Change in equilibrium price	Change in equilibrium quantity
(a) Successful TV advertising for designer trainers	Rise / Fall	Rise / Fall
(b) Report indicates foot damage from wearing designer trainers	Rise / Fall	Rise / Fall
(c) New factories in developing countries reduce costs of producing designer trainers while retaining quality	Rise / Fall	Rise / Fall
(d) Higher rate of VAT applied to designer trainers	Rise / Fall	Rise / Fall

Q8. The supply and demand situation for product X is as follows.

Price of X (£ per unit)	Quantity demanded of X (000 units per week)	Quantity supplied of X (000 units per week)
10	20	80
9	40	70
8	60	60
7	80	50
6	100	40

(a) Draw a diagram showing the demand and supply curves for X and identify the equilibrium price and quantity.

(b) Why is £9 not an equilibrium price? Use your diagram to explain how equilibrium will be restored in a market economy.

(c) The government now introduces a maximum price of £6 per unit. Using your diagram, explore the likely consequences of such a maximum price.

(d) Suppose the government introduced a minimum price of £10 per unit. Using your diagram, explore the likely consequences of such a minimum price.

Chapter summary – pulling it all together

By the end of this chapter you should be able to:

	Confident ✓	Not confident?
Distinguish between *movements along* the demand/supply curve and *shifts in* the demand/supply curve		Revise pages 3–13
Identify the variables causing the demand curve to shift to the right (increase) or to the left (decrease)		Revise pages 4–9
Identify the variables causing the supply curve to shift to the right (increase) or to the left (decrease)		Revise pages 10–13
Using a diagram, explain how price acts as a 'signal' to producers and consumers in bringing about an equilibrium price and output		Revise pages 13–14
Use diagrams to show the impacts of shifts in demand and supply curves on the equilibrium price and output		Revise pages 14–16
Explain how resources are allocated in situations where the market is prevented from achieving an equilibrium price and output		Revise pages 16–21

Now try the **assessment question** at the start of this chapter, using the answer guidelines below.

Answer guidelines

✳ Assessment question

Use market analysis to explain why the price of gold has proved so volatile in recent years.

Approaching the question

The question clearly provides an opportunity to use the demand and supply analysis and diagrams discussed in this chapter, in the particular context of the market for gold. An important characteristic of this market is, of course, the restricted sources of supply for gold and the difficulties of finding new sources of supply.

If this is an assignment question, you can start by investigating and providing empirical evidence of the changes that have occurred in the price of gold in recent years. This will help to demonstrate the volatility in the price of gold that you will be seeking to explain.

Important points to include

- **Data or evidence to indicate price volatility.** Figure 1.8 provides an example of presenting this kind of data in graphical form. It shows the considerable variation in the gold price in a 12-month period from 1 July 2011 to 30 June 2012. As can be seen from the diagram, the gold price reached a high of $1,900 per troy ounce in early September 2011, but had fallen by 16% within days to $1,600 per troy ounce by mid-September 2011.

- **Supply of gold is stable/demand fluctuates widely.** Figures 1.5(a) and (b) are relevant here and you can use them to show that substantial shifts to the right (increase) or left (decrease) in demand for gold will result in sharp rises or falls in the gold price. This is especially so if you draw the supply curve for gold as being vertical or quite steep **(see Chapter 2)**.

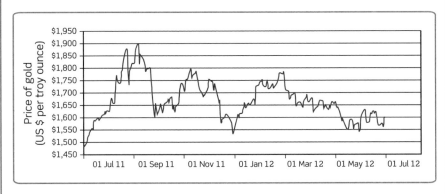

Figure 1.8 Variations in the price of gold over the 12-month period from 1 July 2011 to 30 June 2012.

Source: World Gold Council www.gold.org.

- **Reasons for stability in supply of gold**. When talking about the fixed supply of gold, you could point out that all the gold ever mined could be contained in a single cube-structured container with dimensions for height, width and length of only around 12 metres by 12 metres by 12 metres! At current prices this small stock of global gold would be worth over $9.6 trillion.

- **Reasons for fluctuations in demand for gold:**

– *Gold as a safe haven*: investors switch to gold whenever there are uncertainties in holding alternatives, such as currencies or securities. This can result in sharp rises in the price of gold at such times.

– *Gold as a low-yielding investment*: gold earns no interest and pays no dividends, so when confidence returns, investors switch back to alternatives such as public sector bonds or private sector shares (equities) which do earn interest and dividends. This can result in sharp falls in the price of gold at such times.

– *Gold as a speculative investment*: although the *total* supply of gold is fixed, the amount put onto the market at any one time is variable as private investors and even governments will release gold from their holdings (or add gold to their holdings) if selling gold becomes more (or less) attractive. You can show this as an increase or decrease in supply as in Figure 1.5(c) and (d).

Make your answer stand out

- Presenting and using the diagrams indicated above to support your analysis will help to make your answer stand out. So too will introducing the elasticity concepts **(see Chapter 2)** and their associated diagrams.

- Empirical evidence, as well as good use of diagrams, can help raise your marks. For example, gold suffered the largest two-day drop in price in over 30 years between 24 and 25 August 2011, falling 8.4% from peak to trough in just 48 hours. Investors were taking profits after the 35% surge to a record gold price between April and August 2011, already noted at the start of this chapter.

Read to impress

Here are some books, articles and other sources that you can use to develop your answers on the topic area.

Books

Griffiths, A. and Wall, S. (2011) *Economics for Business and Management*, 3rd edition, Chapter 1, Pearson Education.

Parkin, M., Powell, M. and Matthews, K. (2012) *Economics*, 8th edition, Chapters 1, 2 and 3, Addison Wesley.

Sloman, J. and Garratt, D. (2010) *Essentials of Economics*, 5th edition, Chapter 2, FT/Prentice Hall.

Sloman, J., Wride, A. and Garratt, D. (2012) *Economics*, 8th edition, Chapter 2, Pearson Education.

Journals and periodicals

The following are useful sources of articles and data on many aspects relevant to this and other topics:

Business Review, Philip Allan (quarterly)
Economic Review, Philip Allan (quarterly)
Economics Today, Anforme (quarterly)
Harvard Business Review (monthly)
The Economist (weekly)

Newspapers

Newspapers are important sources of up-to-date information, examples and data. Below are some of the main UK newspaper sources, many of which have websites with search facilities to identify specific topics and articles:

The Guardian
The Times
The Financial Times
The Independent
The Telegraph

Companion website

Go to the companion website at **www.pearsoned.co.uk/econexpress** to find more revision support online for this topic area.

Notes

2

Demand, revenue and elasticity

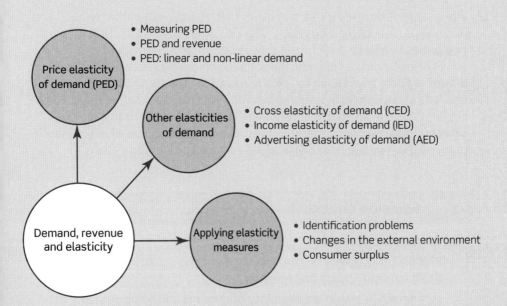

- Measuring PED
- PED and revenue
- PED: linear and non-linear demand

Price elasticity of demand (PED)

Other elasticities of demand

- Cross elasticity of demand (CED)
- Income elasticity of demand (IED)
- Advertising elasticity of demand (AED)

Demand, revenue and elasticity

Applying elasticity measures

- Identification problems
- Changes in the external environment
- Consumer surplus

A printable version of this topic map is available from **www.pearsoned.co.uk/econexpress**

Introduction

'A second-class stamp will cost you 40% more' was the headline on 30 April 2012, when both first- and second-class postage stamps rose sharply in price by 14 pence, costing 60 pence and 50 pence respectively. This was the result of the UK government giving the Royal Mail freedom to set its own prices from that date onwards. Consumers, business groups and postal workers strongly criticised such sharp rises, warning of dramatic slumps in the volume of public-sector mail delivery. Of course, alternative private-sector sources of mail delivery, such as DHL, UPS and TNT, and various Internet providers, saw the benefits to themselves of new revenue streams following sharp price increases by their Royal Mail competitor.

This chapter will help you review the sensitivity ('elasticity') of consumer responses to price and non-price factors, and therefore the outcomes in terms of quantity demanded and revenue received for a range of goods and services. It will also examine the circumstances under which a business can expect its revenue to increase, whether from changes in its own price, in the price of related products or in the real income of households.

The chapter examines these and other factors influencing the demand and revenue prospects for a business. Why do some businesses claim that cutting prices is vital to their future prospects, whilst others insist on raising prices? How should a business respond to the price cuts or price rises of a rival? Is there any reason to link the future prospects of the business to changes in household or national income? We shall see that the 'elasticity' concept plays a key role in determining the firm's response to such questions and will help you understand the economic principles which influence many of the revenue-based strategies adopted by individual firms.

Revision checklist

What you need to know:

- ❑ Explain, using diagrams, the relevance of price elasticity of demand (PED) to pricing policy and revenue.
- ❑ Distinguish between arc elasticity of demand and point elasticity of demand and link these ideas to pricing policy and revenue.
- ❑ Demonstrate the importance of the sign and size of cross-elasticity of demand (CED) for a product to the demand for that product.

❏ Demonstrate the importance of the sign and size of income elasticity of demand (IED) to forecasting future demand for a product.

❏ Review some of the issues involved in interpreting and applying elasticity measures.

❏ Examine the relevance of consumer surplus to resource allocation.

 ## Assessment advice

Use diagrams

You can improve your analysis and gain higher marks in this topic by using diagrams. For example, you can use a demand curve to illustrate the areas of revenue gain and revenue loss from *movements along* the demand curve following a change in the price of the product itself (PED). Diagrams can also be used to show *shifts in* the demand curve for the product following changes in the price of other products, whether substitutes or complements in consumption (CED). Similarly, we can use diagrams to show the extent and direction of shifts in the demand curve for the product following changes in household income (IED).

Use correct definitions and formulae

It will help to remember the definitions and formulae for PED, CED and IED. Try to discuss the importance of sign and size for these formulae.

Use empirical evidence

Try to provide actual examples of situations where price changes have raised or lowered revenue, often in unexpected directions, as with the 'Big Price Drop' policy of Tesco in 2011–12 reducing, rather than increasing, the revenue of Tesco. You can also look at examples where changes in the price of some other product (Y) has influenced the demand for product X, such as changes in the oil price (Y) influencing the demand for air travel (X). Effective use of case-study examples and evidence will strengthen your answers.

 ## Assessment question

Can you answer this essay-type question? Guidelines on answering the question are presented at the end of this chapter.

Examine the reasons why price cutting policies by a business sometimes result in a reduction, rather than increase, in the revenue received.

Price elasticity of demand (PED)

Price elasticity of demand (PED) is a measure of the responsiveness of demand for a product to a change in its own price. PED assumes that as the price of X changes, other things (the conditions of demand) remain equal, so it involves *movements along* the demand curve (expansion/contraction) rather than shifts in the demand curve (increase/decrease).

Key definition

Price elasticity of demand (PED)

Price elasticity of demand (PED) is a measure of the responsiveness of demand for a product to changes in its own price. PED indicates the extent of movement along the demand curve for X in response to a change in price of X:

$$PED = \frac{\% \text{ change in quantity demanded of X}}{\% \text{ change in price of X}}$$

Strictly speaking, the sign of PED for a product is negative, since a fall in the price of X will lead to an expansion of demand for X $(+/- = -)$. For example, if a 3% fall in the price of X results in a 9% expansion in demand, then PED is $+9/-3 = -3$. However, we usually ignore the sign of PED when expressing the numerical values.

Measuring PED

Table 2.1 outlines the different numerical values (ignoring the signs) for price elasticity of demand, together with the terminology used and what it actually means.

Table 2.1 Price elasticity of demand: numerical value, terminology and description.

Numerical value	Terminology	Description
0	Perfectly inelastic demand	Whatever the % change in price, no change in quantity demanded (Figure 2.1(a))
$>0 <1$	Relatively inelastic demand	A given % change in price leads to a smaller % change in quantity demanded (Figure 2.1(b))
1	Unit elastic demand	A given % change in price leads to exactly the same % change in quantity demanded (Figure 2.1(c))

Numerical value	Terminology	Description
$>1 < \infty$	Relatively elastic demand	A given % change in price leads to a larger % change in quantity demanded (Figure 2.1(d))
∞ (infinity)	Perfectly elastic demand	An infinitely small % change in price leads to an infinitely large % change in quantity demanded (Figure 2.1(e))

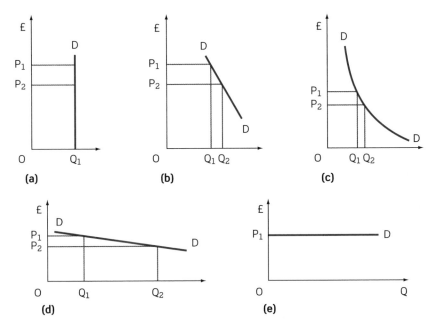

Figure 2.1 Visual presentations of price elasticity of demand.

Source: Griffiths, A. and Wall, S. (2011) *Economics for Business and Management* (3rd ed.) © 2011 Pearson Education. Reproduced with permission.

We use numerical values of PED to avoid being misled by diagrams, since changes in the scale used for the various axes can make a demand curve appear steeper or flatter. Nevertheless it is useful to be aware of the visual presentation of elasticity, as in Figure 2.1.

Factors affecting PED

The numerical value of PED depends on a number of factors.

1 *The availability of substitutes in consumption.* The more numerous and closer the substitutes available, the more elastic the demand. A small percentage change in price of X can then lead to a large percentage change in the quantity demanded of X as consumers switch towards or away from these substitutes in consumption.

2 *The nature of the need satisfied by the product.* The more possible it is to classify the need as being in the luxury category, the more price sensitive

consumers tend to be and the more elastic the demand. The more basic or necessary the need, the less price sensitive consumers tend to be and the less elastic the demand.

3 *The time period.* The longer the time period, the more elastic the demand (consumers take time to adjust their consumption patterns to a change in price).

4 *The proportion of income spent on the product.* The greater the proportion of income spent on the product, the more elastic the demand will tend to be. A given percentage change in the price of a product which plays an important role in the consumer's total spending pattern is more likely to be noticed by the consumer and thereby to influence future purchasing intentions (see also the idea of 'income effect', **Chapter 3, page 69**).

5 *The number of uses available to the product.* The greater the flexibility of the product in terms of the number of uses to which it can be put, the more elastic the demand. Of course, the greater the number of uses available to the product, the more substitute products there will tend to be (point 1 above).

PED and revenue

✳ Assessment advice

Whenever you are considering the pricing strategy for a business, Figure 2.2 can be used to show the linkages between PED and revenue.

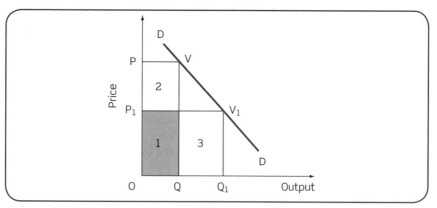

Figure 2.2 Box diagram to show how revenue varies with output for a linear demand curve.

Source: Griffiths, A. and Wall, S. (2011) *Economics for Business and Management* (3rd ed.) © 2011 Pearson Education. Reproduced with permission.

For a business to make sensible decisions as to the price it should charge, it will help to be aware of the linkage between PED and total revenue (turnover). The 'box' diagram shown in Figure 2.2 helps explain this linkage using a straight line (linear) demand curve (DD).

Table 2.2 PED and revenue

Numerical value of PED	Relationship between Area 2 and Area 3
1	Area 3 = Area 2
>1	Area 3 > Area 2
<1	Area 3 < Area 2

We can see that with the initial price at OP, total revenue (price $\times$ quantity) is shown by area OPVQ. A fall in price to OP_1 will lead to an expansion of demand to OQ_1 and a new total revenue indicated by area $OP_1V_1Q_1$. Clearly Area 1 is common to both total revenue situations, but here Area 2 is lost and Area 3 gained. The loss of Area 2 is due to selling the original OQ units at a now lower price; the gain of Area 3 is due to the lower price attracting new $(Q - Q_1)$ consumers for the product.

The relationships listed in Table 2.2 will hold true for the box diagram.

We can now use these relationships to make a number of predictions involving price changes and total revenue.

Price changes and total revenue

- For *price reductions* along a **unit elastic demand** curve (PED = 1) or segment of a demand curve, there will be no change in total revenue (Area 3 = Area 2).
- For *price reductions* along a **relatively elastic demand** curve (PED > 1, PED < ∞) or segment of a demand curve, total revenue will increase as there is a more than proportionate response of extra consumers to the now lower price (Area 3 > Area 2).
- For *price reductions* along a **relatively inelastic demand** curve (PED > 0, PED < 1) or segment of a demand curve, total revenue will decrease as there is a less than proportionate response of extra consumers to the now lower price (Area 3 < Area 2).

Examples & evidence

Pricing strategies and revenue

It will be useful to review two recent pricing strategies, one by Tesco involving price cuts and the other by Royal Mail involving price rises.

In January 2012 there was a major shock to the UK retail sector as Tesco unveiled a poor trading performance over the past year and a warning that profits in the coming year would be lower than previously forecast. This led immediately to a collapse in the Tesco share price, which fell by 16% in one day, wiping £5 billion off the company's value. The 'hypothesis' immediately advanced by analysts was that 'the big price drop' strategy announced in a fanfare by Tesco in September 2011 had failed. This had involved price cuts totalling over £500 million and was seen by many as directly responsible for the profits debacle, many analysts now calling it 'the big profits drop' strategy.

On 30 April 2012, Royal Mail raised the price of second-class stamps from 36 pence to 50 pence (39%), and the price of first-class stamps from 46 pence to 60 pence (30%). Internal Royal Mail memos have been revealed suggesting that senior executives anticipate a 15% fall in volume of second-class letters and analysts are predicting a similar outcome for first-class letters. The intention of the price-raising strategy is to reverse the 25% fall in volume of delivered mail between 2006 and 2012 and the associated 6% fall in revenue.

Questions

1. What might the experiences of Tesco suggest about PED? Explain your reasoning.
2. What PED conditions are required for a successful outcome for the pricing strategy of Royal Mail? Is there any evidence that these conditions apply?

PED: linear and non-linear demand

It is clearly vital that the firm has an accurate estimate of price elasticity of demand over the relevant segment of its demand curve if it is to correctly forecast the revenue consequences of any proposed price change.

So far we have tended to suppose that the *whole* demand curve is relatively elastic, relatively inelastic or unit elastic. However, this is rarely the case, except for the three situations of perfectly inelastic demand, unit elastic demand and perfectly elastic demand curves shown earlier in Figure 2.1(a), (c) and (e) respectively.

In most cases price elasticity of demand *varies along different segments* of the same demand curve. We see below that this is true for both straight-line (linear) and non-linear demand curves.

 Assessment advice

You can use the following analysis to show how (say) price-cutting strategies may raise revenue over price ranges where demand is elastic, but may reduce revenue over price ranges where demand is inelastic.

Variations in PED along a linear demand curve

We first assume a *straight-line (linear) demand curve,* as in Figure 2.3(a).

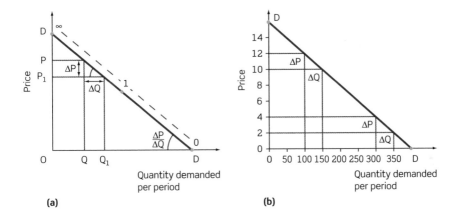

Figure 2.3 Variation of PED along the linear demand curve.

Source: Griffiths, A. and Wall, S. (2011) *Economics for Business and Management* (3rd ed.) © 2011 Pearson Education. Reproduced with permission.

P and Q are the initial price and quantity.

P_1 and Q_1 are the new price and quantity.

Δ indicates the absolute change in the price or quantity.

$$PED = \frac{\text{percentage change in quantity demanded}}{\text{percentage change in price}}$$

$$= \frac{(\Delta Q/Q) \times 100}{(\Delta P/P) \times 100}$$

$$= \frac{\Delta Q}{Q} \div \frac{\Delta P}{P} \quad \text{(100s cancel out)}$$

$$= \frac{\Delta Q}{Q} \times \frac{P}{\Delta P} \quad \text{(change} \div \text{to} \times\text{)}$$

$$= \frac{P}{Q} \times \frac{\Delta Q}{\Delta P} \quad \text{(rearranging)}$$

$$\boxed{PED = \frac{P}{Q} \times K \text{ (a constant)}}$$

- Note that we are multiplying the ratio P/Q by a *constant value (K)*, since the slope of the demand curve does not change over its entire length.
- We can use this expression to show that the value of price elasticity will vary all the way along the demand curve DD from infinity (∞) to zero as we move down the demand curve from left to right.

- At the top end of the demand curve (DD), the ratio P/Q is close to infinity where the demand curve cuts the vertical axis (large P, infinitely small Q), and infinity times a constant (K) is infinity.
- At the bottom end of the demand curve (DD), the ratio P/Q is close to zero where the demand curve cuts the horizontal axis (infinitely small P, large Q), and zero times a constant (K) is zero.

For a straight-line demand curve, PED falls from infinity to zero as price falls, since the ratio P/Q falls and the ratio $\Delta Q/\Delta P$ is a constant.

Variations in PED along a non-linear demand curve

If the demand curve is *not* a straight line (i.e. it is non-linear) then we have a further problem, since the ratio $\Delta Q/\Delta P$ will no longer be a constant. Clearly the ratio $\Delta Q/\Delta P$ in Figure 2.4 will now vary depending on the *magnitude* of the price change from P and the *direction* of the price change from P. This is one of the reasons why alternative measures of price elasticity of demand are used, namely 'arc elasticity' and 'point elasticity'.

 Assessment advice

You can use this analysis to explain how difficult it is for businesses to be sure how elastic (responsive) demand will be to a change in price of their product. Here PED, and therefore the impact of the price change on revenue, will also depend on the size of the price change and the direction (rise or fall) of the price change.

Arc elasticity of demand

As shown in Figure 2.4, this measure is a type of 'average' elasticity between two points (i.e. two different price and quantity situations) on a demand curve. It is particularly useful when the demand curve is not a straight line.

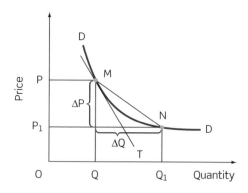

Figure 2.4 Arc and point elasticities for the non-linear demand curve.

Source: Griffiths, A. and Wall, S. (2011) *Economics for Business and Management* (3rd ed.) © 2011 Pearson Education. Reproduced with permission.

Instead of using only the initial price and quantity values in measuring PED, the concept of *arc elasticity of demand* uses the average of the initial and final values. If, using Figure 2.4, P and Q are the initial price and quantity respectively and P_1 and Q_1 are the final price and quantity, then we can write that the arc elasticity of demand

$$= \frac{\dfrac{P + P_1}{2}}{\dfrac{Q + Q_1}{2}} \times \frac{\Delta Q}{\Delta P}$$

$$= \frac{P + P_1}{Q + Q_1} \times \frac{\Delta Q}{\Delta P}$$

- Arc elasticity is a measure of *average* elasticity. In Figure 2.4 it is the elasticity at the mid-point of the chord connecting the two points (M and N) on the demand curve corresponding to the initial and final price levels.
- Arc elasticity is only an approximation to the true elasticity over a particular segment (MN) of the demand curve. The greater the curvature of the segment of the demand curve being measured, the less accurate will this approximation of the true elasticity be.

Point elasticity of demand

- As is also shown in Figure 2.4, this is a measure of the price elasticity of demand *at a single point* (i.e. a single price and quantity situation) on a demand curve. Again it is a particularly useful measure when the demand curve is not a straight line.
- *Point elasticity of demand* involves finding the slope $(-)\Delta Q/\Delta P$ of the straight line that just touches the demand curve at that point (i.e. the slope of the tangent MT) as given by the angle formed at point M in Figure 2.4.

    Point elasticity of demand $= (P/Q) \times$ slope of tangent at point M

The following 'Test yourself' will help to check your understanding of PED and its measurement.

Test yourself

Q1. Look carefully at the data in the table.

Own-price elasticities of demand for tickets at football clubs in England

Club	Price elasticity of demand
Chelsea	−0.40
Everton	−0.97

Club	Price elasticity of demand
Manchester United	−0.12
Newcastle	−0.39
Nottingham Forest	−0.57
Norwich City	−1.15
Stoke City	−1.20
Tottenham Hotspur	−0.44

Briefly comment on what the data suggests and on any policy implications for the clubs involved.

Q2. Using the linear demand curve of Figure 2.3(b), calculate the PED when $P = 12$ and when $P = 4$.

Q3. Suppose that demand for widgets is non-linear and that in 2012, at a price of £4 per widget, the demand was 10 million widgets per annum. In 2013 let us suppose that the price falls to £2 and, other things being equal, the demand expands to 13 million widgets per annum.

    (a) Calculate the *arc elasticity of demand* over the price range £2 to £4.

    (b) Calculate the *point elasticity of demand* at the price of £2, assuming the slope of the tangent to the demand curve at this price is (−)0.5.

    (c) Compare the two types of elasticity.

Other elasticities of demand

Here we consider a number of other elasticities which can have important impacts on the demand for a product and therefore the revenue of the firm.

Key definitions

Cross-elasticity of demand (CED)

Cross-elasticity of demand (CED) is the responsiveness of demand for a product to changes in the price of some other product.

$$CED = \frac{\%\ \text{change in quantity demanded of X}}{\%\ \text{change in price of Y}}$$

The CED for *substitutes in consumption* is positive $(-/-)$. The CED for *complements in consumption* is negative $(+/-)$. CED involves shifts in demand.

Income elasticity of demand (IED)

Income elasticity of demand (IED) is the responsiveness of demand for a product to changes in consumer (national) income. Here, as for CED, we are considering shifts in the demand curve of the product.

$$IED = \frac{\%\ \text{change in quantity demanded of X}}{\%\ \text{change in real income}}$$

Advertising elasticity of demand (AED)

Advertising elasticity of demand (AED) is a measure of the responsiveness of demand for product X to a change in advertising expenditure on the product. The intention of most forms of advertising is to reinforce the attachment of existing consumers to the product and to attract new consumers. In this latter case the advertising is seeking to change consumer tastes in favour of the product, i.e. shift the demand curve to the right with more of X bought at any given price.

$$AED = \frac{\%\ \text{change in quantity demanded of X}}{\%\ \text{change in advertising expenditure on X}}$$

Cross-elasticity of demand (CED)

Cross-elasticity of demand (CED) is a measure of the responsiveness of demand for a product (X) to a change in price of *some other product* (Y). It involves shifts in a demand curve (increase/decrease) for X rather than movements along a demand curve (expansion/contraction).

The CED for product X is given by the equation:

$$CED = \frac{\%\ \text{change in quantity demanded of X}}{\%\ \text{change in the price of Y}}$$

- The *sign* of CED will indicate the direction of the shift in demand for X (D_X) in response to a change in the price of Y (P_Y), which in turn will depend upon the relationship in consumption between products X and Y.

(i) Where X and Y are **substitutes in consumption**, a fall in P_Y will result in an expansion of demand for Y and a decrease in demand for X, i.e. a leftward shift in D_X as some consumers switch to the now relatively cheaper substitute for X. Here the sign of CED will be positive $(-/- = +)$.

(ii) Where X and Y are **complements in consumption**, a fall in P_Y will result in an expansion of demand for Y and an increase in demand for X, i.e. a rightward shift in D_X as consumers require more of X to complement their extra purchases of Y. Here the sign of CED will be negative $(+/- = -)$.

Substitutes and complements in consumption were defined in the previous chapter **(page 5).**

● The *magnitude* of the shift in D_X will depend upon how close X and Y are as substitutes or complements in consumption. The closer the two products are as substitutes or complements, the greater will be the numerical value of cross-elasticity of demand. In other words, a given fall in price of Y will cause a larger shift to the left of D_X for close substitutes, and a larger shift to the right of D_X for close complements.

 Assessment advice

The sign and size of CED will be useful to the business in deciding whether or not to react to changes in the pricing policy of a rival. The sign and size of CED is also relevant to the use of game theory **(Chapter 7, page 179).**

Income elasticity of demand (IED)

Income elasticity of demand (IED) is a measure of the responsiveness of demand for a product to a change in income (household income or national income). Usually we use real income rather than nominal income for this measurement. IED involves shifts in a demand curve (increase/decrease) rather than movements along a demand curve (expansion/contraction).

The IED for product X is given by the equation:

$$IED = \frac{\% \text{ change in quantity demanded of X}}{\% \text{ change in income}}$$

● For a *normal product* the sign of IED will be positive: for example, a rise in income increases demand for X, i.e. a rightward shift in D_X, with more of X demanded at any given price.

● For an *inferior product* the sign will be negative over certain ranges of income: for example, a rise in income beyond a certain 'threshold' level may decrease demand for X as consumers use some of the higher income to switch away from the relatively cheap but poor-quality product X to a more expensive, better-quality substitute.

As a broad rule of thumb, some people regard income elasticity of demand as useful in classifying products into 'luxury' and 'necessity' groupings. A product is often considered a luxury if IED > 1 and a necessity if IED is significantly <1.

Factors affecting IED

Factors affecting the numerical value of IED for a commodity include the following:

1 *The nature of the need satisfied by the commodity.* For some basic needs, e.g. 'Engel's law' concerning certain types of foodstuffs, the proportion of household income spent on products satisfying these needs falls as income increases. For other needs, the proportion of household income spent on products satisfying these needs rises as income increases, e.g. services such as healthcare and education.
2 *The time period.* The longer the time period, the more likely it is that consumer expenditure patterns will have adjusted to a change in income, implying a higher IED.
3 *The initial level of national income.* At low levels of national income, certain products will still be largely unattainable for the majority of the population. Changes in national income around such a low level will therefore have little effect on the demand for these products, implying a lower IED.

Test yourself

Q4. Look at the data in Table 2.3 which refers to household expenditure in the UK in 2011 on various goods and service products.

Table 2.3 Percentage of UK average weekly expenditure on various products

Product	Weekly expenditure (£)	Percentage of average weekly expenditure (%)
Telephone	10.80	2.4
Electricity	12.20	2.2
Gas	9.70	2.1
Water	6.50	1.4

Product	Weekly expenditure (£)	Percentage of average weekly expenditure (%)
TV and Internet	5.90	1.3
Chocolate	2.20	0.5
Postal services	0.40	0.1

Using the data, suggest which products you would expect to have the highest and lowest income elasticity of demand. Explain your reasoning.

Advertising elasticity of demand (AED)

Advertising elasticity of demand (AED) is a measure of the responsiveness of demand for product X to a change in advertising expenditure on the product. The intention of most forms of advertising is to reinforce the attachment of existing consumers to the product and to attract new consumers. In this latter case the advertising is seeking to change consumer tastes in favour of the product, i.e. shift the demand curve to the right with more of X bought at any given price.

$$AED = \frac{\% \text{ change in quantity demanded of } X}{\% \text{ change in advertising expenditure on } X}$$

Table 2.4 shows the percentage of total advertising expenditure in the UK on various media outlets. Internet advertising has now overtaken both TV and press advertising and, with Direct Mail, is the fastest growing media outlet for advertising.

A firm may also be interested in *cross-advertising elasticity,* which measures the responsiveness of demand for product X to a change in advertising expenditure on some other product Y. If X and Y are substitutes in consumption and extra advertising on the rival Y decreases demand for X substantially, then some counter-strategy by X to restore its fortunes (i.e. shift its demand curve to the right) might be of high priority, perhaps including an aggressive advertising campaign of its own.

Table 2.4 Advertising expenditure in 2012

Advertising source	Percentage of total advertising expenditure	Percentage change in advertising expenditure, 2011–12
Internet	29.7%	+8.9%
TV	25.8%	+2.0%
Press	24.5%	−0.9%
Direct Mail	10.7%	+18.4%
Outdoor	5.5%	+5.0%
Radio	2.7%	+3.5%
Cinema	1.1%	+3.43%

Test yourself

Match each *lettered* term to its correct *numbered* description.

Q5. Terms

   (a) Price elasticity of demand

   (b) Cross-elasticity of demand

   (c) Income elasticity of demand

   (d) Inferior good (product)

   (e) Unit elastic demand

Descriptions

   (1) Responsiveness of demand for a product to changes in consumer income

   (2) Rise in real income over certain ranges may cause demand to shift to the left

   (3) A given percentage change in the own price of the product leads to the same percentage change (in the opposite direction) in the quantity demanded

   (4) Responsiveness of demand for a product to changes in its own price

   (5) Responsiveness of demand for a product to changes in the price of some other product

Q6. Terms

    (a) Negative cross-elasticity of demand

    (b) Positive cross-elasticity of demand

    (c) Unit elastic demand

    (d) Relatively elastic demand

    (e) Relatively inelastic demand

Descriptions

    (1) Any change in price leaves total revenue unchanged

    (2) Two products are substitutes in consumption

    (3) A fall in price will reduce total revenue

    (4) Two products are complements in consumption

    (5) A fall in price will raise total revenue

Q7. Terms

    (a) Point elasticity of demand

    (b) Arc elasticity of demand

    (c) Engel's Law

    (d) Perfectly elastic demand

    (e) Perfectly inelastic demand

Descriptions

    (1) An infinitely small change in price will lead to an infinitely large change in quantity demanded

    (2) It is predicted that the proportion of income spent on food declines as income rises

    (3) A measure of average elasticity over a range of the demand curve

    (4) There will be no change in quantity demanded whatever the change in price

    (5) A measure of elasticity of demand which involves an infinitely small change from some initial price

The next 'Examples & evidence' uses transport to review the various elasticities covered in this chapter.

Examples & evidence

Transport and elasticities of demand

Evidence from the developed economies suggests that for every 10% increase in real fuel prices, the demand for fuel will fall by around 6%. This consumer response to higher fuel prices may take several years to fully work through.

The demand for car ownership and for travel (and therefore the derived demand for fuel) is also closely related to the level of household income. Again, studies suggest that for every 10% increase in real income the demand for fuel eventually increases by around 12% within two years of the rise in real income.

Of course, the demand for fuel depends not only on its own price and the level of real household income, but also on other factors. For example, whereas the real cost of motoring per kilometre travelled (fuel costs, car purchase, repairs, road tax, etc.) has barely changed over the past 20 years (e.g. more efficient engines result in more kilometres per litre of petrol), the real costs of rail and bus per kilometre travelled have risen by more than 30% and 35% respectively over the same 20-year period. Clearly this change in *relative* costs has given a boost to demand for car ownership and travel, and therefore to the demand for fuel.

Many people argue that fuel taxes should rise even higher than they are now, since the private motorist imposes costs on society that he or she does not actually pay for. Extra motorists bring about congestion on our roads and increased journey times, increase the need for more road building with the inevitable loss of countryside, and result in more carbon dioxide (CO_2) and other toxic gas emissions which damage the ozone layer and lead to global warming. In other words, many believe that the *private costs* of the motorist do not fully reflect the *social costs* imposed by the motorist.

Higher taxes on fuel will, as we have seen, raise the price of motoring and discourage road travel. For example, it has been estimated that a 10% increase in the price of fuel will lead to an extra 1% of rail passengers on rail services and an extra 0.5% of bus passengers on bus services.

Of course, demand for some products may actually *decrease* as fuel prices rise. With less car usage there may be a decrease in demand for garage-related services and products.

The *net* effect of a rise in fuel prices will depend on the sign and size of all these elasticities, namely own-price, income and cross-elasticities of demand.

Questions

1. Can you calculate any own-price, income and cross-elasticities of demand from the information given above?
2. Why do some people believe that fuel taxes and fuel prices are too low?
3. Can you suggest why governments might be wary of making the motorist pay the full private and social costs of any journey?

Applying elasticity measures

While the various measures of elasticity of demand play a key role in business decision making and business outcomes, it may be useful to introduce a note of caution when using such estimates.

Identification problems

Essentially the identification problem results from the fact that our 'other things being equal' assumption rarely applies in practice. This makes it difficult to be sure that our PED measure really does represent a movement along the demand curve for the product.

Figure 2.5 usefully illustrates this identification problem, where we have four observations E_1 to E_4 on a scatter diagram relating price to quantity. If only the supply curve had been shifting from S_1 to S_4, then these points would indeed trace out the true demand curve. If, however, both demand and supply curves had been shifting, then the line through (or nearest to) these points would give an inaccurate estimate of demand. In Figure 2.5 we would be underestimating the true own-price elasticity along a given demand curve. The firm might therefore raise price, expecting total revenue to rise (PED < 1), only to find total revenue falling due to the higher than expected responsiveness of demand to price.

Changes in the external environment

Again we are challenging the rather simplistic assumption that 'other things are equal' when moving along the demand curve. For example, a firm may

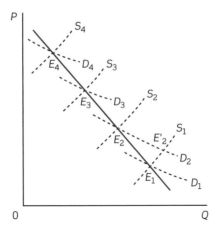

Figure 2.5 Problems in identifying the demand curve when both demand and supply curves are shifting.

Source: Griffiths, A. and Wall, S. (2012) *Intermediate Microeconomics* (2nd ed.) © 2000 Pearson Education. Reproduced with permission.

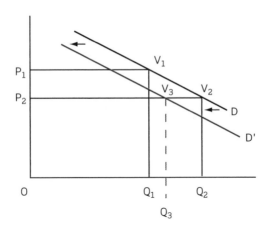

Figure 2.6 Price reduction and decrease in demand.

cut the price of a product for which consumers really have shown them-selves to be price sensitive in the past. However, if that product also has a high income elasticity of demand and we are in a time of 'austerity', with real incomes decreasing sharply, then we might be in the situation shown in Figure 2.6.

Instead of the price cut from P_1 to P_2 resulting in an expansion of demand from Q_1 to Q_2, the leftward shift (decrease) in demand from the real income reduction means the expansion of demand from the price cut is much smaller, from Q_1 to Q_3 only.

Test yourself

Q8. Use Figure 2.6 to explain what has happened to total revenue before and after the price cut.

Q9. Can you think of other changes in the external environment which might also result in the situation shown in Figure 2.6?

Consumer surplus

Key definition

Consumer surplus

Consumer surplus is the benefit to consumers of paying a price for a product which is less than the amount they are willing to pay.

In its most widely used form, **consumer surplus** measures in value terms the difference between the amount of money that a consumer *actually pays* to buy a certain quantity of product X and the amount that he or she would be *willing to pay* for this quantity of X. In Figure 2.7 it is given by the area APC, where quantity X_1 is purchased at price P.

✳ Assessment advice

The idea of consumer surplus is sometimes used when trying to put a value on the economic welfare from using resources in a particular way. It is also closely related to the idea of *producer surplus* **(Chapter 4, page 107)**.

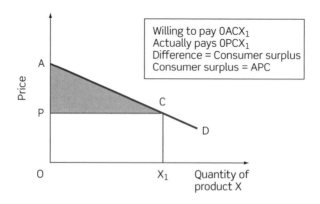

Willing to pay $OACX_1$
Actually pays $OPCX_1$
Difference = Consumer surplus
Consumer surplus = APC

Figure 2.7 Consumer surplus.

Source: Griffiths, A. and Wall, S. (2011) *Economics for Business and Management* (3rd ed.) © 2011 Pearson Education. Reproduced with permission.

Chapter summary – pulling it all together

By the end of this chapter you should be able to:

	Confident ✓	Not confident?
Explain, using diagrams, the relevance of price elasticity of demand (PED) to pricing policy and revenue		Revise pages 30–34
Distinguish between arc elasticity of demand and point elasticity of demand and link these ideas to pricing policy and revenue		Revise pages 34–38
Demonstrate the importance of the sign and size of cross-elasticity of demand (CED) for a product to the demand for that product		Revise pages 38–40
Demonstrate the importance of the sign and size of income elasticity of demand (IED) to forecasting future demand for a product		Revise pages 40–42
Review some of the issues involved in interpreting and applying elasticity measures		Revise pages 45–48
Examine the relevance of consumer surplus to resource allocation		Revise pages 48–49

Now try the **assessment question** at the start of this chapter, using the answer guidelines below.

Answer guidelines

✳ Assessment question

Examine the reasons why price cutting policies by a business sometimes result in a reduction, rather than an increase, in the revenue received.

Approaching the question

The elasticity concept is clearly relevant to this question, especially price elasticity of demand (PED) and its links to revenue. However, PED assumes that we move along the demand curve 'other things being equal'. But other things may not be equal and the demand curve may also be shifting because of changes in the external environment. This brings the other elasticities, such as CED and IED, into play.

Important points to include

- Define PED and apply it to changes in price and revenue. Figure 2.1 will be relevant here.

- Show how, where PED > 1, a fall in price can be expected to increase revenue (area of revenue gain > area of revenue loss). Figure 2.2 will be relevant here.

- Suggest why firms often make errors in estimating PED for their products.

- PED varies along a straight-line (linear) demand curve (Figure 2.3) – may be elastic (PED > 1) over some price ranges, inelastic (PED < 1) over other price ranges.

- PED is even more variable when the demand curve is non-linear, depending on the size and direction of price change (Figure 2.4).

- Problems with identifying 'true' demand curve and therefore in estimating PED (Figure 2.5).

- Changes in the external environment may offset the expected effect on demand of any price fall, thereby resulting in little or no extra demand and reducing, rather than increasing, total revenue (Figure 2.6):

  - price falls but decline in real income for product with high and positive IED;

  - price falls but rivals retaliate by cutting their prices too, which will be particularly important for products with a high and positive CED.

- Examples/case studies will also help here.

Make your answer stand out

As already indicated above, the effective use of diagrams will gain you the highest marks, especially if you use them in the text of your answer.

Read to impress

Here are some books, articles and other sources that you can use to develop your answers on this topic area.

Books

Griffiths, A. and Wall, S. (2011) *Economics for Business and Management,* 3rd edition, Chapter 2, Pearson Education.

Parkin, M., Powell, M. and Matthews, K. (2012) *Economics,* 8th edition, Chapter 4, Addison Wesley.

Sloman, J. and Garratt, D. (2010) *Essentials of Economics,* 5th edition, Chapter 3, FT/Prentice Hall.

Sloman, J., Wride, A. and Garratt, D. (2012) *Economics,* 8th edition, Chapter 2, Pearson Education.

Journals and periodicals

The following are useful sources of articles and data on many aspects relevant to this and other topics:

Business Review, Philip Allan (quarterly)
Economic Review, Philip Allan (quarterly)
Economics Today, Anforme (quarterly)
Harvard Business Review (monthly)
The Economist (weekly)

Newspapers

Newspapers are important sources of up-to-date information, examples and data. Below are some of the main UK newspaper sources, many of which have websites with search facilities to identify specific topics and articles:

The Guardian
The Times
The Financial Times
The Independent
The Telegraph

Companion website

Go to the companion website at **www.pearsoned.co.uk/econexpress** to find more revision support online for this topic area.

Notes

3 Consumer behaviour

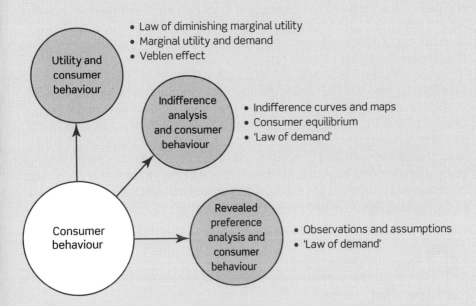

- Law of diminishing marginal utility
- Marginal utility and demand
- Veblen effect

Utility and consumer behaviour

Indifference analysis and consumer behaviour
- Indifference curves and maps
- Consumer equilibrium
- 'Law of demand'

Consumer behaviour

Revealed preference analysis and consumer behaviour
- Observations and assumptions
- 'Law of demand'

A printable version of this topic map is available from **www.pearsoned.co.uk/econexpress**

Introduction

In 2012 smart phones, apps and dating agency fees were added to the official UK shopping basket when calculating price indices, reflecting the increasing importance of the digital economy to consumer spending. Being aware of changing consumer tastes over time will be a key part of forecasting future demand for a wide range of businesses involved in the supply chain of household products. Winners and losers in such forecasts become apparent each year when the Office for National Statistics (ONS) reports on changes in the UK 'shopping basket'. The ONS monitors the most popular household products bought each year with some 650 goods and services identified as being purchased by a typical household over the last 12 months. Each year some new products appear and some existing products are dropped.

In 2011 cereal bars, allergy tablets, blu-ray players, lip gloss and liquid soap appeared for the first time in the shopping basket, but lipstick, bars of soap, pitta bread, small fruit drink cartons and various other products disappeared from the 'basket'. Vending machines for cigarettes and prime cuts of meat were also removed from the shopping basket as cigarette smoking is declining and oven-ready prepared meats become more popular. Businesses which were able to forecast such shifts in consumer behaviour *before* they happened will have been much better placed to benefit from these shifts in consumer tastes than those which did not predict them!

This chapter will help you review the economic principles which underpin such changes in consumer behaviour. We see that theories involving consumers seeking to maximise utility (satisfaction) can help explain the so-called 'law of demand', whereby we expect more of a product to be purchased as its price falls. The concepts of indifference curves and budget lines are used in developing such theories, although we note that the same 'law of demand' can also be developed by observations of how consumers actually behave, in this case using the so-called 'revealed preference' approach.

 Revision checklist

What you need to know:

- ❑ How the so-called *'law of demand'* can be derived from the assumption that consumers seek to maximise utility.
- ❑ How you can use indifference curves and budget lines in analysing consumer behaviour, especially as regards the 'substitution effect' and 'income effect' following a price change.

- ❑ How the 'law of demand' can also be derived from observations of actual consumer behaviour, using revealed preference analysis.
- ❑ Circumstances under which the 'law of demand' can be violated, as in the case of the so-called 'Veblen effect'.

Assessment advice

Use diagrams

You can improve your analysis and gain higher marks in this topic by using diagrams involving indifference curves and budget lines. These can be used to identify the so-called 'income effect' and 'substitution effect' of a price change and to show why the 'law of demand' will normally apply. Diagrams also play a key role when using revealed preference analysis.

Use consistent terminology

Terms such as expansion and contraction of demand **(encountered in Chapters 1 and 2)** for movements along a demand curve will be important here, as will terms such as normal and inferior products. New terms will also be encountered, such as substitution and income effects, cardinal and ordinal utility, and these should be carefully defined and consistently applied.

Use empirical evidence

The theoretical analysis of consumer behaviour can be taken further by the use of appropriate examples and case studies.

Assessment question

Can you answer this essay-type question? Guidelines on answering the question are presented at the end of this chapter.

Use *either* indifference curve analysis *or* revealed preference analysis to explain the so-called 'law of demand'.

Utility and consumer behaviour

Utility refers to the satisfaction consumers derive from the consumption of goods and services (products). Utility is important because only those products which possess utility, i.e. which provide satisfaction, will be demanded. Of course, the amount of utility or satisfaction gained from consuming a product is different for different people. To begin, we simplify the situation by assuming that utility can be measured in 'units of satisfaction' as in Table 3.1.

Total and marginal utility

Key definitions

Total utility
Total utility is the overall satisfaction from consuming a given amount of a product.

Marginal utility
Marginal utility is the change in satisfaction from consuming an extra unit of the product.

Table 3.1 An individual's utility schedule.

Drinks consumed	Total utility (units of satisfaction)	Marginal utility (units of satisfaction)
0	0	
1	27	27
2	39	12
3	47	8
4	52	5
5	55	3
6	57	2
7	58	1
8	58	0
9	56	−2

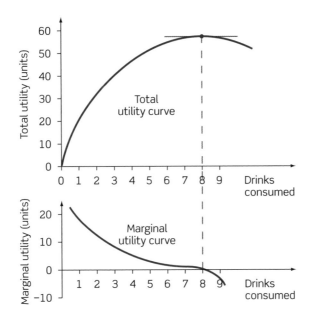

Figure 3.1 Total and marginal utility curves.
Source: Griffiths, A. and Wall, S. (2011) *Economics for Business and Management* (3rd ed.) © 2011 Pearson Education. Reproduced with permission.

Table 3.1 shows the different levels of **total utility** and **marginal utility** from consuming different amounts of drink. We can see that total utility rises up to seven drinks consumed, remains unchanged for the eighth drink and actually falls for the ninth drink. However, marginal utility falls continuously after the first drink.

Figure 3.1 plots the data of Table 3.1 on a diagram showing the total utility curve and the marginal utility curve.

Law of diminishing marginal utility

This simply states that as extra units of a product are consumed, each extra (marginal) unit adds less and less to total utility (satisfaction). The second cold drink on a hot day may certainly increase your satisfaction, but *by less* than you gained from consuming the first cold drink! In other words, the marginal utility of the second cold drink was less than that of the first, and so on. Indeed the marginal utility of the eighth drink is zero in Table 3.1 and that of the ninth drink is actually negative (i.e. results in *disutility*).

Utility and the demand curve

The *law of diminishing marginal utility* helps to explain the general relationship between an individual's demand for a good or service and the price of that good or service. If each extra unit of a product gives less satisfaction to an individual than the previous unit, then it follows that the individual will often need the incentive of a lower price if he or she is to be encouraged to consume an extra unit. Because of this it is reasonable to assume that for an individual, as the price of a good or service falls, the amount demanded will rise (expand).

A further assumption about utility is usually made, namely that consumers will choose between the different goods and services they might purchase in order to gain as much utility as possible, i.e. to *maximise total utility*. Of course, the different combinations of goods and services actually available to consumers will depend upon their levels of income and the prices of the goods and services.

Marginal utility and demand

Since consumers aim to maximise their total utility, it follows that consumer equilibrium exists when a consumer cannot increase total utility by reallocating his or her expenditure. This occurs when the following condition is satisfied:

$$\frac{MU_A}{P_A} = \frac{MU_B}{P_B} = \cdots \frac{MU_n}{P_n}$$

In other words, utility is maximised when the ratios of marginal utility and price are equal for all products consumed.

✳ Assessment advice

This marginal utility approach is one approach you can use to explain why the demand curve slopes downwards from left to right, i.e. the so-called 'law of demand' whereby more of a product is demanded as its price falls.

When this condition is satisfied, it is impossible for the consumer to increase total utility by rearranging his or her purchases, because the last pound spent on each product yields the same addition to total utility in all cases. This must maximise total utility because, for example, if the last pound spent on product B yielded more utility than the last pound spent on product A, then the consumer could increase total utility by buying more of B and less of A. This is impossible when the ratios of marginal utility and price are equal (see Table 3.2).

It is assumed that only two products, A which costs £2 per unit and B which costs £4 per unit, are available, and that the consumer has a total budget of £18.

Table 3.2 Marginal utility and demand.

Quantity consumed	Product A			Product B		
	Price (£)	Total utility	Marginal utility	Price (£)	Total utility	Marginal utility
1	2	15	15	4	25	25
2	2	27	12	4	48	23
3	2	37	10	4	68	20
4	2	46	9	4	86	18
5	2	53	7	4	102	16
6	2	56	3	4	116	14
7	2	57	1	4	128	12
8	2	55	-2	4	139	11

Given the consumer's budget, the existing prices and the levels of utility available from consumption, equilibrium is achieved when 3 units of product A and 3 units of product B are purchased.

$$\frac{MU_A}{P_A} = \frac{MU_B}{P_B} \text{ with } \frac{10}{2} = \frac{20}{4}$$

With a budget of £18 it is impossible to achieve a higher level of utility.

Test yourself

Q1. Use Table 3.2 to explain why 2 units of product A and 5 units of product B, with a total budget of £18, does not maximise utility.

Q2. Suppose the price of product B now falls from £4 to £2 per unit, other things equal. Use the equilibrium condition to show that the demand for B must expand if utility is to be a maximum.

So far we have assumed that a fall in price will lead to an expansion of demand, and vice versa; in other words, the demand curve slopes downwards from left to right. Later in this chapter we use indifference curves to explain why this so-called 'law of demand' generally applies to most products.

Veblen effect

However, it is worth noting at this point that there has long been a recognition that in some circumstances the demand curve might actually slope upwards from left to right. In other words, a rise in price results in an expansion of demand, and a fall in price results in a contraction of demand. For example, Thorstein Veblen, in his book *Theory of the Leisure Class* in 1899, pointed out that the key characteristic of some products is that they are ostentatious ('showy') and intended to impress. For such 'conspicuous consumption products', the satisfaction derived from their consumption derives largely from the effect this has on other people rather than from any inherent utility in the product itself. This is known as the **'Veblen effect'**.

Key definition

'Veblen effect'

The psychological association of price with quality by consumers, with a fall in price taken to imply a reduction in quality and therefore greater reluctance to purchase.

Instead of an expansion of demand, the fall in price may therefore result in a contraction of demand, giving an upward-sloping demand curve. The 'Veblen effect' is more likely to operate for high- priced products in 'prestige' markets where accurate information on the true quality of these products is highly imperfect.

Examples & evidence

University fees and prestige pricing

Here price is itself associated with *quality* by users of the product. In situations where the information available to users is imperfect, price is often used as a proxy variable for quality. Student and parent assessment of educational courses characterised by differential top-up fees is an obvious candidate for such a 'Veblen effect', reinforced by the fact that most of the 'older' universities in the UK (widely perceived by the general public to be of the highest quality) are charging the full £9,000 annual tuition fee for most of their courses.

A major cross-country study into higher education by IDP Education Australia in association with the British Council strongly supported the existence of this Veblen effect as regards international student demand for higher education. Senior researcher Anthony Bohm commented: 'Students cannot make an informed choice about the exact quality of comparable products, so they use price as a proxy for understanding the value they will get out of an international programme.'

Questions

1. Suppose you were responsible for setting the top-up fees to be charged for the course you are studying. Use the ideas in the case study to suggest how you might go about making your decision.

2. Can you explain how the above might provide some support for an upward-sloping demand curve for higher education?

Indifference analysis and consumer behaviour

So far we have assumed that we can actually measure satisfaction (**cardinal utility**). In practice, many observers believe that there is no such thing as a 'unit of satisfaction (utility)' that is common to everybody, so that utility cannot be measured. If that is the case then we need a different approach to consumer behaviour. An alternative approach does exist which can also explain the downward-sloping demand curve but using the much 'weaker' and more realistic assumption that consumers need only be able to *order* their preferences between different combinations (bundles) of products, preferring some bundles to other alternative bundles (**ordinal utility**). This is the essential feature of indifference curve analysis.

Key definitions

Cardinal utility

Cardinal utility can be measured, e.g. in 'utiles' of utility.

Ordinal utility

Ordinal utility cannot be measured, though different combinations of products can be ranked in order as regards the utility they provide for an individual.

Indifference curves and maps

Indifference curves

Indifference curves are lines representing different combinations (bundles) of products that yield a constant level of utility or satisfaction to the consumer. The consumer is therefore indifferent to the various consumption possibilities denoted by the line.

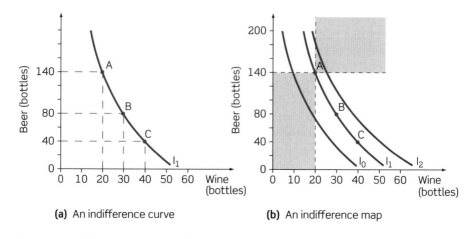

(a) An indifference curve   **(b)** An indifference map

Figure 3.2 Indifference curves and maps.
Source: Griffiths, A. and Wall, S. (2011) *Economics for Business and Management* (3rd ed.) © 2011 Pearson Education. Reproduced with permission.

Figure 3.2(a) can be used to illustrate the properties of an indifference curve.

In addition to diminishing marginal utility, suppose our consumer is indifferent between three different combinations of bottles of wine and beer, namely A (20 wine, 140 beer), B (30 wine, 80 beer) and C (40 wine, 40 beer). In other words, these three combinations of wine and beer yield the same level of utility to the consumer as in fact do all the combinations of wine and beer on the curve I_1. We call this curve connecting all the combinations (bundles) of products that yield a constant level of utility an indifference curve.

Indifference maps

As we can see from Figure 3.2(b), indifference maps show *all* the indifference curves that rank the preferences of our consumer for either of the two products. Indifference maps are drawn on the basis of three key assumptions:

1 *Non-satiation*. The consumer is not totally satisfied (satiated) with the amounts of the products already obtained, but prefers to have more of either. In other words, 'a good is a good', with any extra units of either product (good or service) adding some positive amount to total utility.
2 *Transitivity*. Consumers are consistent in their ranking of various consumption bundles.
3 *Diminishing marginal rate of substitution between products*. This assumption is related to our earlier idea of 'diminishing marginal utility'. However, this time it refers to the fact that as more of any one product (X) is consumed, the consumer will be willing to sacrifice progressively less of some other product (Y) for utility to remain unchanged.

Let us now examine the relevance of these assumptions to our indifference map.

1 The first assumption of *non-satiation* implies that more of one product and no less of some other product is a preferred position, so that indifference curves above and to the right must represent higher levels of utility/satisfaction. In Figure 3.2(b) the indifference curve I_2 includes consumption bundles in the shaded box above and to the right of consumption bundle A on indifference curve I_1. These shaded consumption bundles all include having more beer and no less wine, or more wine and no less beer, or more beer and more wine than A, and are therefore preferred consumption bundles to A. It follows that all the consumption bundles on I_2 that go through this shaded area must correspond to a higher level of satisfaction than the consumption bundles on I_1.

2 The second assumption, that consumers are *consistent* in their preference orderings, implies that it is impossible for separate indifference curves to intersect one another. For example, suppose we have the following consumer ranking of three bundles of products A, B and C:

A > B
B > C

Then, via consistent consumer behaviour we can say that

A > C

If this assumption holds true, then indifference curves could not intersect. However, if consumer preferences are *not* consistent, then indifference curves can intersect, as they do in Figure 3.3.

In Figure 3.3:

A > B (more of Y, same X)
A = C (on same indifference curve)
B = D (on same indifference curve)
C > D (via consistency assumption)
But D > C (more of Y, same X)!

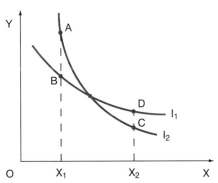

Figure 3.3 Indifference curves intersect if preferences not consistent.

Source: Griffiths, A. and Wall, S. (2011) *Economics for Business and Management* (3rd ed.) © 2011 Pearson Education. Reproduced with permission.

Clearly, when indifference curves intersect this indicates that consumers are *not* exercising consistency in their ranking of different bundles of product.

3 The third assumption of *diminishing marginal rate of substitution* between the products implies that we draw indifference curves convex to (bowed towards) the origin. In other words, the more of one product you are consuming, progressively less of the other product you are willing to give up in order to consume an extra unit of that product. This means that the slope of an indifference curve diminishes as we move from left to right along its entire length.

Consumer equilibrium

We can use indifference curve analysis to predict the downward-sloping demand curve, just as we used marginal utility analysis previously. However, before doing this we must become familiar with the idea of the *budget line* of the consumer.

Budget line

In much of the analysis involving indifference curves we assume that consumers wish to maximise utility subject to a number of constraints, such as the level of household income and the prices of the products bought. These particular constraints can be represented by the budget line showing the various combinations of two products, X and Y, which can be purchased if the whole household income is spent on these products.

● The *slope* of the budget line will depend upon the relative prices of the two products.

● The *position* of the budget line will depend on the level of household income.

Figure 3.4 usefully illustrates these points.

Let us suppose the following:

Household income = £200

Price of product X (P_x) = £20

Price of product Y (P_y) = £25

In Figure 3.4(a), if all the income is spent on X, then we are at point B (10X, 0Y); if all the income is spent on Y then we are at point A (0X, 8Y). The line AB is therefore the budget line and represents the various combinations of X and Y that could be purchased if the *whole* household income was spent on these products.

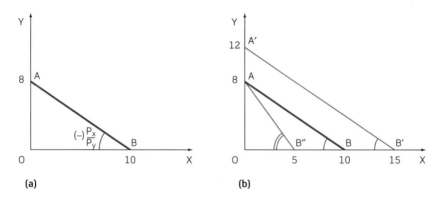

Figure 3.4 The budget line. Slope depends on relative prices; position depends on household income.

Source: Griffiths, A. and Wall, S. (2011) *Economics for Business and Management* (3rd ed.) © 2011 Pearson Education. Reproduced with permission.

The *slope* of this budget line depends on the relative price ratio:

$$\text{Slope} = (-)\frac{8}{10} = (-)\frac{20}{25} \ i.e. (-)\frac{P_x}{P_y}$$

The *position* of this budget line depends on the level of household income.

We can use Figure 3.4(b) to make this last point clear:

- A'B' shows what happens to the budget line AB if there is a 50% increase in household income from £200 to £300. Notice that a rise in household income leads to a *parallel* outward shift in the budget line. The new and old budget lines have the same slope because the price ratio is unchanged.

- AB'' shows what happens to the budget line AB if the household income remains at the original £200 but the price of product X (P_x) rises from £20 to £40 with the price of the product Y (P_y) unchanged at £25. Notice that a change in the relative price ratio means that the slope of the new budget line is different from that of the old budget line. In this case the slope is steeper, since only five units of X can now be purchased from an income of £200 if its price rises from £20 to £40, whilst it is still possible to purchase eight units of Y at its unchanged price of £25. Notice that a rise in the price of product X leads to the budget line pivoting inwards around point A.

Consumer equilibrium

We assume that the consumer seeks the maximum utility (highest indifference curve) subject to the constraints imposed on him or her. These constraints involve the level of household income (the *position* of the budget line) and the relative prices of the products (the *slope* of the budget line).

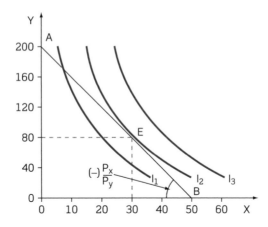

Figure 3.5 Consumer equilibrium: reaching the highest indifference curve attainable, at point E.

Source: Griffiths, A. and Wall, S. (2011) *Economics for Business and Management* (3rd ed.) © 2011 Pearson Education. Reproduced with permission.

Figure 3.5 brings together our work on indifference curves and budget lines to identify the particular consumption bundle that corresponds to maximum consumer utility subject to these constraints.

Given the position of the budget line AB in Figure 3.5 and its slope $(-)P_x/P_y$, the highest indifference curve the consumer can reach is I_2 at point E. By consuming 30 units of X and 80 units of Y, the consumer has maximised utility subject to the constraints he or she faces. I_3 is, of course, an indifference curve yielding still higher satisfaction, but is unattainable under present circumstances.

Notice that this consumption bundle of 30X and 80Y, which corresponds to 'consumer equilibrium', represents a situation of *tangency* between the budget line and the highest attainable indifference curve. In other words, consumer utility is maximised when the slope of an indifference curve is exactly equal to the slope of the budget line (i.e. the price ratio).

Examples & evidence

Technology and consumer behaviour

In many types of face-to-face retailing, it pays to size up your customer and tailor your offering accordingly. In a 2006 study of Fulton fish market in New York, Kathryn Graddy of Oxford University found that dealers regularly charged Asian buyers less than whites because the Asian buyers had proved, over time, more willing to reject high prices and readier to band together to boycott dealers who ripped them off.

The Internet, by allowing anonymous browsing and rapid price comparison, was supposed to mean low, and equal, prices for all. Now, however, online retailers are being offered software that helps them detect shoppers who can afford to pay more or are in a hurry to buy, so as to present pricier options to them or simply charge more for the same stuff.

Source: Adapted from *The Economist*, 30 June 2012, p. 75, 'How deep are your pockets?'.

Question

1. How might these Internet-related developments affect consumer behaviour and the consumer equilibrium shown in Figure 3.5?

Price–consumption line

Figure 3.6 uses this idea of 'consumer equilibrium' to derive the so-called *price–consumption line*, showing tangency points between budget lines with different prices of product X (P_x) and the highest attainable indifference curves.

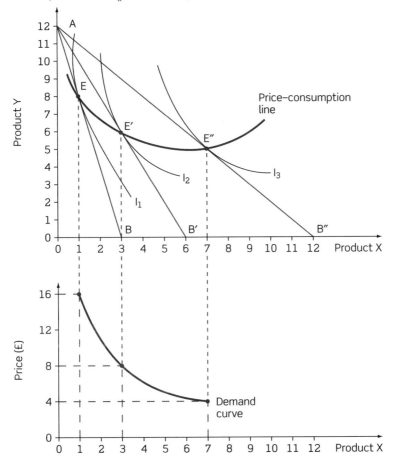

Figure 3.6 The price–consumption line and the individual demand curve.

Source: Griffiths, A. and Wall, S. (2011) *Economics for Business and Management* (3rd ed.) © 2011 Pearson Education. Reproduced with permission.

Suppose our household has a weekly income of £48, with the initial price of X (P_x) at £16 and the price of Y (P_y) at £4. This gives us the initial budget line AB and the equilibrium point at E for maximum utility of I_1. At P_x = £16, one unit of good X is demanded. Suppose now that P_x falls first to £8 and then to £4, other things being equal (i.e. household income and P_y). We can represent this by pivoting the budget line to AB' (P_x = £8) and AB'' (P_x = £4) respectively. This gives us new equilibrium points of E', and E'' where the consumer reaches the highest attainable indifference curves of I_2 and I_3 respectively.

From this, we can derive the individual demand curve in the bottom part of Figure 3.6. So at P_x = £16 we have one unit of X demanded, at P_x = £8 we have three units of X demanded, and at P_x = £4 we have seven units of X demanded.

As we shall see, the demand curve for normal commodities will always have a negative slope, denoting the law of demand, namely that the quantity demanded rises (expands) as price falls.

'Law of demand'

A reduction in the price of X has, in our analysis, resulted in an overall rise in the quantity demanded of good X, as for instance in the move from E to E' along the price–consumption line in Figure 3.6 and along the corresponding demand curve. However, this rise in the quantity demanded is the **total price effect** which may be split into two separate parts, the **substitution effect** and the **income effect**. We now examine each part in turn (see Figure 3.7).

- *Substitution effect.* This refers to the extra purchase of product X now that it is, after the price fall, relatively cheaper than other substitutes in consumption.

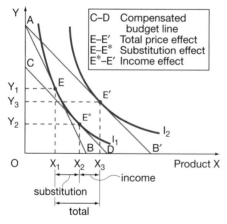
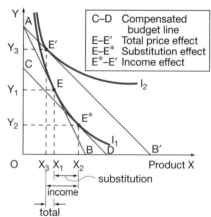

(a) Law of demand supported – i.e. downward sloping demand curve

(b) Law of demand violated – i.e. upward sloping demand curve

Figure 3.7 Income and substitution effects.

Source: Griffiths, A. and Wall, S. (2011) *Economics for Business and Management* (3rd ed.) © 2011 Pearson Education. Reproduced with permission.

- *Income effect.* This refers to the rise in real income (purchasing power) now that the price of one product is lower within the bundle of products purchased by the consumer. This extra real income can potentially be used to buy more of all products, including X.

For analytical purposes it is helpful to deal separately with each effect and we do this by making use of the '**compensated budget line**'. In Figure 3.7 the fall in P_x has caused the budget line to pivot from AB to AB′, representing the new price ratio between X and Y.

The total price effect is shown in the movement from E to E′, i.e. the rise in quantity demanded of X from X_1 to X_3. To derive the compensated budget line we reduce the consumer's real income but retain the new price ratio after the fall in P_x so that the consumer is still only able to achieve the same level of utility as before. We show this by shifting the budget line AB′ inwards and parallel to itself (thereby retaining the new price ratio) until it is a tangent to the original indifference curve I_1. This occurs with the budget line CD at point E*.

Key definitions

Substitution effect

The extra purchase of a product X now that it is, after the price fall, relatively cheaper than other substitutes in consumption is called the substitution effect.

Income effect

The rise in real income (purchasing power) now that the price of one product is lower within the bundle of products purchased by the consumer is called the income effect.

Total price effect

The total price effect is the sum of the substitution effect and the income effect.

Compensated budget line

This is the budget line which reflects reducing the consumer's real income, but retaining the new price ratio after the fall in P_x so that the consumer is only able to achieve the same level of utility as before the price fall.

We can now say that the movement from E to E* is the pure *substitution effect*, i.e. the extra amount $(X_2 - X_1)$ of X purchased solely as a result of X being cheaper relative to Y, the income effect having been compensated, i.e. eliminated.

If we now allow the income effect to be restored, the budget line returns to AB' moving outwards and parallel to CD. We can now say that the movement from E* to E' is the *income effect*. In this case the income effect is positive ($X_3 - X_2 > 0$), with still more of X being purchased as a result of a rise in the consumer's real income.

We can therefore state that:

| Total price effect $\equiv$ Substitution effect + Income effect |

The income effect can be positive, zero or negative, depending on the type of product in question. For *normal* products, the income effect will be positive; for *inferior* products, the income effect may be negative over certain ranges of income. Inferior products are cheap but poor-quality substitutes for other products. As real incomes rise beyond a certain level, consumers will tend to replace such inferior products with more expensive but better-quality alternatives.

We can now explore the situation which will result in the law of demand operating in the conventional manner, i.e. more of X being demanded at a lower price.

- Clearly, when *both* substitution and income effects are positive, as in Figure 3.7(a), the total price effect will be positive and the law of demand holds.
- However, if the product is inferior, then the total price effect may include a positive substitution effect but a negative income effect, and the overall outcome will be in doubt.
- Where the product is so inferior that the income effect is sufficiently negative to more than outweigh the positive substitution effect, the total price effect will be negative. In this case a fall in P_x will result in a fall in the demand for X and the law of demand will be violated, with the demand curve sloping upwards from left to right.

Just such an occurrence is shown in Figure 3.7(b). The negative income effect ($X_2 - X_3$) more than outweighs the positive substitution effect ($X_1 - X_2$). The fall in price of X causes demand to contract from X_1 to X_3.

Inferior products and Giffen products

- **Inferior products.** These are cheap but poor-quality substitutes for other products. As real incomes rise above a certain threshold, consumers tend to substitute the more expensive but better-quality alternatives for them. In other words, inferior products have negative income elasticities of demand over certain ranges of income.
- **Giffen products.** These are named after the nineteenth-century economist Sir Robert Giffen, who claimed to identify an upward-sloping demand curve for certain inferior products. Not all inferior products are Giffen products.

We should now be in a position to explain exactly when an inferior product will become a Giffen product. The total price effect will be negative when the positive substitution effect is more than outweighed by the negative income effect. This has already been illustrated in Figure 3.7(b) so that this inferior product is also a Giffen product. For an inferior product where the degree of inferiority is rather small, however, the negative income effect may be outweighed by the positive substitution effect, so that the law of demand will still hold. In other words, a fall in P_x will still result in a rise (expansion) in the quantity of X demanded and this inferior product is not a Giffen product.

Key definitions

Inferior product

An inferior product is a cheap but poor-quality substitute for another product.

Giffen product

A Giffen product (or Giffen good) is an inferior product which has a positive substitution effect but a negative income effect such that the total price effect is negative.

Table 3.3 summarises the various possibilities.

Table 3.3 Inferior and Giffen products.

Type of product	Substitution effect	Income effect	Total effect
Normal	Positive	Positive	Positive
Inferior (but not Giffen)	Positive	Negative	Positive
Giffen	Positive	Negative	Negative

Examples & evidence

Luxury products sell, despite austerity

Sales of luxury and premium products are still increasing, despite economic recession. Bain, the consultancy company, undertook a major survey of UK shopping behaviour in late 2011 and found that over half the population had purchased at least one luxury product over the past 12 months. The survey of over 6,000 shoppers found that younger people aged 25–44 years made up the biggest market for luxury products, accounting for 40% of all sales but 58% of all luxury sales. Nor were the purchasers necessarily rich – people earning between £25,000 and £50,000 per year accounted for over 30% of all luxury sales.

'Family and friends' were identified as the most important influence on luxury purchases, linked to over 35% of all such purchases, much higher than adverts, whether in the press (8%), via the Internet (7%) or TV (6%), via company websites (5%), catalogues (4%), etc. Shop displays were linked to some 15% of luxury sales.

Premium and luxury brands are seen as appealing to the emotions, providing comfort and reassurance when life is difficult. The report also noted that premium products were increasingly sold through specialist stores. As people 'trade up' to luxury brands they are more likely to shop at specialist stores in order to get better service and advice.

A 2012 report from CLSA forecast that over half of the global growth in luxury products during that year will come from Chinese consumers. China is already the world's largest market for jewellery after the UK, and for gold after India. One-third of the global sales of Prada and Gucci come from China.

Question

1. How might our work on indifference analysis help explain these findings for sales of luxury products?

Revealed preference analysis and consumer behaviour

Revealed preference analysis does not even require the consumer to rank his preferences, as in indifference analysis, or indeed to provide any information at all about his or her tastes. Under this analysis we can establish the 'law of demand' by making three rather straightforward assumptions.

Key definition

Revealed preference

If a consumer chooses some bundle of goods A, in preference to other bundles B, C and D which were also available, then if none of the latter bundles is more expensive than A, we can say that A has been revealed preferred to the other bundles.

Observations and assumptions

To establish that consumers will usually purchase more of a product when its price falls, we require only the following three assumptions using revealed preference analysis:

1 *Non-satiation.* The consumer prefers bundles of commodities that include more of some commodities and no less of any other commodities
2 *Consistency.* The consumer behaves consistently in choosing bundles of commodities. In other words, if bundle A is chosen in preference to bundle B which was also available, then he or she will not subsequently choose B in any other situation where A is also available. Using notation, if A > B then B < A.
3 *Transitivity.* The consumer chooses bundles of commodities in such a way that if bundle A is revealed as preferred to bundle B, and in another situation bundle B is revealed as preferred to bundle C, then we can assume that bundle A will be revealed as preferred to bundle C in any situation where A and C are available. Using notation, if A > B and B > C then A > C.

However, we have not yet introduced the price of commodities into our analysis.

Budget line and revealed preferences

As we have seen, the budget line reflects the income of the consumer and the relative prices of commodities. We can now use the budget line to explore further this idea of revealed preference.

Suppose that the consumer facing the budget constraint given by line B_1 in Figure 3.8(a) chooses bundle A. We can state that A is revealed preferred to bundle C, since C has been rejected in favour of A in a situation where C is no more expensive than A, being on the same budget line. By extension, A is revealed preferred to all other bundles *on* the budget line and to all other bundles *inside* the budget line, since each point inside the budget line represents smaller amounts of both commodities than some point on the budget line. Here the consumer is revealing that bundle A maximises the utility of the consumer under present circumstances.

Suppose now that the relative prices of commodities X and Y change, a fall in P_x and a rise in P_y causing the budget line to pivot to B_2 in Figure 3.8(b). Suppose also that the consumer chooses bundle D in a situation where bundle C was still available. Although bundles A and D are on different budget lines, we can still compare them: namely, we can say that bundle A is revealed preferred to bundle D, using our earlier assumption of transitivity of consumer choices.

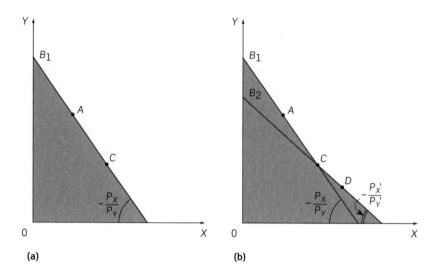

Figure 3.8 Revealed preference approach.
Source: Griffiths, A. and Wall, S. (2012) *Intermediate Microeconomics* (2nd ed.) © 2000 Pearson Education. Reproduced with permission.

'Law of demand'

Here we use revealed preferences to derive the individual consumer demand curve, drawing on the ideas of income and substitution effects mentioned previously.

Assume that the consumer has the budget line AB in Figure 3.9(a) and reveals his preference for the bundle of commodities denoted by point C. Suppose that the price of X now falls so that the consumer faces the budget line AB_1. We now make a compensating variation of consumer income, i.e. we reduce income so that the consumer has just enough income to continue purchasing the original bundle C if he so wishes, at the new set of relative prices (i.e. the compensated budget line is A_1B_2 through C and parallel to AB_1). Since the bundle C is still available, the consumer will not choose any bundle to the left of C on the segment A_1C because this would be inconsistent, given that in the original situation all these bundles along A_1C were revealed less-preferred (inferior) to C. It follows that the consumer will either continue to buy C (i.e. substitution effect = zero) or choose a bundle on the segment CB_2, such as D, which includes a larger quantity of X (i.e. substitution effect = positive). Note here that under revealed preference analysis the substitution effect can be zero or positive, whereas under indifference curve analysis it is always positive, given the convexity of the indifference curves to the origin.

If we now restore income to the consumer, allowing the budget line to return to AB_1, he will choose a bundle of commodities (such as E) somewhere to the right of D, provided that commodity X is normal with a positive income effect. The new revealed equilibrium position (E) includes a larger quantity of X (i.e. X_3)

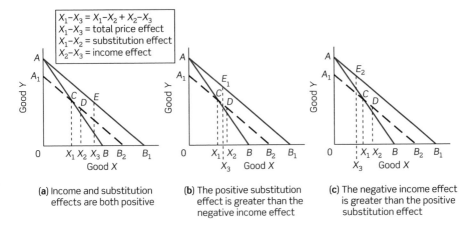

$$X_1-X_3 = X_1-X_2 + X_2-X_3$$
$$X_1-X_3 = \text{total price effect}$$
$$X_1-X_2 = \text{substitution effect}$$
$$X_2-X_3 = \text{income effect}$$

(a) Income and substitution effects are both positive

(b) The positive substitution effect is greater than the negative income effect

(c) The negative income effect is greater than the positive substitution effect

Figure 3.9 Income and substitution effects using revealed preference analysis.

Source: Griffiths, A. and Wall, S. (2012) *Intermediate Microeconomics* (2nd ed.) © 2000 Pearson Education. Reproduced with permission.

resulting from the fall in its price. As with indifference analysis, revealed preference indicates the validity of the law of demand for normal goods; as the price of X falls, more of X is purchased.

As before, the upward-sloping demand curve could be explained for an inferior good in which the negative income effect more than offsets the (zero or positive) substitution effect, which is the case with the Giffen good in Figure 3.9(c). Even though the good is inferior in Figure 3.9(b), the law of demand still applies since the negative income effect is outweighed by the positive substitution effect.

Chapter summary – pulling it all together

By the end of this chapter you should be able to:

	Confident ✓	Not confident?
Explain how the so-called 'law of demand' can be derived from the assumption that consumers seek to maximise utility		Revise pages 56–61
Demonstrate how you can use indifference curves and budget lines in analysing consumer behaviour, especially as regards the 'substitution' and 'income effects' following a price change		Revise pages 61–72

	Confident ✓	Not confident?
Explain how the 'law of demand' can also be derived from observations of actual consumer behaviour, using revealed preference analysis		Revise pages 72–75
Assess the circumstances under which the 'law of demand' can be violated, as in the case of the so-called 'Veblen effect'		Revise pages 60–61

Now try the **assessment question** at the start of this chapter, using the answer guidelines below.

Answer guidelines

✳ Assessment question

Use *either* indifference curve analysis *or* revealed preference analysis to explain the so-called 'law of demand'.

Approaching the question

The 'law of demand' is that the demand curve is negatively sloped, with a fall in price resulting in an expansion of demand. This question asks you to explain the theoretical basis for this 'law'. You are asked to use either indifference curve analysis or revealed preference. You therefore cannot use diminishing marginal utility analysis and must choose one of the alternatives. Here we will use indifference curve analysis and try to make use of the diagrams and analysis we covered earlier.

Important points to include

- After defining the concepts of indifference curves and budget lines, use the consumer equilibrium diagram (Figure 3.5) and explain how utility is maximised at point E.

- Show how a price fall will cause the budget line to pivot (Figure 3.6) from AB to AB′′, resulting in the negatively sloped demand curve.

- Now define and demonstrate the substitution effect and the income effect (Figure 3.7(a)) using the idea of the compensated budget line.

- The conditions for the 'law of demand' applying or being violated can be explained:

  – using the income and substitution effects (Figure 3.7(b)) where the product is so inferior that the negative income effect outweighs the positive substitution effect, then the demand curve will be positively sloped and the 'law of demand' violated;

  – using the 'Veblen effect', where price is associated with quality, then the demand may also be positively sloped.

- You might use examples to illustrate when these violations might occur.

Make your answer stand out

As already indicated above, the effective use of diagrams for such a theory-based question will gain you the highest marks. In particular it will help you to draw Figures 3.6 and 3.7 carefully and clearly, and then use them to demonstrate the income and substitution effects. You can then establish that for a normal product for which the 'Veblen effect' does not apply, we can expect the usual downward-sloping demand curve – i.e. the 'law of demand' will apply.

If you can illustrate with examples of normal, inferior and Veblen-related products, this will further strengthen your answer.

Read to impress

Here are some books, articles and other sources that you can use to develop your answers on the topic area.

Books

Griffiths, A. and Wall, S. (2011) *Economics for Business and Management*, 3rd edition, Chapter 2, Pearson Education.

Parkin, M., Powell, M. and Matthews, K. (2012) *Economics*, 8th edition, Chapter 8, Addison Wesley.

Sloman, J. and Garratt, D. (2010) *Essentials of Economics*, 5th edition, Chapter 3, FT/Prentice Hall.

Sloman, J., Wride, A. and Garratt, D. (2012) *Economics*, 8th edition, Pearson Education.

Journals and periodicals

The following are useful sources of articles and data on many aspects relevant to this and other topics:

Business Review, Philip Allan (quarterly)
Economic Review, Philip Allan (quarterly)
Economics Today, Anforme (quarterly)
Harvard Business Review (monthly)
The Economist (weekly)

Newspapers

Newspapers are important sources of up-to-date information, examples and data. Below are some of the main UK newspaper sources, many of which have websites with search facilities to identify specific topics and articles:

The Guardian
The Times
The Financial Times
The Independent
The Telegraph

Companion website

Go to the companion website at **www.pearsoned.co.uk/econexpress** to find more revision support online for this topic area.

Notes

Notes

4

Supply, production and cost

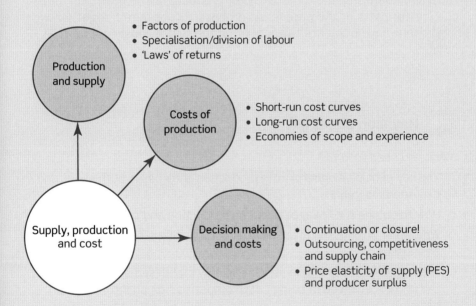

- Factors of production
- Specialisation/division of labour
- 'Laws' of returns

Production and supply

Costs of production

- Short-run cost curves
- Long-run cost curves
- Economies of scope and experience

Supply, production and cost

Decision making and costs

- Continuation or closure!
- Outsourcing, competitiveness and supply chain
- Price elasticity of supply (PES) and producer surplus

A printable version of this topic map is available from **www.pearsoned.co.uk/econexpress**

Introduction

The importance of reliable supply chains in an increasingly globalised economy was sharply highlighted by the Japanese earthquake and tsunami in March 2011. Some 90% of the world's specialist resins used in the semiconductor industry came from a single Japanese factory close to the Fukoshima nuclear power plant, with the loss of output from this plant resulting in the global production of cars and many other products being halted or cut back in the months following the tsunami. The increasing frequency of 'unexpected happenings' has resulted in major companies sourcing from many suppliers in many locations. In attempting to more effectively risk-manage supply chains, business processes are now more likely to involve larger numbers of smaller businesses operating within more geographically dispersed and more flexible supply chains.

This chapter will help you review the production and cost issues which underpin movements along and shifts in the supply curves **encountered in Chapter 1**. We also assess the benefits to businesses from growing in size and operating at a larger scale of production. The growth of 'outsourcing' for parts of the production process is considered, together with more recent developments towards repatriating previously outsourced activities.

 ### Revision checklist

What you need to know:

- ❑ The key principles underpinning production activities in both short- and long-run time periods.
- ❑ How to outline the linkages between production and cost.
- ❑ Why larger businesses often have a cost advantage over smaller businesses.
- ❑ The role of outsourcing in an increasingly globalised supply chain and the factors involved in being cost-competitive on an international basis.
- ❑ The relevance of costs to business decision making in both short- and long-run time periods.
- ❑ The relevance of ideas such as price elasticity of supply and producer surplus to resource allocation.

Assessment advice

Use diagrams

You can improve your analysis and gain higher marks in this topic area by using carefully constructed diagrams to represent production and cost, in both short- and long-run time periods. You can use diagrams to demonstrate the (different) levels of output at which diminishing marginal product and diminishing average product set in. The shape of the marginal and average cost curves can then be related to the marginal and average product curves for labour and other variable factors.

Use consistent terminology

Time periods are particularly important when reviewing production and cost. The short-run time period is that for which at least one factor of production is fixed for that industry or sector of economic activity. The long-run time period is that for which all factors can be varied.

Use empirical evidence

It will always help to illustrate issues of production and cost by using case study examples and by using other empirical evidence. This could include cost and productivity data for different companies and countries.

 ## Assessment question

Can you answer this stimulus-based question? Guidelines on answering the question are presented at the end of this chapter.

Car output per plant per year	Index of unit average production costs (per car)
100,000	100
250,000	83
500,000	74
1,000,000	70
2,000,000	66

Optimum output per year (cars)	
Advertising	1,000,000
Sales	2,000,000
Risks	1,800,000
Finance	2,500,000
Research and Development	5,000,000

Q1. What does the data suggest about the benefits of size in the car industry?

Q2. Explain the reasons for these benefits of size.

Q3. What implications does the data have for production and supply chain issues in the car industry?

Q4. What other production and cost data would be useful for a car company which is considering further outsourcing of elements of its supply chain?

Production and supply

Production and cost issues always involve two key time periods.

Key definitions

Long-run

The long run is that period of time in which all factors of production can be varied. New firms can enter an industry only in the long-run time period in which they can bring together *all* the resources (land, labour, capital, etc.) needed for production to begin.

Short-run

The short run is that period of time in which at least one factor of production is fixed.

Factors of production

Factors of production are those inputs required to produce a particular product, and are often thought to include land, labour, capital and enterprise.

- *Land*: 'all the free gifts of nature', i.e. all the natural resources with some economic value which do not exist as a result of any effort by human beings.

- *Labour:* not only the number of people available for the production of goods or services, but also including their physical and intellectual abilities. The labour force of a country is the number of people in employment plus the number unemployed.
- *Capital:* any man-made asset which can be used to support the production of goods and services. Fixed capital can be used time and again in the production process and includes machinery and factory buildings, the road and rail networks, hospital and educational buildings and so on. Circulating capital (also known as working capital) consists of raw materials and other intermediate inputs into the production process.
- *Enterprise:* sometimes referred to as entrepreneurship, with the entrepreneur seen as performing two important roles:
  - hiring and combining factors of production;
  - risk-taking by producing goods and services in anticipation of demand which may, or may not, materialise.

Specialisation/division of labour

'Division of labour' or 'specialisation' is relevant to many questions involving productivity and cost. These terms refer to the ways in which economic activities can be broken down into their various component parts so that each worker performs only a small part of the entire operation. The idea was developed as early as 1776 by Adam Smith in his *Wealth of Nations* when he demonstrated how the production of pins could be greatly increased by splitting the process down into separate tasks, each performed by a single person.

Advantages of specialisation

- *Increased productivity.* Greater specialisation leads to a greater output per worker:
  - performing the same task results in higher productivity ('practice makes perfect');
  - less time is wasted in moving from work area to work area or in changing one set of tools for another;
  - breaking production down to a small number of repetitive tasks makes possible the use of specialist machinery which can also raise productivity;
  - workers can specialise in performing tasks for which they are well suited.

- *Increased standard of living.* The greater levels of productivity have led to an increase in the volume of total output and value of total money income. Greater productivity also helps to reduce prices, raising 'real' income still higher.
- *Increased range of products available.* Increased standards of living have increased the effective demand for a wide range of goods and services.

Disadvantages of specialisation

- *Increased boredom.* Greater specialisation results in boredom as workers perform the same tasks, which can lead to low morale, poor labour relations and higher absenteeism as well as carelessness and an increased number of accidents.
- *Lack of variety.* Output is standardised and large numbers of identical products are produced.
- *Increased worker interdependence.* Each worker in the production process now depends upon all other workers and a stoppage by a small group of workers can cause considerable disruption.
- *Limited market size.* Division of labour is only possible if there is a sufficiently large market to purchase the larger quantities produced.

Examples & evidence

Specialisation in bread making

Bread making by major producers such as Warburton has adopted the ideas of Adam Smith's division of labour in pin-making. Some 10 separate processes have been identified in bread making over a four-hour production period.

Preparation

Bulk mix of dough

Divide dough into pieces

Mould pieces into shape

Cut dough

Baking

Place in tin

Smooth surface of dough in tin

De-tin (remove from tin)

Packing

Cool

Slice

Wrap

Of course, an 11th process is then involved, namely distribution to supermarkets and bread shops.

Some 11 million loaves are sold every day in the UK, with the UK bread market having a daily value of £3.6bn. Of this some £1.9bn involves pre-packaged bread, £0.9bn croissants and other 'morning' breads, and £0.8bn flour and other home-baking products.

The 10-stage process above produces bread with a four-day shelf-life. However, European consumers eat less pre-packed bread and more fresh bread than in the UK. Shops expect pre-packed bread to have a longer 12-day shelf-life in Europe so that it can be sold as a reserve option when local consumers are not able to buy their preferred 'fresh' bread at the local bread shop. To secure sales in Europe, Warburton and other UK pre-packed bread producers have added an extra process, namely injecting extra preservatives into the dough to give a 19-day shelf-life, giving enough time to transport and distribute the bread to Europe.

Questions

1. How might splitting the process of bread-making into separate activities help increase productivity (output per person)?
2. What extra activities will be required when producing pre-packed bread in the UK for European consumers?

'Laws' of returns

All production requires the input of factors of production, which can be combined in a variety of ways, sometimes by using more of one factor relative to another, and vice versa. Profit-maximising firms, i.e. firms which aim to make as large a profit as possible, will combine the factors of production so as to achieve the maximum output from a given amount of factor inputs or, put another way, to minimise the cost of producing any given output.

It will be useful to remember the key definitions of **total product**, **average product** and **marginal product**.

Key definitions

Total product (TP)

Total product is the total output a firm produces within a given period of time.

Average product (AP)
Average product is usually measured in relation to a particular factor of production, such as labour or capital.

$$\text{Average product of labour} = \frac{\text{Total product}}{\text{Total labour input}}$$

Marginal product (MP)
Marginal product is the change in total product when one more unit of the factor is used.

$$\text{Marginal product of labour} = \frac{\text{Change in total product}}{\text{Change in labour input}}$$

Law of variable proportions

This 'law' applies to the *short-run time period* when at least one factor of production (usually capital) is fixed. It follows that as the variable factor is progressively increased, the *proportions* in which it is combined with the fixed factor will change. Table 4.1 illustrates this 'law'.

Table 4.1 Changing nature of returns to a variable factor.

No. of workers	Total product	Average product	Marginal product
1	3	3	3
2	10	5	7
3	21	7	11
4	36	9	15
5	50	10	14
6	63	10.5	13
7	70	10	7
8	72	9	2
9	63	7	–9

Figures rounded to one decimal place

Increasing returns to the variable factor

Up to some optimum proportion of the variable to fixed factor (e.g. one person to one machine), we initially have too little of the variable factor. Extra units of the variable factor, here labour, will then be highly productive, making fuller use of 'spare capacity' in the fixed factor. Output rises more than in proportion to the extra input of variable factor, and we say that *increasing returns* have set in.

Diminishing returns to the variable factor

Beyond the optimum proportion of variable to fixed factor, additional units of the variable factor, here labour, will be progressively less productive. We now say that *diminishing returns* have set in.

Test yourself

Q1. Use Table 4.1 to identify:

(a) Diminishing average returns to labour

(b) Diminishing marginal returns to labour

Q2. What do you notice?

Figure 4.1 presents a stylised diagram to highlight some of these relationships between total, average and marginal product of the variable factor, here labour. We can see that the marginal product of labour curve starts to fall after five units of labour, but that the average product of labour keeps rising until six units of labour are employed, after which it falls. In other words, diminishing marginal returns set in before diminishing average returns.

Note that when the last worker neither adds to, nor subtracts from, output (i.e. the marginal product is zero), then total product is a maximum (point C).

✳ Assessment advice

It is important to be aware of the linkages between the output at which diminishing marginal product of the variable factor sets in and the output at which marginal costs begin to rise. The same relationship holds for the output at which diminishing average product of the variable factor sets in and the output at which average variable costs begin to rise.

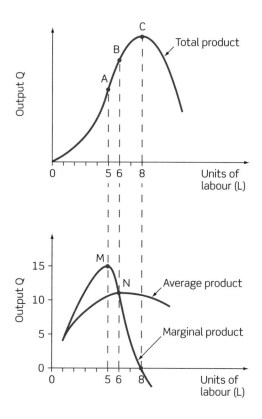

Figure 4.1 Total, average and marginal product curves for the variable factor (labour).
Source: Griffiths, A. and Wall, S. (2011) *Economics for Business and Management* (3rd ed.) © 2011 Pearson Education. Reproduced with permission.

Costs of production

It is important that you can link the ideas discussed for production to the determination of **cost**, particularly in the *short-run* time period when the law of variable proportions applies.

Short-run cost curves

In the short-run time period, costs are usually defined as either fixed or variable costs corresponding to the fixed or variable factors of production previously discussed.

Fixed costs

It is impossible to vary the input of fixed factors in the short run, therefore fixed costs do not change as output increases. Fixed costs are incurred even when the firm's output is zero, and might include mortgage or rent on premises, hire purchase repayments, business rates, insurance charges, depreciation on assets, and so on. Since none of these costs are directly related to output, they are therefore sometimes referred to as *indirect costs* or *overheads*.

Variable costs

Unlike fixed costs, variable costs are directly related to output. When firms produce no output they incur no variable costs, but as output is expanded extra variable costs are incurred. Variable costs include costs of raw materials and components, power to drive machinery, wages of labour and so on.

Key definitions

Total cost

Total cost = Total fixed cost + Total variable cost

i.e.   TC = TFC + TVC

Average total cost

$$\text{Average total cost (ATC)} = \frac{\text{Total cost}}{\text{Total output}} = \frac{TC}{Q}$$

i.e. $$ATC = \frac{TFC + TVC}{Q} = \frac{TFC}{Q} + \frac{TVC}{Q}$$

$$ATC = AFC + AVC$$

Marginal cost

This is the addition to total cost from producing one extra unit of output. Marginal cost is entirely variable cost.

$$\text{Marginal cost (MC)} = \frac{\text{Change in total cost}}{\text{Change in total output}} = \frac{\Delta TC}{\Delta Q} \text{ where } \Delta Q = 1$$

It is often helpful to plot the values for total, average and marginal costs on diagrams as in Figure 4.2.

Total cost curves

In Figure 4.2(a), the total cost (TC) curve is obtained by adding (vertically) the total fixed cost (TFC) and total variable cost (TVC) curves. TFC is a horizontal straight line at some given value V, since the fixed costs do not vary with output. However, TVC is usually drawn as an inverted letter 'S', suggesting that *increasing returns* to the variable factor initially mean that total variable costs

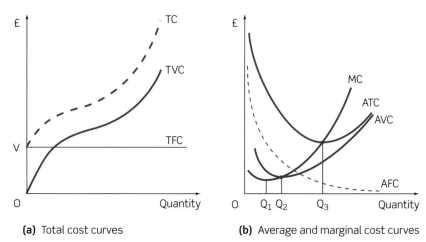

(a) Total cost curves   **(b)** Average and marginal cost curves

Figure 4.2 Short-run cost relationships.
Source: Griffiths, A. and Wall, S. (2011) *Economics for Business and Management* (3rd ed.) © 2011 Pearson Education. Reproduced with permission.

rise relatively slowly with output. However, as *diminishing returns* set in, the total variable costs rise at an increasingly rapid rate with output.

 Assessment advice

Being able to link cost diagrams involving production (Figure 4.1) with diagrams involving costs (Figure 4.2) will demonstrate a high level of understanding to examiners.

Examples & evidence

Theatre costs

Some interesting data have been made available on theatre costs for performances at the New London Theatre, owned by the Really Useful Theatre (RUT) Company, in London. The producer of the shows paid rent of £25,000 a week to the New London Theatre.

The 'contra' costs (i.e. the costs of running the theatre, including wages of performers, cleaning and maintenance) were estimated to be between £30,000 and £35,000 per week.

A more general breakdown of the typical costs of putting on a West End show is presented in the table opposite, which reflects estimates of where the money received on each ticket actually goes.

Of course, as well as ticket revenue, extra revenue is possible to the producers of shows via the sales of merchandising. Even here, however, merchandising staff were required to pay a 25% commission to RUT, the owners of the New London Theatre.

Type of cost	Source	% of total costs
Fixed costs	Theatre rent and 'contra' costs (i.e. cost of running and maintenance of theatre)	Up to 50%
Variable costs	Ticketmaster (booking fees)	4%
	Ticket commission per ticket	10%
	Creative team pay (commission-based contracts)	8%
	VAT	20%
Profit	(depending on attendance)	8%

Questions

1. Why are performers' wages regarded as a fixed cost in the table? Is this a usual practice?
2. Comment on the items placed under the variable cost heading.

Average and marginal cost curves

Figure 4.2(b) on page 92 presented the various average cost curves and the marginal cost curve.

- Note that average fixed costs (AFC) fall continuously as we divide an unchanged TFC with a progressively increasing quantity. (This is often referred to as 'spreading the overheads'.)
- Note that the marginal cost (MC) curve slopes downwards initially, with falling marginal costs the mirror image of *increasing marginal returns* to the variable factor in the short run (see the rising part of the marginal product curve in Figure 4.1). At output Q_1 *diminishing marginal returns* set in (see the falling part of the marginal product curve in Figure 4.1) and the MC curve begins to rise.

- Note that we initially have increasing average returns to the variable factor with the result that AVC falls. At output Q_2 *diminishing average returns* set in (again see Figure 4.1) and the AVC curve begins to rise.

- Note that the ATC curve is the vertical sum of the AFC and AVC curves and this starts to rise after output Q_3 when the rise in AVC outweighs the fall in AFC.

- Note also that, for reasons identical to those previously explained, the MC curve cuts the AVC and ATC curves at their respective minima. As soon as the marginal is above the average, then of course the average must rise, the analogy with a game being that if your last (marginal) score is greater than your average, then your average must rise.

Test yourself

Q3. Look carefully at Figure 4.3 which shows production and cost curves in the short-run time period.

    (a) Explain what is happening in the top diagram where MP is marginal product and AP is average product.

    (b) Explain what is happening in the bottom diagram where MC is marginal cost and AVC is average variable cost.

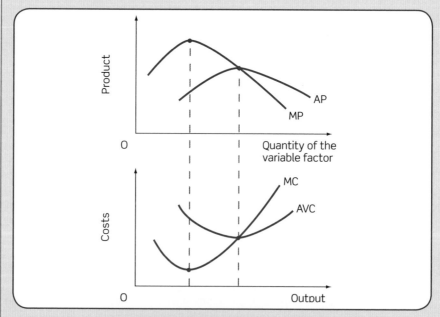

Figure 4.3 Production and cost curves.

Source: Griffiths, A. and Wall, S. (2011) *Economics for Business and Management* (3rd ed.) © 2011 Pearson Education. Reproduced with permission.

(c) How are the two diagrams linked? In other words, explain the relationship between marginal product (MP) and marginal cost (MC), and between average product (AP) and average variable cost (AVC).

Q4. Complete the following table (round, where needed, to 1 decimal place):

Output	TFC	TVC	TC	AFC	AVC	ATC	MC
0	50	0					
1	50	40					
2	50	75					
3	50	108					
4	50	138					
5	50	170					
6	50	205					
7	50	243					
8	50	286					
9	50	335					
10	50	390					

Q5. Now draw a diagram which includes the AFC, AVC, ATC and MC curves. What do you notice?

Long-run cost curves

In the *long-run* time period we no longer add units of a variable factor to a fixed factor, since there is no fixed factor! In other words, in the long-run time period all factors are variable. However, you need to know the linkages between the short-run average cost curves (SRACs) of Figure 4.2(b) and the long-run average cost curve (LRAC) of Figure 4.4.

Long-run average cost (LRAC)

Figure 4.4 shows the long-run average cost (LRAC) curve as an *envelope* to a family of short-run average cost curves (SRACs).

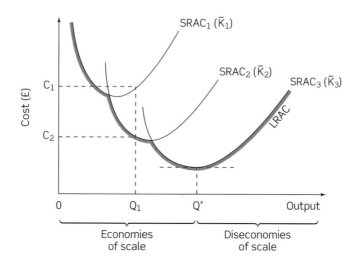

Figure 4.4 The long-run average cost (LRAC) curve as the outer 'envelope' to a family of short-run average cost (SRAC) curves.

Source: Griffiths, A. and Wall, S. (2011) *Economics for Business and Management* (3rd ed.) © 2011 Pearson Education. Reproduced with permission.

Each of the short-run average cost (SRAC) curves shows how costs change with output at some given value or level of the fixed factor, here capital. For example, with capital fixed at $\bar{K}_1$, the lowest cost of producing output Q_1 would be C_1. However, in the long run we can vary all factors, including capital. The lowest cost of producing output Q_1 in the long run would be to change capital to $\bar{K}_2$ when it would be possible to produce Q_1 at cost C_2. So C_2 (and not C_1) is a point on the *long-run average cost curve* (LRAC) which shows the lowest cost of producing any output, given that all factors (here including capital, $\bar{K}$) can be adjusted to their optimal level.

In fact, the outer envelope to the family of short-run average cost curves in Figure 4.4 will constitute the long-run average cost curve (LRAC). Up to output Q^* the LRAC is falling, and we refer to *economies of scale*; beyond output Q^* the LRAC is rising, and we refer to *diseconomies of scale*.

Reasons for economies of scale

In the long run the firm can increase all its factors of production and grow in size (scale) of output. This greater size may allow it to combine the factors of production in ways that reduce long-run average cost and yield economies of scale.

> ### ✳ Assessment advice
>
> Being able to explain the reasons for a larger scale of production reducing long-run average costs is a key element in many questions set on this topic. Figure 4.4 can be drawn and both technical and non-technical reasons explained, using examples, to account for the shape of Figure 4.4.

The economies of scale are many and varied, but they are usually grouped into certain categories.

Technical economies

These are related to an increase in size of the plant or production unit. Reasons include the following:

- *Specialisation of labour and capital* becomes more possible as output increases. Specialisation raises productivity per unit of labour/capital input, so that average variable costs fall as output increases. We have already seen that specialisation is 'limited by the size of the market' so that as output grows, more specialisation is possible.
- *'Engineers' rule'* whereby material costs increase as the square but volume (capacity) increases as the cube, so that material costs per unit of capacity fall as output increases. Wherever volume is important, as in sizes of containers, lorries, ships, aircraft, etc., this 'rule' is important.
- *Dovetailing of linked processes* may be feasible only at high levels of output. For example, if the finished product needs processes A, B and C respectively, each with specialised equipment producing 10, 24 and 30 items per hour, then only at high levels of output do processes 'dovetail' in the sense that each process divides exactly into this level of output (120 is the lowest common multiple of 10, 24 and 30).
- *Indivisibility of large-scale, more efficient processes.* Certain processes of production, e.g. mass assembly techniques, can be operated efficiently only at large output volumes and cannot be operated as efficiently at lower outputs, even if all factor inputs are scaled down in proportion to one another. We call this inability to scale down the processes of production, without affecting their efficiency of operation, *indivisibility* of the production process.

Take, for example, the three production processes outlined in Table 4.2. For all three processes, the ratio of capital to labour is the same at 1:1 and each process is a scaled-down (or scaled-up) version of one of the other processes. However, the larger-scale processes are clearly more productive or efficient than the smaller-scale processes.

Table 4.2 Indivisibility in the production process.

Type of process	Factor inputs		Output
	L (workers)	K (machines)	X (units)
A Small-scale process	1	1	1
B Medium-scale process	100	100	1,000
C Large-scale process	1,000	1,000	20,000

Non-technical (enterprise) economies

These are related to an increase in size of the *enterprise as a whole* rather than simply an increase in size of the plant or production unit. Reasons include the following:

- *Financial economies.* Larger enterprises can raise financial capital more cheaply (lower interest rates, access to share and rights issues via Stock Exchange listings, etc.).
- *Administrative, marketing and other functional economies.* Existing functional departments can often increase throughput without a pro-rata increase in their establishment.
- *Distributive economies.* More efficient distributional and supply-chain operations become feasible with greater size (lorries, ships and other containers can be despatched with loads nearer to capacity, etc.).
- *Purchasing economies.* Bulk buying discounts are available for larger enterprises.

Examples & evidence

Technical and enterprise economies

Technical economies result from an increase in the size of the production unit. When Kraft, the US food giant, acquired Cadbury, the UK confectioner, for £11.9 billion in 2010, becoming the world's largest confectioner, cost savings of £675 million per year were identified from more efficient operations via scale economies. Similarly the huge fabricated chip manufacturing plants ('Fabs') cost over $3 billion each, roughly twice as much as previous plants, but are able to produce over three times as many silicon chips per time period, with such 'plant economies' reducing the unit cost per chip by over 40%.

Enterprise economies result from the growth in size of the whole enterprise, permitting economies via bulk purchase, the spread of administrative costs over greater output, and the cheaper cost of finance, etc. The renamed and expanded Air France-KLM airline formed in 2004 estimated cost savings from such 'enterprise economies' of around £200 million over the following five years, mainly from economies in functional areas such as sales, distribution, IT and procurement.

Question

1. Select a company and identify examples of these various economies.

Cost gradient

As can be seen from Figure 4.5, where economies of scale exist for these various reasons, then the long-run average cost (LRAC) curve will fall as output rises over the range $O–Q_1$. The *more substantial* these economies of scale, the *steeper* the fall in the LRAC curve, which then means that any firm producing less output than Q_1 is at a considerable cost disadvantage vis-à-vis its competitors.

The *cost gradient* is an attempt to measure the steepness of the fall in LRAC up to the minimum efficient size (MES). Sometimes this 'cost gradient' is expressed over the range of the LRAC from ½MES to MES and sometimes from ⅓MES to MES.

For example, suppose the cost gradient for an industry is expressed as 40% from ½MES to MES. This means that a firm that is at output Q_2 in Figure 4.5 will have average costs at C_2 which are some 40% higher than a firm which has an output that is twice as large as Q_2 and which is benefiting from all the economies of scale available. Clearly the steeper (higher value) the cost gradient, the greater the disadvantages for a business in operating below the MES for that industry.

Also note that the larger MES (Q_1) is relative to total industry output, the fewer efficient firms the industry can sustain. For example, if Q_1 is 50% of the usual UK output of cement, then arguably the UK can sustain only two efficient cement producers.

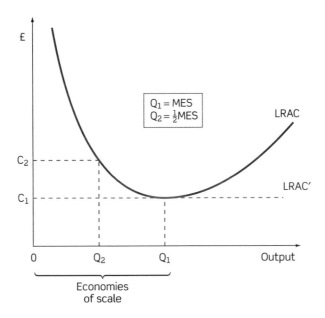

Figure 4.5 Economies of scale and minimum efficient size (MES).

Source: Griffiths, A. and Wall, S. (2011) *Economics for Business and Management* (3rd ed.) © 2011 Pearson Education. Reproduced with permission.

Assessment advice

The idea of the cost gradient, and its associated diagram, is an effective way of showing the advantages of reaching a certain size for a firm, and the disadvantages of failing to reach that size.

Diseconomies of scale

Some surveys suggest that if a firm attempts to produce beyond the MES (Q_1), then average costs will begin to rise and we have the U-shaped LRAC curve in Figure 4.5. These higher average costs are called *diseconomies of scale* and are usually attributed to managerial problems in handling output growth efficiently.

However, other surveys suggest that while LRAC ceases to fall, there is little evidence that it actually rises for levels of output beyond Q_1. In other words, it flattens out to look less like the letter 'U' and more like the letter 'L', shown by LRAC′ in Figure 4.5.

We also need to distinguish between **internal economies of scale** and **external economies of scale**.

Key definitions

Internal economies of scale

These are the cost advantages from a growth in the *size of the business* itself over the long-run time period.

External economies of scale

These are the cost advantages to a business from a growth in the *size of the sector of economic activity* of which the business is a part. In other words, the sources of the cost reductions are external to the business itself.

Economies of scope and experience

We have considered costs that depend mainly on the size of output and the time period in question. Here we consider two other types of cost which may be important to the business.

Economies of scope

This refers to changes in average costs as a result of changes in the *mix* of production between two or more products. The suggestion here is that there may be benefits from the joint production of two or more products.

Examples & evidence

Ethanol, corn and economies of scope

In the six years since the global financial crisis began in 2007, only gold has matched corn in terms of the percentage return on investment (140%+). This reflects the rapid rise in the price of corn, with a major factor being the increasing demand for ethanol as a 'clean' fuel, which in turn has increased the demand for a key input to ethanol, namely corn. In fact the US government has passed legislation which requires 40% of the US annual corn crop to be used in ethanol production. However, corn is also a staple foodstuff itself as well as an important input for milk, meat, packaged food, soda and even petrol. In 2012 the sharp rise in the world price of corn from $6 to $8 per bushel raised costs of producing all these products substantially – for example, the $2 rise in price increased the cost of producing a pound weight of chicken by 7 cents. *Economies of scope* would suggest that ethanol producers might consider adding corn to their product mix, as might producers of a wide range of products for which corn is an important input

Question

1. Suggest another example of economies of scope.

Economies of experience

This refers to a fall in average costs as *cumulative output* rises (see Figure 4.6). For example, a small firm producing an average output of 5,000 units over 20 years has a cumulative output of 100,000 units. It may have learnt many useful 'lessons' over time to help it reduce costs and compete effectively with larger rivals.

✱ Assessment advice

Questions are regularly set in examinations and assignments which involve the reasons why firms seek to grow in size. It will help if you can explain economies of scale (technical and non-technical), economies of scope and economies of experience in some detail. Do use diagrams where appropriate to support your argument. Recent case-study examples will also help to 'deepen' your argument.

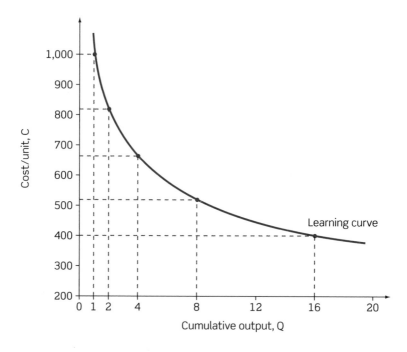

Figure 4.6 The experience or learning curve: declining average costs as a function of cumulative output.

Source: Griffiths, A. and Wall, S. (2011) *Economics for Business and Management* (3rd ed.) © 2011 Pearson Education. Reproduced with permission.

Decision making and costs

Continuation or closure

The distinction between fixed costs and variable costs is important in deciding whether firms should cease production. The firm must cover its fixed costs whether it undertakes production or not. For example, even when the firm produces no output it still incurs costs such as insurance charges, depreciation on assets, mortgage repayments, rent on premises, and so on. However, unlike these fixed costs, variable costs are incurred only when the firm undertakes production. When the firm produces no output it incurs no costs from purchasing raw materials, from charges for energy to drive the machinery, from overtime payments to existing workers or extra labour costs for hiring new workers, etc. All of these costs tend to rise only as output increases.

Once a firm has incurred fixed costs, its decision about whether to continue producing is therefore determined by the relationship between revenue and costs incurred over the time period in question.

Short-run decision making

- If total revenue *just covers* the total variable (running) costs incurred by producing, then the firm is neither better off nor worse off if it continues production.
- If total revenue is *greater than* total variable costs, then the firm makes at least some contribution towards covering the fixed costs already incurred by continuing in production.
- If total revenue is *less than* total variable costs, then the firm will be better off by ceasing production altogether. If the firm shuts down, its total loss is equal to its fixed cost compared with a loss equal to its fixed costs *plus* the ongoing losses from failing to cover its variable costs.

Firms will therefore undertake production, in the short run, if the *price* (average revenue) at which their product is sold is at least equal to the *average variable cost* of production. When price (average revenue) and average variable cost are equal, total revenue is exactly equal to total variable cost.

Figure 4.7(a) shows the short-run 'shutdown point', i.e. the level of output (Q_1) below which the firm cannot cover its variable costs in the short run.

The firm will shut down in the short run if the AVC is above, or the AR curve below, that shown in Figure 4.7(a).

Long-run decision making

In the long run, unless *price* (average revenue) at least covers the *average total cost,* firms will experience a loss. In other words, total revenue must cover total cost in the long run, including total variable costs and total fixed costs. When price (average revenue) and long-run average total cost (LRATC) are equal, total revenue is exactly equal to total cost in the long run.

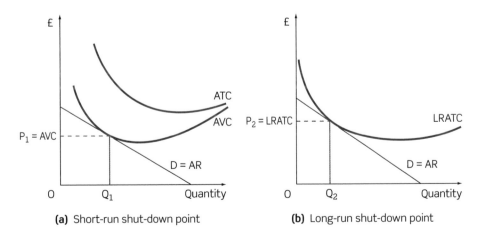

(a) Short-run shut-down point   **(b)** Long-run shut-down point

Figure 4.7 (a) Short-run shutdown point; (b) long-run shutdown point.

Figure 4.7(b) shows the long-run 'shutdown point', i.e. the level of output (Q_2) below which the firm cannot cover all its costs, both variable and fixed, in the long run.

The firm will shut down in the long run if the LRATC curve is above, or the AR curve below, that shown in Figure 4.7(b).

 Assessment advice

Remember to mention that in the long run the total revenue of the firm must also cover 'normal profit', i.e. that level of profit regarded as just sufficient to keep a firm in that industry or sector of economic activity in the long run. Normal profit is often thought of as a long-run 'cost' of production in that if it is not made then the firm will move its scarce resources into another sector of economic activity.

While they may be prepared to accept losses in the short run (as long as total variable costs are covered), firms cannot accept losses in the long run. If firms are to continue in production in the long run, the price at which their product is sold must at least equal the average total cost of production.

Outsourcing, competitiveness and the supply chain

Costs of production depend not only on the size of the production unit (plant) or enterprise (firm) but also on the geographical location of different elements of the supply chain. In an increasingly global economy, new opportunities are available for many multinational enterprises (MNEs) to outsource activities which can reduce the costs of producing any given level of output.

The examples here usefully illustrate the attraction of outsourcing.

Examples & evidence

Outsourcing car assembly

While car assembly includes robotic and highly automated systems, it still requires labour, and Renault estimate that wage costs account for around 15% of the value of a car. When, in February 2012, Renault announced it would open a new €1.1bn plant in Tangier, Morocco, to produce a new 'people carrier', it contrasted the €4.50 per hour it would pay workers in Morocco with the €30 per hour it would need to pay in France. The factory in Tangier will employ 6,000 workers by 2015, making 400,000 lower-priced 'people carriers'.

Responding to sharp criticism of outsourcing jobs at a time when 2.87 million are unemployed in France, Renault argue that every car made in Morocco will still generate €800 for the French economy – €400 in parts and €400 in engineers' salaries.

Questions

1. What are the advantages and disadvantages to Renault of outsourcing the 'people carrier'?
2. What are the advantages and disadvantages to France of Renault outsourcing the 'people carrier'?

Of course, there are sometimes some surprises in outsourcing, with countries which once received substantial inward investment themselves becoming relatively expensive over time. As a result, businesses in those countries begin to look for lower-cost sources of manufacture and supply, as can be seen in the case of China.

Examples & evidence

China outsources clothes

Vancl, China's largest independent online clothing retailer by sales, has started shifting production overseas in an effort to cut labour rates and beat the country's rapidly rising production costs. Vancl is sourcing part of its products from Bangladesh and plans to increase the proportion of clothes made outside China. Vancl said the main incentive for the move was cheaper labour costs. 'One Bangladesh worker's monthly salary would be Rmb500 to Rmb600 ($80 to $95), while one Chinese worker now costs at least Rmb2,000 per month', it said, noting that even after paying higher transport and other costs it could save 5–10% of total costs by outsourcing. In fact, monthly pay for Chinese workers has risen by over 30% in the past three years.

Difficulty in recruiting workers was another reason for the move, Vancl said, noting that the 'new generation' of Chinese workers did not like factory jobs. A Vancl official said the company was contacting manufacturers in Indonesia, Cambodia and other south-east Asian countries as part of the outsourcing effort, although it has not yet decided how significant a proportion of its production it will source overseas. 'The production cycle can be as long as four to six months (in Bangladesh)', said a company official, while domestic suppliers are required to deliver in 30 to 45 days. The online retailer said it also felt proud of its traditional 'made in China' label.

'Vancl only sells to the China market', said Shaun Rein of China Market Research in Shanghai. One of the reasons they win is they can introduce new products, tailored specifically for China, very quickly. Mr Rein added that sourcing from Bangladesh could jeopardise that.

FT *Source*: Waldmeir, P., 'China's Vancl trials production overseas', *Financial Times*, 9 August 2012.

Questions

1. What are the advantages to Vancl of outsourcing clothing production to Bangladesh and other south-east Asian countries?

2. What are the disadvantages of such outsourcing?

Relative unit labour cost (RULC)

This whole issue of outsourcing can be more clearly understood in the context of **relative unit labour cost (RULC)**. This measurement is the most widely accepted indicator of international competitiveness that will ultimately determine whether and where any particular part of a firm's value chain will be outsourced.

Labour costs per unit of output (unit labour costs) depend on both the wage and non-wage (e.g. employer National Insurance contributions in the UK) costs of workers and the output per worker (labour productivity). For example, if the total (wage and non-wage) costs per worker double, but productivity more than doubles, then labour costs per unit will actually fall.

However, the exchange rate must also be taken into account when considering international competitiveness and this also is included in the definition of RULC here. For example, for any given value for labour costs per unit, if the exchange rate of that country's currency falls against a competitor's, then its exports become more competitive (cheaper) abroad and its imports less competitive (dearer) at home.

Key definition

Relative unit labour cost (RULC)

The calculation of RULC is as follows:

$$\text{RULC} = \frac{\text{Relative labour costs}}{\text{Relative labour productivity}} \times \text{Relative exchange rate}$$

This formula emphasises that (compared with some other country) lower RULC for, say, the UK could be achieved by reducing the UK's relative labour costs, or by raising the UK's relative labour productivity, or by lowering the UK's relative exchange rate, or by some combination of all three.

Price elasticity of supply (PES) and producer surplus

Key definitions

Price elasticity of supply (PES)

This measures the responsiveness of the supply of product X to a change in its own price.

Producer surplus

This is the excess payment to producers over and above the amount required for them to supply the product.

Price elasticity of supply

Price elasticity of supply (PES) refers to a movement along the supply curve (expansion or contraction) rather than a shift in the supply curve (increase or decrease):

$$PES = \frac{\% \text{ change in quantity supplied of X}}{\% \text{ change in price of X}}$$

The numerical value, terminology and descriptions used for price elasticity of demand (PED) apply equally to supply, though for supply all the signs are strictly positive, since when the price of X rises the quantity supplied of X also rises (+/+ = +).

Table 4.3 presents the numerical values, terminology and descriptions for price elasticity of supply.

Figure 4.8 presents diagrams to capture some of these PES situations.

Factors affecting the numerical value of PES for a product include the following:

- *The mobility of factors of production.* The more easily the factors of production can be moved between product X and the supply of other products, the more elastic the supply.
- *The time period in question.* The longer the time period under consideration, the more elastic the supply (producers take time to redirect factors of production).
- *The producer's attitude towards risk.* The less risk-averse the producer, the more elastic the supply. In other words, if producers are more willing to take risks, they will be more responsive in redirecting factors of production to alternative uses in response to price changes in product X.
- *The existence of natural constraints on production.* The less inhibited is production as regards natural constraints (such as fertile land, climate, mineral deposits, etc.), the more elastic the supply is likely to be.

Table 4.3 Price elasticity of supply, terminology and description.

Numerical value of PES	Terminology	Description
0	Perfectly inelastic supply	Whatever the % change in price (Figure 4.8(a)), no change in quantity supplied
>0 < 1	Relatively inelastic supply	A given % change in price leads to a smaller % change in quantity supplied
1	Unit elastic supply	A given % change in price leads to exactly the same % change in quantity supplied (Figure 4.8(b))
>1 <∞	Relatively elastic supply	A given % change in price leads to a larger % change in quantity supplied
∞ (infinity)	Perfectly elastic supply	An infinitely small % change in price leads to an infinitely large % change in quantity supplied (Figure 4.8(c))

Producer surplus

Producer surplus is an idea similar to that of consumer surplus **considered in Chapter 2 (page 48)**. Whereas consumer surplus involves the idea of individuals being willing to pay more than the market price for units of a product, here producers are seen as being willing to offer units of the product at less than market price.

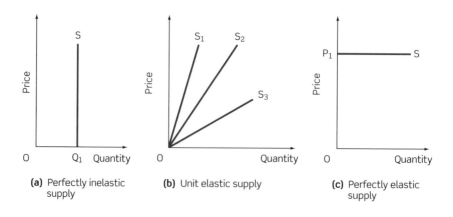

(a) Perfectly inelastic supply

(b) Unit elastic supply

(c) Perfectly elastic supply

Figure 4.8 Some important price elasticities of supply.

Source: Griffiths, A. and Wall, S. (2011) *Economics for Business and Management* (3rd ed.) © 2011 Pearson Education. Reproduced with permission.

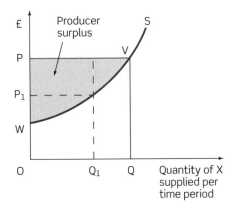

Figure 4.9 Producer surplus.

Source: Griffiths, A. and Wall, S. (2011) *Economics for Business and Management* (3rd ed.) © 2011 Pearson Education. Reproduced with permission.

In Figure 4.9 the OQ_1th unit would have been supplied at a price of P_1, but the producer actually receives the higher market price of OP, giving a producer surplus of $P - P_1$ on that unit.

Over all the OQ units, the shaded area PVW corresponds to the *excess* of revenue received by producers over and above the amount required to induce them to supply OQ units of the product.

Chapter summary – pulling it all together

By the end of this chapter you should be able to:

	Confident ✓	Not confident?
Outline the key principles underpinning production activities in both short- and long-run time periods		Revise pages 84–90
Outline the linkages between production and cost		Revise pages 90–95
Explain why larger businesses often have a cost advantage over smaller businesses		Revise pages 95–102
Examine the role of outsourcing in an increasingly globalised supply chain and the factors that are involved in being cost-competitive on an international basis		Revise pages 104–106

	Confident ✓	Not confident?
Explain the relevance of costs to business decision making in short- and long-run time periods		Revise pages 102–104
Examine the relevance of ideas such as price elasticity of demand and producer surplus to resource allocation		Revise pages 107–109

Now try the **assessment question** at the start of this chapter, using the answer guidelines below.

Answer guidelines

✱ Assessment question

Look again at the data in the assessment question at the start of this chapter.

Q1. What do the data suggest about the benefits of size in the car industry?

Q2. Explain the reasons for these benefits of size.

Q3. What implications do the data have for production and supply chain issues in the car industry?

Q4. What other production and cost data would be useful for a car company which is considering further outsourcing of elements of its supply chain?

Approaching the question

When you are given stimulus materials (here data), try to *use* the materials in your answer, wherever appropriate. When there are several parts to a question (or several questions), assume that they give equal marks, unless you are told otherwise.

Important points to include

Q1. You are given information in the two tables that you can use to discuss the benefits of size in the car industry. For example, any small car manufacturer producing only 100,000 cars per year will have average production costs 34% higher than a large car maker producing

2,000,000 or more cars per year. You can use other data in the first table to discuss the advantages and disadvantages of different volumes of output, comparing rival car producers.

The second table provides data on the 'optimum' output for a range of non-production activities, where 'optimum' means at the lowest average cost (i.e. 'minimum efficient size' **- see page 99**). You can again discuss the benefits of size for large car producers.

Q2. You can use the earlier discussion **(pages 96–98)** on technical and non-technical economies of scale here.

Q3. Growth in size via organic growth, merger, acquisition, joint venture, etc., would be important for smaller car producers. This would also apply to the range of 'service' functions in the second table, as well as to plant size in the first table. You could link the data to empirical and case study evidence, such as rival car producers collaborating on engines and other parts but competing on design.

Q4. The idea of relative unit labour cost **(pages 104–106)** would be relevant here, explaining that it is not just labour costs that are important, but also labour productivity and the exchange rate.

Make your answer stand out

Diagrams can be used to support your points, e.g. Figures 4.4 and 4.5 when discussing benefits of size and Figure 4.6 when discussing economies of experience. Draw your diagrams neatly, label them fully and use them in your answer. Up-to-date case-study examples and empirical evidence will also help to make your answer stand out.

Read to impress

Here are some books, articles and other sources that you can use to develop your answers on the topic area.

Books

Griffiths, A. and Wall, S. (2011) *Economics for Business and Management*, 3rd edition, Chapter 3, Pearson Education.

Parkin, M., Powell, M. and Matthews, K. (2012) *Economics*, 8th edition, Chapters 9 and 10, Addison Wesley.

Sloman, J. and Garratt, D. (2010) *Essentials of Economics*, 5th edition, Chapter 4, FT/Prentice Hall.

Sloman, J., Wride, A. and Garratt, D. (2012) *Economics*, 8th edition, Pearson Education.

Journals and periodicals

The following are useful sources of articles and data on many aspects relevant to this and other topics:

Business Review, Philip Allan (quarterly)

Economic Review, Philip Allan (quarterly)

Economics Today, Anforme (quarterly)

Harvard Business Review (monthly)

The Economist (weekly)

Newspapers

Newspapers are important sources of up-to-date information, examples and data. Below are some of the main UK newspaper sources, many of which have websites with search facilities to identify specific topics and articles:

The Guardian

The Times

The Financial Times

The Independent

The Telegraph

Companion website

Go to the companion website at **www.pearsoned.co.uk/econexpress** to find more revision support online for this topic area.

Notes

Notes

5 Firm objectives and firm behaviour

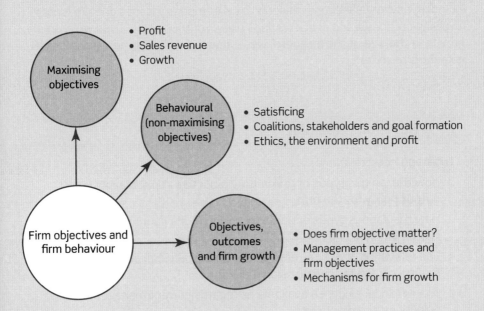

Maximising objectives
- Profit
- Sales revenue
- Growth

Behavioural (non-maximising objectives)
- Satisficing
- Coalitions, stakeholders and goal formation
- Ethics, the environment and profit

Firm objectives and firm behaviour

Objectives, outcomes and firm growth
- Does firm objective matter?
- Management practices and firm objectives
- Mechanisms for firm growth

A printable version of this topic map is available from **www.pearsoned.co.uk/econexpress**

Introduction

When, in April 2012, Philip Clarke, the Chief Executive Officer (CEO) of Tesco, gave a specific undertaking to shareholders that it would quit the USA unless its 'Fresh and Easy' stores at least 'broke even' by February 2013, this was regarded by many observers as 'astonishingly candid'! CEOs are rarely so specific with business objectives, whether for their overall group activities or for those of particular operating divisions within the group. In this case the grocery giant had just announced its first group profit warning in over 20 years and revealed losses in the US of over £700m in the previous five years, despite over £1 billion of capital investment there over that period.

This chapter will help you examine a number of alternative objectives open to the firm, including those of a *maximising* type, whether for profit, sales revenue or growth. The implications for firm price and output of different objectives are examined. A number of *non-maximising* or behavioural objectives are also reviewed, including recent research into actual firm behaviour. We note that although profit is important, careful consideration must be given to a number of other objectives if we are accurately to predict firm behaviour, including how organisations respond to contemporary issues and pressures involving corporate and social responsibility. For those objectives which imply growth in the size of the business, we review the different mechanisms available for firm growth.

 Revision checklist

What you need to know:

- ❏ How the various types of maximising objective impact on price and output policy for the firm.
- ❏ How the various types of non-maximising (behavioural) objectives impact on price and output policy for the firm.
- ❏ The relevance of ethical, environmental and ecological considerations for firm objectives and decision making.
- ❏ The empirical evidence available as regards current management objectives and practices.
- ❏ The mechanisms available for achieving growth-related objectives, whether organic or non-organic (mergers and acquisitions).

Assessment advice

Use diagrams

As in earlier topics, diagrams can be used to show how different firm objectives will lead to different decisions as regards the price and output policy of the firm. For example, revenue and cost curves can be used to show how the profit-maximising firm will usually charge a higher price and produce a lower level of output than the firm seeking other objectives, such as maximising sales revenue or growth.

Use consistent terminology

It will help to distinguish between maximising objectives and non-maximising objectives. The latter are often referred to as 'behavioural' objectives, since they more closely reflect how businesses and organisations actually respond to a range of market pressures.

Use empirical evidence

Using actual case study examples and evidence to illustrate your points is important in this topic area.

 Assessment question

Can you answer this stimulus-based question? Guidelines on answering the question are presented at the end of this chapter.

Look carefully at Table 5.1 which presents the results from a major questionnaire survey on firm objectives.

Table 5.1 Important objectives identified by the firms surveyed (%).

Objectives	Per cent
No single objective	30
Maximising profit	26
Maximising sales revenue	10

Objectives	Per cent
Increasing shareholder value	15
Growing the size of the business	12
Other	7
Total	**100**

Q1. What do the results of the survey suggest as regards firm objectives? Examine the various objectives and explain your reasoning.

Q2. How might a knowledge of the objectives of a particular firm help to predict its price and output behaviour? Explain your reasoning.

Maximising objectives

The objectives of an organisation can be grouped under two main headings: *maximising objectives* and *non-maximising objectives*. We shall see that marginal analysis is particularly important when reviewing maximising objectives.

Profit

For most firms, *profit* is a major concern. **Total profit** is defined as total revenue minus total cost, **average profit** as average revenue minus average total cost, and **marginal profit** as marginal revenue minus marginal cost. Profit is an important objective because:

• it ensures the long-term survival of the business;
• it provides a source of finance for future investment;
• it provides rewards for stakeholders (dividends for shareholders, wage increases for employees, price reductions or improved products for the consumer);
• it provides a measure of the efficiency and effectiveness of management policies;
• it allows comparison with other forms of investment.

Key definitions

Total profit

Total profit is total revenue minus total cost (TP = TR − TC).

Average profit

Average profit is average revenue minus average total cost (AP = AR − ATC).

Marginal profit

Marginal profit is marginal revenue minus marginal cost (MP = MR − MC).

✳ Assessment advice

Figure 5.1 shows the output (Q_p) at which total profit is a maximum. This diagram will also be useful when considering other maximising objectives, such as sales revenue maximisation and constrained sales revenue maximisation.

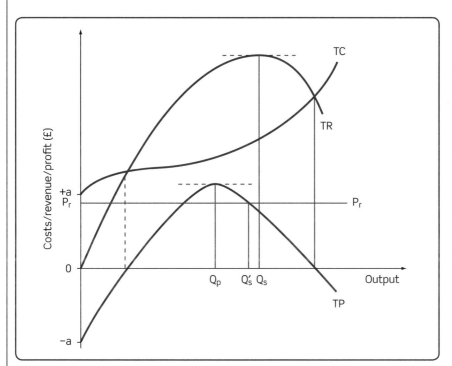

Figure 5.1 Variation of output with firm's objective.

Source: Griffiths, A. and Wall, S. (2011) *Economics for Business and Management* (3rd ed.) © 2011 Pearson Education. Reproduced with permission.

Test yourself

Q1. Had the marginal revenue and marginal cost curves been presented in Figure 5.1, where would they have intersected?

Q2. Had the marginal revenue curve been presented, where would it have intersected the horizontal axis when total revenue (TR) was a maximum?

Profit maximisation and marginal analysis

In Figure 5.2 we show that total profit can be a maximum only when MR = MC.

- In Figure 5.2, for every unit of output up to Q_p, MR > MC and each unit adds something to total profit (i.e. marginal profit is positive).
- In Figure 5.2, for the Q_p th unit of output, MR – MC = 0 and that unit adds nothing to total profit (i.e. marginal profit is zero).
- In Figure 5.2, for every unit of output beyond Q_p, MR < MC and each extra unit reduces total profit (i.e. marginal profit is negative).
- It follows that only at output Q_p is total profit (area RVC) a maximum. If we draw the total profit (TP) curve, it will have reached a maximum value (TP_1) at output OQ_p.

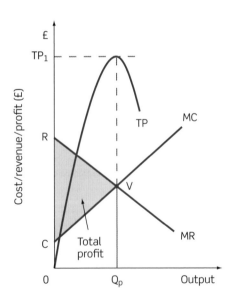

Figure 5.2 Total profit is a maximum (RVC) at the output (Q_p) for which MR = MC.
Source: Griffiths, A. and Wall, S. (2011) *Economics for Business and Management* (3rd ed.)
© 2011 Pearson Education. Reproduced with permission.

Assessment advice

Drawing a diagram such as Figure 5.2 can help indicate why profit maximisation requires marginal revene (MR) to equal marginal cost (MC). It is also useful in showing that at output Q_p the rate of change of total profit (i.e. marginal profit) is zero. We can see this from the fact that the gradient to the TP curve is horizontal at output Q_p (i.e. TP has reached a maximum turning point).

The profit-maximising theory is based on two key assumptions:

1 that owners are in control of the day-to-day management of the firm, so that there is no 'principal–agent' problem (see below);
2 that the main desire of owners is for higher profit.

The case for profit maximisation as 'self-evident' is, as we shall see, undermined if either of these assumptions fails to hold.

Principal–agent problem

To assume that it is the owners who control the firm neglects the fact that the dominant form of industrial organisation is the public limited company (plc) which is usually run by managers rather than by owners. This may lead to conflict between the owners (shareholders) and the managers whenever the managers pursue goals which differ from those of the owners. This conflict is referred to as a type of *principal–agent problem* and emerges when the shareholders (principals) contract a second party, the managers (agents), to perform some tasks on their behalf. In return, the principals offer their agents some compensation (wage payments and bonuses). However, because the principals are divorced from the day-to-day running of the business, the agents may be able to act as they themselves see fit. This independence of action may be due to their superior knowledge of the company as well as their ability to disguise their actions from the principals. Agents, therefore, may not always act in the manner desired by the principals.

The following example highlights an attempt by a particular company, Royal Bank of Scotland (RBS), to align the interests of its executives (agents) more closely with those of its principals (owners).

Examples & evidence

Principal–agent issues at RBS

In March 2010 Royal Bank of Scotland (RBS) unveiled a new tougher reward scheme for senior executives built around a range of performance measures, as the state-backed bank moved to introduce a more balanced pay structure. It was developed after extensive discussions with

UK Financial Investments (UKFI), the body responsible for managing the government's stakes in banks, and with other shareholders.

UKFI had previously supported a pay scheme that focused solely on RBS's share price performance as this was aligned with the government's interest in selling its 70% stake in the bank at a profit. However, UKFI has been keen for RBS to introduce a broader set of performance criteria. Under the new scheme's terms:

- 50% of executive pay will be linked to the bank's economic profit, which factors in its cost of capital.
- 25% of executive pay will be based on the total shareholder return, a measure of the share performance of RBS relative to its competitors, with the maximum awarded for a top quartile performance by RBS.
- 25% of executive pay will be based on the RBS share price performance. Executives will gain a full entitlement if the shares hit 75p; RBS shares were trading at 42p when the scheme was introduced.

FT *Source:* Goff, S. and Jones, A., 'RBS outlines reward scheme to shareholders', *Financial Times*, 19 March 2010.

Questions

1. What contribution might these changes in the remuneration packages for senior executives at RBS make to the principal–agent problem?

2. What are the arguments for including a target share price in the remuneration package?

3. Why include elements other than share price performance?

When it is the agents' objectives that predominate, there may be a shift of focus away from profit. This has led to a number of managerial theories of firm behaviour, such as the maximisation of sales revenue (turnover), the maximisation of firm growth, and a range of non-maximising objectives.

Sales revenue

It has been suggested that the manager-controlled firm is likely to have sales revenue (turnover) maximisation as its main goal rather than the profit maximisation favoured by shareholders. W. J. Baumol argued that the salaries of top managers and other perquisites (perks) are more closely correlated with sales revenue than with profits, giving managers an incentive to prioritise sales revenue in situations where managers have effective control of the firm.

If management seeks to maximise sales revenue without any thought of profit at all (i.e. *pure sales revenue maximisation*), this would lead to output Q_s in Figure 5.1. This Q_s th unit of output is neither raising nor lowering total revenue, i.e. its marginal revenue is zero and total revenue is a maximum.

 Assessment advice

You will gain extra credit if you can present diagrams and use them to explain why different objectives will lead to different levels of output and price.

Constrained sales revenue maximisation

Both Baumol and Williamson recognised that some constraint on managers is often exercised by shareholders. The shareholders might demand at least a certain level of distributed profit, so that sales revenue can only be maximised subject to this profit constraint.

The difference a profit constraint makes to firm output is shown in Figure 5.1:

- If P_r is the minimum profit required by shareholders, then Q_s' is the output that permits the highest total revenue while still meeting the profit constraint.
- Any output beyond Q_s' would raise total revenue TR – the major objective – but reduce total profit TP below the minimum required (P_r).
- Therefore Q_s' represents the *constrained sales revenue maximisation* output.

Other analysts suggest that firms will seek to maximise the rate at which they grow their business.

Test yourself

Q3. Use Figure 5.1 to explain how the target level of output varies with different firm objectives.

Growth

Some of the main reasons for firms seeking growth include the following:

- *Cost savings*: large firms can benefit from economies of scale.
- *Diversification of product*: larger firms can reduce the risk of dependence on one product or service.
- *Diversification of market*: larger firms can reduce their dependence on one market or on one set of customers.

- *Market power*: larger firms have increased power in the market, which allows them to influence prices and to obtain better profit margins through reduced competition.
- *Risk reduction*: larger firms are less likely to suffer in market downturns as they can spread their 'risk' over a broader portfolio of products and of market outlets.

The Marris model of growth

So far we have assumed that the goals of owners (profits) have been in conflict with the goals of management (sales revenue). R. Marris, however, argues that the overriding goal which *both* managers and owners have in common is growth:

- Managers seek growth in demand for the firm's products or services, to raise sales revenue and firm size, and thereby managerial income, power and status.
- Owners seek growth in the capital value of the firm to increase personal wealth.

Marris suggests that it is only through the growth of the firm that the goals of both managers and owners can be achieved.

Central to the analysis of Marris is the ratio of retained to distributed profits, i.e. the 'retention ratio':

- If managers distribute most of the profits (*low retention ratio*), shareholders will be content and the share price will be sufficiently high to deter takeover.
- If managers distribute less profit (*high retention ratio*), then the retained profit can be used for investment, stimulating the growth of the firm. In this case shareholders may be less content, and the share price lower, thereby increasing the risk of a takeover bid.

The major objective of the firm, with which both managers and shareholders are in accord, is therefore seen by Marris as maximising the rate of growth of both the firm's demand and the firm's capital ('*balanced growth*') subject to an acceptable retention ratio. Figure 5.3 shows the trade-off between higher balanced growth and the average profit rate.

In Figure 5.3, point Z is where the balanced growth rate is at a maximum (G1), with an implied retention ratio so high that all profitable investment projects have been pursued, giving an average profit rate Pr_1. Risk avoidance by managers may, however, enforce a lower retention ratio with more profits distributed.

Point Y is a constrained growth-maximising position (G_2), with a lower retention ratio, lower investment and higher average profit (Pr_2) than at point Z.

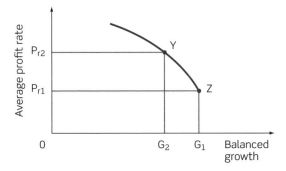

Figure 5.3 Trade-off between average profit and balanced growth.
Source: Griffiths, A. and Wall, S. (2011) *Economics for Business and Management* (3rd ed.) © 2011 Pearson Education. Reproduced with permission.

How close the firm gets to its major objective, Z, will depend on how constrained management feels by the risk of disgruntled shareholders, or of a takeover bid, should the retention ratio be kept at the high rates consistent with points near to Z.

Behavioural (non-maximising objectives)

The traditional (owner control) and managerial (non-owner control) theories of the firm assume that a single goal (objective) will be pursued. The firm then attempts to achieve the highest value for that goal, whether profits, sales revenue or growth.

The *behaviouralist* viewpoint is rather different and sees the firm as an organisation with various groups, such as workers, managers, shareholders and customers, each of which has its own goal, or set of goals. The group that achieves prominence at any point in time may be able to guide the firm into promoting its 'goal set' over time. This dominant group may then be replaced by another giving greater emphasis to a totally different 'goal set'.

The traditional and managerial theories which propose the maximisation of a single goal are seen by behaviouralists as being remote from the organisational complexity of modern firms.

Satisficing

One of the earliest behavioural theories was that of H. A. Simon who suggested that, in practice, managers cannot identify when a marginal point has been reached, such as maximum profit with marginal cost equal to marginal revenue. Consequently, managers set themselves *minimum acceptable levels of achievement*. Firms which are satisfied in achieving such limited objectives are said to 'satisfice' rather than 'maximise'.

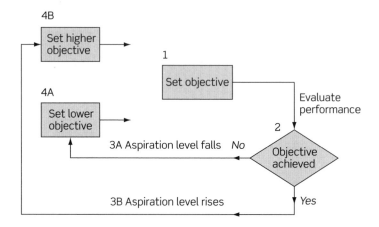

Figure 5.4 Development of aspiration levels through goal achievement.
Source: Griffiths, A. and Wall, S. (2011) *Economics for Business and Management* (3rd ed.) © 2011 Pearson Education. Reproduced with permission.

This is not to say that satisficing leads to some long-term performance which is less than would otherwise be achieved. The achievement of objectives has long been recognised as an incentive to improving performance and is the basis of the management technique known as management by objectives (MBO).

Figure 5.4 illustrates how the attainment of initially limited objectives might lead to an improved long-term performance. At the starting point 1, the manager sets the objective and attempts to achieve it. If, after evaluation, it is found that the objective has been achieved, then this will lead to an increase in aspirational level (3B). A new and higher objective (4B) will then emerge. Thus, by setting achievable objectives, what might be an initial minimum target turns out to be a prelude to a series of higher targets, perhaps culminating in the achievement of some maximum target or objective.

If, on the other hand, the initial objective is *not* achieved, then aspirational levels are lowered (3A) until achievable objectives (4A) are set.

Simon's theory is one in which no single objective can be presumed to be the inevitable outcome of this organisational process. In fact, the final objective may be far removed from the initial one.

✳ Assessment advice

Being able to compare and contrast a range of non-maximising (behavioural) objectives with maximising objectives will gain extra credit. This demonstrates an awareness of how organisations actually behave and the objectives which result from that behaviour.

Coalitions, stakeholders and goal formation

If a firm is 'satisficing', then who is being satisficed – and how? R. M. Cyert and J. G. March were rather more specific than Simon in identifying various groups or coalitions within an organisation. A *coalition* is any group that, at a given moment, shares a consensus on the goals to be pursued.

- Workers may form one coalition, wanting good wages and work conditions and some job security.
- Managers may form another coalition and want power and prestige as well as high salaries.
- Shareholders may form yet another coalition and want high profits.

These differing coalitions with differing goals may well result in group conflict, e.g. higher wages for workers may mean lower profits for shareholders.

The behavioural theory of Cyert and March, along with that of Simon, does not then view the firm as having *one* outstanding objective (e.g. profit maximisation) but rather *many*, often conflicting, objectives.

Cyert, March and others have suggested that different coalitions will be in effective control of firms (i.e. be *dominant*) at different times. For example, in times of recession the dominant coalition may be that which has formed around the cost and management accountants with the agreed objective of avoiding bankruptcy. In more prosperous times the dominant coalitions may involve marketing or promotion directors and others seeking objectives such as higher turnover, market share or growth. Clearly, different objectives may be followed depending on the coalitions that are dominant at any point in time.

The following are just some of the multiple objectives or goals identified by Cyert and March:

- *profit goals* (e.g. rate of return on capital employed);
- *sales goals* (e.g. growth of turnover or market share);
- *production goals* (e.g. to achieve a given level of capacity or to achieve a certain unit cost of production);
- *financial goals* (e.g. to achieve a sustainable cash flow).

Within the organisation different groups will pursue different priorities. In order to achieve success, the firm's managers have to compromise and trade off some goals or objectives against others. For example, a single-minded pursuit of production goals can obviously conflict with sales goals (if the production levels exceed market demand), inventory goals (if the unsold production piles up in warehouses), financial goals (if the firm's cash is tied up in unsold output) and profit goals (if, in order to sell the output, prices are slashed to below cost).

Examples & evidence

TESCO changes tack

In January 2012 there was a major shock to the UK retail sector as Tesco unveiled a poor trading performance over the past year and a warning that profits in the coming year would be lower than previously forecast. This led immediately to a collapse in the Tesco share price, which fell by 16% in one day, 12 January 2012, wiping £5 billion off the company's value. The 'hypothesis' immediately advanced by analysts was that 'the big price drop' strategy announced in a fanfare by Tesco in September 2011, involving price cuts totalling over £500 million, had in fact been directly responsible for the profits debacle, many analysts now calling it 'the big profits drop' strategy.

The Chief Executive Officer of Tesco, Philip Clarke, made a number of observations as to its future direction. 'What we must do is improve relative to the competition, because that's how consumers make a choice between one shop and another. Retail is always a game of loyalty – we need to earn their lifetime loyalty' (Walsh, K., *Sunday Times*, 15 January 2012, 'Business', p. 7).

Tesco announced a series of new initiatives aimed at countering the 2% loss of market share to its rivals. These included attempts to reduce costs (e.g. cutting back on planned out-of-town stores) and to increase revenue (e.g. more expenditure on online sales platforms).

Questions

1. What business objectives might have been behind Tesco's 'big price drop' strategy?
2. Why might that strategy have failed to achieve those objectives?
3. What new objectives would Tesco seem to be setting for the future?

Stakeholder approaches

It is not just internal groups that need to be satisfied. There is an increasing focus by leading organisations on *stakeholders*, i.e. the range of both internal and external groups which relate to that organisation. Stakeholders have been defined as any group or individual who can affect or be affected by the achievement of the organisation's objectives. Cyert and March suggest that the aim of top management is to set goals that resolve conflict between these opposing stakeholder groups.

Ethics, the environment and profit

It is often suggested that firm behaviour which seeks to be more than usually ethical or to give considerable weight to environmental concerns must do so at the expense of profit. However, many firms are now seeing ethical and environmentally responsible behaviour as being in their own self-interest.

Examples & evidence

Fairtrade

It was reported in 2012 that annual sales of *Fairtrade* food and drink in Britain have reached over £600m, having grown at over 40% per year over the past decade. It has expanded from one brand of coffee 10 years ago to around 1,000 foodstuffs, including chocolate, fruit, vegetables, juices, snacks, wine, tea, sugar, honey and nuts. A Mori poll found that two-thirds of UK consumers claim to be green or ethical and actively look to purchase products with an environmental/ethical association.

Question

1. Can you give examples of those who might benefit and those who might lose from the growth of Fairtrade?

Various 'kitemarks' exist for firms to certify that their product conforms to ethical standards in production, such as the Rug-Mark for carpets and rugs, the Forest Stewardship Council mark to certify wood derived from sustainable forestry extraction methods, and the Fairtrade mark which guarantees a higher return to developing country producers.

Corporate governance

Corporate governance refers to the various arrangements within companies which provide both authority and accountability in its operations; in other words, the various rules and procedures which are in place to direct and control the running of the company. However, there has been much concern in recent years as to the ways in which the larger public limited companies have been governed, especially in view of high-profile company collapses such as those of Enron in the US in 2001 and Parmalat in Italy in 2004.

Executive remuneration

The issue of *executive remuneration* has also been a major source of concern to shareholders and other corporate investors.

In Europe 84% of companies place decisions about executive pay in the hands of their compensation or remuneration committee, so ultimately it is remuneration committees that are as responsible as anyone when executive pay appears to bear little relationship to corporate performance.

Stock options have been a particular source of criticism – the practice whereby senior executives have been given the 'option' of buying company shares at a heavily discounted price (i.e. lower than the market price) and then selling them at a profit should they succeed in raising the share price above an agreed target. Often, exercising these options has given far more income to executives than their basic salaries.

Examples & evidence

Executive pay

Table 5.2 shows the average CEO compensation across the FTSE 100 companies over the period 1998–2011, the average employee earnings across those companies, and the multiple between the two. Clearly the general trend has been one whereby the multiple is rising, though with some reduction in the recessionary period 2007–2011. However, there has been a major change from a situation where the average CEO salary of FTSE 100 companies was 47 times the average employee salary in 1998 to one in which it was 118 times that salary in 2011.

Table 5.2 Executive and average employee compensation in FTSE 100 companies, 1998–2011.

Year	Average CEO earnings (£)	Average employee earnings (£)	Multiple
1998	1,012,380	21,540	47
1999	1,235,401	20,939	59
2000	1,684,900	24,070	70
2001	1,812,750	24,170	75
2002	2,587,474	24,182	107
2003	2,773,904	24,767	112
2004	3,121,435	25,955	119

Year	Average CEO earnings (£)	Average employee earnings (£)	Multiple
2005	3,312,285	27,254	121
2006	3,339,421	30,828	107
2007	3,935,820	25,677	151
2008	3,950,642	30,994	128
2009	3,710,440	32,521	115
2010	3,740,628	32,019	117
2011	3,820,501	32,320	118

Source: FT (various).

Questions

1. What do the data suggest in terms of firm objective?
2. How might the issue of executive pay be resolved?

Objectives, outcomes and firm growth

Does firm objective matter?

The analyst is continually seeking to predict the output and price behaviour of the firm. Figure 5.1 has already indicated that *firm output* does indeed depend upon firm objective, with the profit-maximising firm having a lower output than the sales-revenue-maximising firm (pure and constrained).

Price, output and firm objective

If we remember that price is average revenue (i.e. total revenue/total output), we can see from Figure 5.5 that *firm price* will also vary with firm objective.

Price in the pure sales-maximising firm $= \tan \theta_s = R_1/Q_s$

Price in the profit-maximising firm $= \tan \theta_p = R_2/Q_p$

$$\tan \theta_s < \tan \theta_p$$

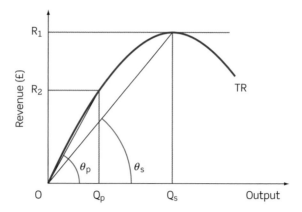

Figure 5.5 Variation of price with firm's objective.

Source: Griffiths, A. and Wall, S. (2011) *Economics for Business and Management* (3rd ed.) © 2011 Pearson Education. Reproduced with permission.

Price of the pure sales-maximising firm is below that of the profit-maximising firm. It is clear that it really does matter what objective we assume for the firm, since both output and price depend on that objective.

Test yourself

Look carefully at Figure 5.6.

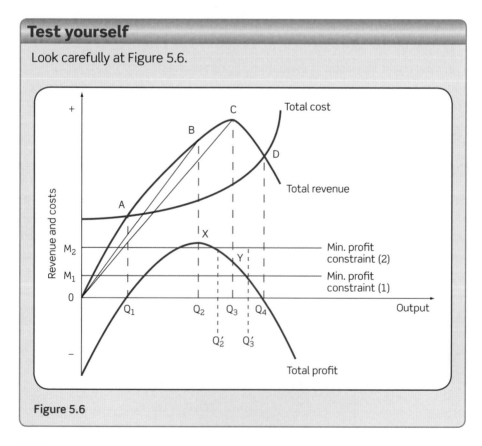

Figure 5.6

Q4. At what output is total profit a maximum? What is the value of total profit at this output?

Q5. At what output is total revenue a maximum? What is the value of total revenue at this output?

Q6. What is the situation at both output Q_1 and output Q_4?

Q7. If the firm is seeking to maximise sales revenue subject to the minimum profit constraint (1), what output should it produce? Would anything change if the minimum profit constraint rises from (1) to (2)?

Management practices and firm objectives

Recent evidence on management practice broadly supports the behavioural contention, namely that it is unhelpful to seek a single firm objective as a guide to actual firm behaviour.

Portfolio planning

Work in the US by the Boston Consulting Group known as 'portfolio planning' suggests that firms, especially the larger ones, can be viewed as having a collection or 'portfolio' of different products at different stages in the product life cycle. If a product is at an early stage in its life cycle, it will require a large investment in marketing and product development in order to achieve future levels of high profitability. At the same time another product may have 'matured' and, already possessing a good share of the market, be providing high profits and substantial cash flow.

The usual strategy in portfolio planning is to attempt to balance the portfolio so that existing profitable products are providing the funds necessary to raise new products to maturity. This approach has become a classic part of strategic decision making.

- If a firm is using the portfolio approach in its planning, it may be impossible to predict the firm's behaviour for individual products or market sectors on the basis of a single firm objective.

- This is because the goals of the firm will change for a given product or market sector depending on the relative position of that product or market sector within the overall portfolio.

'Managing for value' (MFV)

The non-maximisation behaviour of large companies can be seen clearly in the 'managing for value' approach taken by some large companies. For example, between 1997 and 2000 Cadbury Schweppes, the chocolate and confectionery multinational, prior to its acquisition by Kraft, explained its objectives in terms of 'managing for value' (MFV). To meet the MFV criterion the company stressed the importance of the following:

- increasing earnings per share by at least 10% every year;
- generating £150m of free cash flow every year;
- doubling the value of shareholders' investment in the four years to 2000;
- competing in the world's growth markets by effective internal investment and by value-enhancing acquisitions;
- developing market share by introducing innovations in product development, packaging and routes to market;
- increasing commitment to value creation in managers and employees through incentive schemes and share ownership;
- investing in key areas of air emissions, water, energy and solid waste.

From the above list it is clear that the first three preoccupations were related to the profit objectives while the fourth and fifth were related to company growth and market share. In addition, the final two objectives encompassed both human resource and environmental issues. In this context, it can be seen that maximising a single corporate goal seems unrealistic in the dynamic world of multinationals.

 Assessment advice

Being able to explain organisational constraints on management decision making will gain extra credit, as will using examples and evidence for the ways in which firms seek to fulfil specific objectives, such as firm growth.

Mechanisms for firm growth

Firms grow by either **organic growth** or **non-organic growth**. Four major forms of non-organic growth are often identified: horizontal integration, vertical integration, conglomerate integration, and lateral integration.

Key definitions

Organic growth

Organic growth occurs when firms use their own resources to grow in size, such as by ploughing back profits.

Non-organic growth

Non-organic growth occurs when firms seek to grow in size by merger, acquisition or joint venture.

Horizontal integration

Horizontal integration occurs when firms combine at the same stage of production, involving similar products or services. Some 80% of mergers are of this type. The acquisition of Cadbury by Kraft in 2010 was an example of horizontal integration resulting in the world's largest confectioner.

Horizontal integration may provide a number of economies at the level of both the plant (productive unit) and the enterprise (business unit).

- *Plant economies* may follow from the rationalisation made possible by horizontal integration. For instance, production may be concentrated at a smaller number of enlarged plants, permitting the familiar technical economies of greater specialisation, the dovetailing of separate processes at higher output, and the application of the 'engineers' rule' whereby material costs increase as the square but capacity as the cube. All these lead to a reduction in cost per unit as the size of plant output increases.

- *Enterprise economies* may also follow from the growth in size of the whole enterprise, permitting economies via bulk purchase, the spread of similar administrative costs over greater output, the cheaper cost of finance, etc.

Examples & evidence

Horizontal integration

- In 2012 *Walgreen*, America's largest drugstore chain, took a 45% stake in *Alliance Boots* which owns *Boots* chemist shops. The deal is worth $6.7 billion and gives Walgreen the option of buying the remaining shares in Boots by late 2015. The combined company will be the world's biggest buyer of prescription drugs.

- Japanese *Shiseido*, the cosmetics company, bought Californian rival *Bare Escentuals* for $1.7bn (£1bn) in 2010. This made Shiseido the world's fourth largest cosmetics company behind L'Oréal, Procter & Gamble, and Unilever.

- In the UK, the *Co-operative Society* took over *Somerfield* stores in 2009 to give it an 8% share of the UK's grocery market. The £1.6bn takeover makes the Co-operative Society the fifth largest food chain in the UK.

- *Lafarge SA*, the leading French global cement company, acquired the Egyptian company *Orascom Cement*, the leading cement group in the Middle East and Mediterranean, for $12.8bn in 2008, in order to strengthen its presence in the region.

Question

1. Can you give an example of horizontal integration in the past 12 months?

Vertical integration

This occurs when firms combine at different stages of production of a common good or service. Only about 5% of UK mergers are of this type.

- *Backward vertical integration.* Firms might benefit by being able to exert closer control over quality and delivery of supplies if the vertical integration is 'backwards', i.e. towards the source of supply. Factor inputs might also be cheaper, obtained at cost instead of cost + profit.
- *Forward vertical integration.* Alternatively, vertical integration could be 'forwards' – towards the retail outlet. This may give the firm merging 'forward' more control of wholesale or retail pricing policy, and more direct customer contact.

Vertical integration can often lead to increased control of the market, infringing monopoly legislation. This is undoubtedly one reason why it is so infrequent. Another is the fact that, as Marks & Spencer has shown, it is not necessary to have a controlling interest in suppliers in order to exert effective control over them. Textile suppliers of Marks & Spencer send over 75% of their total output to the company. Marks & Spencer have been able to use this reliance to its own advantage. In return for placing long production runs with these suppliers, Marks & Spencer has been able to restrict supplier profit margins while maintaining their viability. Apart from low costs of purchase, Marks & Spencer is also able to insist on frequent batch delivery, cutting stockholding costs to a minimum.

Examples & evidence

Vertical integration

- An example of backward vertical integration can be seen in the case of the US aircraft company *Boeing*, which bought out its parts suppliers *Vought Aircraft* in 2009 and *Global Aeronautics* in 2008, in order to control the supply chain for its 787 Dreamliner plane which had fallen behind in terms of its production schedule.
- An example of forward vertical integration is the acquisition in 2012 by *Dell*, a maker of personal computers, of *Quest*, which provides corporate business management systems. The $2.4bn acquisition reflects Dell's strategy to push beyond hardware into higher-margin software.

Question

1. Can you give an example of vertical integration in the past 12 months?

Conglomerate integration

This refers to the adding of different products to each firm's operations. Diversification into products and areas in which the acquiring firm was not previously directly involved accounted for over 30% of mergers and acquisitions in the UK. The major benefit is the spreading of risk for the firms and shareholders involved. Giant conglomerates like Unilever (with interests in food, detergents, toilet preparations, chemicals, paper, plastics, packaging, animal feeds, transport and tropical plantations – in 75 countries) are largely cushioned against any damaging movements which are restricted to particular product groups or particular countries. The various *enterprise economies* outlined above may also result from a conglomerate merger. The ability to buy companies relatively cheaply on the stock exchange, and to sell parts of them off at a profit later is another important reason for some conglomerate mergers.

Examples & evidence

Conglomerate integration

Procter & Gamble (P&G), the US multinational, is the world's largest consumer group conglomerate, owning brands such as Pringles crisps, Pampers nappies and Crest toothpaste. In recent years it has broadened its portfolio of products still further into haircare, acquiring Nioxin, a US scalp care company, in 2009, Gillette hair care products in 2005, the German haircare company, Wella, in 2003, and Clairol in 2001.

Question

1. Can you give an example of conglomerate integration in the past 12 months?

Lateral integration

This is sometimes given separate treatment, though in practice it is difficult to distinguish from a conglomerate merger. The term 'lateral integration' is often used when the firms which combine are involved in different products, but in products which have *some element of commonality*. This might be in terms of factor input, such as requiring similar labour skills, capital equipment or raw materials; or it might be in terms of product outlet.

Examples & evidence

Lateral integration

- In 2012 *Starbucks* developed a joint venture with *Square*, a pioneer in technology, that enables payments through smartphones. Square's GPS-based system will eventually allow Starbucks customers to pay for their latte by simply saying their name.

- In 2012 *Microsoft* took a major step into digital books by acquiring a 17.6% stake in *Barnes & Noble*'s Nook e-reader business. The pair will develop a Nook app for Microsoft's Windows 8 operating system and share revenue from e-book sales. The alliance will seek to challenge Amazon's Kindle and Apple's i-Book.

Question

1. Can you give an example of lateral integration in the past 12 months?

Chapter summary – pulling it all together

By the end of this chapter you should be able to:

	Confident ✓	Not confident?
Examine how the various types of maximising objectives impact on price and output policy for the firm		Revise pages 114–121 and 127–129
Examine how the various types of non-maximising (behavioural) objectives impact on price and output policy for the firm		Revise pages 121–124
Assess the relevance of ethical, environmental and ecological considerations for firm objectives and decision making		Revise pages 125–127
Review the empirical evidence available as regards current management objectives and practices		Revise pages 129–130
Explain the mechanisms available for achieving growth-related objectives, whether organic or non-organic (mergers and acquisitions)		Revise pages 130–134

Now try the **assessment question** at the start of this chapter, using the answer guidelines below.

Answer guidelines

✳ Assessment question

Look again at the data in the assessment question at the start of this chapter and answer the following questions.

Q1. What do the results of the survey suggest as regards firm objectives? Examine the various objectives and explain your reasoning.

Q2. How might a knowledge of the objectives of a particular firm help to predict its price and output behaviour? Explain your reasoning.

Approaching the question

This question requires you to *use* the data presented in responding to the questions, especially Q1. Try to think in terms of the various maximising and non-maximising (behavioural) objectives you have studied and relate these to the data in the table. Remember to explain any interpretation you give to the data.

Important points to include

For Q1, you could identify profit as clearly an important objective as 26% of respondents claim to seek to maximise profit. However, you might argue that profit is also implied by 'increasing shareholder value' (15%) since, for example, share price is often closely related to dividend payout. It may also be that profit is one of several objectives identified by the 30% who responded with 'no single objective'.

The data would, however, seem to imply other maximising objectives and non-maximising (behavioural) objectives, such as maximising sales revenue (10%) and growth of the business (12%). The 30% with 'no single objective' may include firms which are satisficers or who have established coalitions with the predominant objectives varying according to which coalition is dominant at any particular time or which stage of the product life cycle has been reached for products in the firm's portfolio.

For Q2, diagrams will be particularly important and you could make use of Figures 5.1 and 5.5 especially. You can use these to show that price and output will vary depending on firm objective – for example a profit maximising objective will tend to have lower levels of output and higher prices than would the other possible objectives.

Make your answer stand out

The careful drawing, labelling and use of diagrams will make your answer stand out and gain higher marks, especially in Q2. So too will your awareness of actual management practices (portfolio planning, managing for value, etc.). You might make the point that a particular firm may have different objectives at different times, depending on the stage of the product life cycle, the coalition which is dominant at any particular time or the stakeholders it is seeking to support, and so on.

Read to impress

Here are some books, articles and other sources that you can use to develop your answers on the topic area.

Books

Griffiths, A. and Wall, S. (2011) *Economics for Business and Management*, 3rd edition, Chapter 4, Pearson Education.

Parkin, M., Powell, M. and Matthews, K. (2012) *Economics*, 8th edition, Chapter 9, Addison Wesley.

Sloman, J. and Garratt, D. (2010) *Essentials of Economics*, 5th edition, Chapters 4 and 5, FT/Prentice Hall.

Sloman, J., Wride, A. and Garratt, D. (2012) *Economics*, 8th edition, Pearson Education.

Journals and periodicals

The following are useful sources of articles and data on many aspects relevant to this and other topics:

Business Review, Philip Allan (quarterly)
Economic Review, Philip Allan (quarterly)
Economics Today, Anforme (quarterly)
Harvard Business Review (monthly)
The Economist (weekly)

Newspapers

Newspapers are important sources of up-to-date information, examples and data. Below are some of the main UK newspaper sources, many of which have websites with search facilities to identify specific topics and articles:

The Guardian
The Times
The Financial Times
The Independent
The Telegraph

Companion website

Go to the companion website at **www.pearsoned.co.uk/econexpress** to find revision support online for this topic area.

Notes

Notes

6

Perfect competition, monopoly and contestable markets

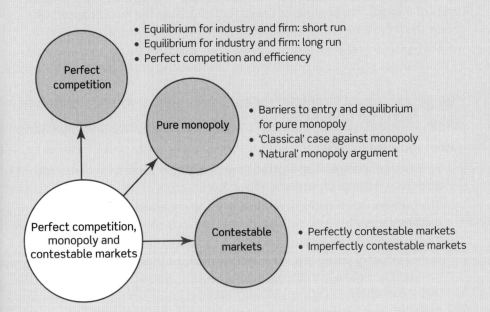

- Equilibrium for industry and firm: short run
- Equilibrium for industry and firm: long run
- Perfect competition and efficiency

Perfect competition

Pure monopoly

- Barriers to entry and equilibrium for pure monopoly
- 'Classical' case against monopoly
- 'Natural' monopoly argument

Perfect competition, monopoly and contestable markets

Contestable markets

- Perfectly contestable markets
- Imperfectly contestable markets

A printable version of this topic map is available from **www.pearsoned.co.uk/econexpress**

Introduction

With UK energy prices soaring in recent years in some cases by up to 20% per annum, there have been widespread calls for increased competition in the gas, electricity and other energy-related sectors. The public outcry for lower energy prices even led the UK government to propose regulations to force the energy companies to identify and provide the lowest tariff available for each household, responding to consumer complaints that there are over 500 separate tariffs for electricity alone. Such information overload is widely seen as acting as a disincentive for consumers to find and then switch to the lowest-cost source available.

This chapter will help you examine the allocation of resources under perfect competition and pure monopoly, widely regarded as types of market structure at the opposite ends of the competition spectrum. We also review the so-called 'contestable' markets hypothesis, which suggests that the mere *threat* of new firm entry will cause existing firms in an imperfect market to act as though they were in a competitive market. The formal definition of monopoly in the UK is where more than one-third of the output of an industry is in the hands of a single firm or group of linked firms. Later, **in the next chapter,** we review the more intermediate competitive market structures of monopolistic competition and oligopoly.

 Revision checklist:

What you need to know:

- ❑ Why perfect competition is often regarded as the 'ideal' form of market structure in terms of resource allocation.
- ❑ The barriers which deter new firm entry and generate 'market power' for existing firms.
- ❑ The basis for the so-called 'classical' case against monopoly, namely higher industry prices and lower industry output than would exist under competitive market structures, and other criticisms of welfare loss under monopoly.
- ❑ The 'natural monopoly' argument with only one firm seen as the most efficient outcome.
- ❑ How 'contestable market' analysis can still be used to predict competitive outcomes in industries which are anything but competitive!

Assessment advice

Provide a clear structure

Whenever you are referring to perfect competition, monopoly or contestable markets, you should carefully define those terms. For example, are you referring to 'pure' monopoly, where a single firm controls all the output, or to a 'technical' monopoly, where a single firm controls one-third or more of the output? Remember to outline the key characteristics of each market structure and to explain how these influence the equilibrium price and output for the industry. You will often need to compare and contrast price, output and welfare (consumer surplus + producer surplus) outcomes of these different markets with those of perfect competition.

Use diagrams

For this topic you can use side-by-side diagrams (see Figures 6.6(a) and (b)) to show the equilibrium price and output in the long run both for the perfectly competitive industry and for the individual firm. You can also use a diagram (Figure 6.8) to explain why the 'classical' case suggests a higher price and lower output for a (pure) monopoly industry as compared with a perfectly competitive industry, or Figure 6.9 to show how monopoly results in less economic welfare than a competitive market. Yet another diagram (Figure 6.10) can be used to explain the circumstances under which the 'natural monopoly' argument might apply in which only a single firm can exist if average costs are to be a minimum for that industry. A range of other diagrams can also be used to compare and contrast industry and firm outcomes under the different types of market structure covered in this chapter.

Use empirical evidence

There are many useful case studies of actual firms and industries you can use from newspapers, textbooks and reports by competition authorities in the UK, EU and elsewhere, providing evidence of monopoly power being applied to the disadvantage of consumers. Referring to carefully selected empirical evidence of this kind and using it to support your arguments will gain higher marks.

 Assessment question

Consider the suggestion that monopoly will invariably operate to the disadvantage of consumers.

Perfect competition

Figure 6.1 shows that perfect competition and monopoly fall at the opposite ends of the spectrum of market structures. Perfect competition is often said to represent the 'ideal' market structure in which producers have no control over price and competitive behaviour arguably results in resources being allocated most efficiently. The further to the right on the spectrum in Figure 6.1, the less competitive the market structure and the greater the extent to which the firm can influence price and output.

In this type of market structure, there are a large number of small firms producing identical products with none of these firms having any 'market power', in the sense of being able to influence market price or output. Strictly speaking, for a market to be defined as 'perfectly competitive' a number of conditions must all be met simultaneously:

- *large number of small firms* supplying the product, none of which is able, by itself, to influence overall (market) supply;
- *each small firm is a 'price taker'* in the sense that it recognises that it is too small to influence the ruling market price, which must therefore simply be accepted;
- *large number of buyers*, none of whom is sufficiently large to influence overall (market) demand;
- *perfect information* for both sellers and buyers;
- *homogeneous product* so that the product offered by one firm is identical in all respects to the product offered by the other firms;
- *freedom of entry and exit* so that firms can either enter or leave the market at will, with no 'barriers' to discourage such entry or exit.

These assumptions are extremely restrictive and it would be difficult to find an example of a market structure that fulfils all these assumptions simultaneously. However, some markets display many of the features of perfect competition and it is often argued that the Internet is helping to move markets in the direction of perfect competition.

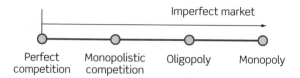

Figure 6.1 Spectrum of market structures.

Source: Griffiths, A. and Wall, S. (2011) *Economics for Business and Management* (3rd ed.) © 2011 Pearson Education. Reproduced with permission.

Examples & evidence

Perfect competition and the Internet

The importance of the Internet in providing important price-comparison data is well known. In November 2012 a major audit of the NHS identified losses of over £500 million per annum as a result of a failure to use Internet-related technologies to communicate between hospitals when purchasing supplies. Identical products were found to be purchased at prices 30% to 105% higher than necessary because of lack of shared information as to the least-cost source available. Indeed it has been argued in recent years that the explosive growth of retailing on the Internet has been largely due to the ready availability of price and other product information, which has made Internet retailing resemble an almost perfectly competitive market. Consumers appear to have perfect information about both prices and products at their fingertips by merely logging on to the net in search of the best deals. In a perfectly competitive market products are identical; there are a large number of buyers and sellers; there are no search costs; customers are perfectly informed; there is free entry into and exit out of the industry; and profit margins would be 'normal' in the long run.

The Internet does seem to have some of these attributes of a perfect market. For example, studies have shown that online retailers tend to be cheaper than conventional retailers and that they adjust prices more finely and more often. The Internet has also led to the growth of people who use 'shopbots', i.e. computer programs that search rapidly over many websites for the best deal. These provide customers with a more complete knowledge of the market, hence minimising search costs. In addition, entry and exit from Internet sites is relatively easy for sellers, so there are no obvious barriers to entry. Under these conditions one would expect prices for the same or similar products to be virtually identical on the Internet, as under perfect competition.

However, a closer study of the Internet retail market shows that there may still be important elements of imperfection in the market. Studies in the USA by the Sloan School of Management have shown that there is still an element of price dispersion (i.e. difference between the highest and lowest prices for a given product or service) in Internet retail markets. This would tend to indicate that the Internet retail market is inefficient, with some retailers still being able to charge more than others. For example, price dispersion for identical books and for CDs and software among different online retailers can differ by as much as 33% and 25% respectively. Researchers at the Wharton School in Pennsylvania found that airline tickets from online travel agents differed by an average of 28%!

Questions

1. Why does a degree of price dispersion suggest that we do not have a perfect market?

2. What factors might explain why various retailers can still charge different prices for the same product over the Internet, despite the claim that it resembles a perfect market?

As we shall see, the perfectly competitive market structure makes certain predictions as to firm and industry price and output in both **short-run** and **long-run** time periods.

Equilibrium for industry and firm: short run

Key definitions

Short run

The short run is that period of time in which at least one factor of production is fixed.

Long run

The long run is that period of time in which all factors of production can be varied. New firms can enter an industry only in the long-run time period in which they can bring together *all* the resources (land, labour, capital, etc.) needed for production to begin.

Before undertaking this analysis it will be useful to consider the individual firm's *demand curve* in rather more detail.

Firm's demand curve

We have noted that each perfectly competitive firm recognises that, by itself, it cannot influence market supply and therefore market price. The situation is thus as shown in Figure 6.2.

The equilibrium price (P_1) is determined in Figure 6.2(a) by the intersection of the market demand curve (D_M) with the market supply curve (S_M) for this identical product. At this market price P_1 the small firm can reasonably suppose that it can sell *all* its output, knowing that it is so small that any extra output will have no impact on market supply and therefore no impact on price. It is as though the firm's demand curve is perfectly elastic at the going market price P_1, as we can see in Figure 6.2(b).

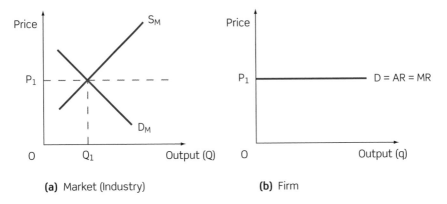

Figure 6.2 The firm as a 'price taker'.

Source: Griffiths, A. and Wall, S. (2011) *Economics for Business and Management* (3rd ed.) © 2011 Pearson Education. Reproduced with permission.

✳ Assessment advice

It is really important to draw and use Figure 6.2 to explain why the small competitive firm is regarded as a 'price taker'.

When the firm sells all its product at an identical price, its demand curve tells us the revenue per unit or average revenue (AR) from any given output. When the firm's demand (D = AR) curve is horizontal or perfectly elastic **(see Chapter 2, pages 30–32)**, each additional unit of output adds exactly the same amount to total revenue as did each previous unit. In other words, the marginal revenue (MR) is constant at the going market price P_1. We can say that:

$$D = AR = MR$$

This perfectly elastic demand curve for the firm will ensure that it charges an identical price for its product to that charged by other firms. Since the product is homogeneous, consumers will have no preference for a particular firm's product, so that if a firm sets a price *above* that of its competitors it will face a total loss of sales.

Alternatively, the firm has no incentive to set a price *below* that of its competitors, since it can sell its entire output at the existing market price. The firm in perfect competition is therefore a 'price taker', i.e. it accepts the market price as given and beyond its control.

Firm's supply curve

We noted **(Chapter 5, page 118)** that the profit-maximising firm must equate marginal cost with marginal revenue (MC = MR). It follows that, under perfect competition, the *marginal cost curve* will, in effect, be the firm's supply curve. This is shown in Figure 6.3.

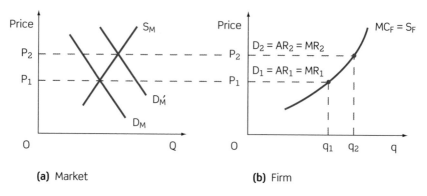

(a) Market   **(b)** Firm

Figure 6.3 Under perfect competition the firm's supply curve (S_F) is the firm's marginal cost curve (MC_F).

Source: Griffiths, A. and Wall, S. (2011) *Economics for Business and Management* (3rd ed.) © 2011 Pearson Education. Reproduced with permission.

We start with market demand D_M and market supply S_M in Figure 6.3(a), giving an initial market price P_1. At this price P_1 the price-taking small firm in Figure 6.3(b) is faced with the horizontal demand curve $D_1 = AR_1 = MR_1$. The profit-maximising firm will then produce output q_1, where marginal cost equals marginal revenue.

However, should market demand increase to D_M' in Figure 6.3(a), then market price rises to P_2 and the price-taking small firm in Figure 6.3(b) is faced with the horizontal demand curve $D_2 = AR_2 = MR_2$. The profit-maximising firm will now produce output q_2, where marginal cost equals marginal revenue.

What we can see in Figure 6.3(b) is that at each price the small firm will *supply* that output where price (= AR = MR) = marginal cost (MC). Put another way, the *firm's marginal cost curve* is the *firm's supply curve*, telling us how much output the profit-maximising firm will supply at each and every price.

✳ Assessment advice

Knowing that under perfect competition the MC curve of the firm is the firm's supply curve, and therefore that the MC curve of the industry is the industry supply curve, is a key element in being able to answer questions on the 'classical' case against monopoly, namely that price is higher and output lower than in competitive market structures.

Having identified the firm's supply curve, we can now identify the industry (market) supply curve.

Industry supply curve

Clearly, segments of the MC curve of the firm constitute the supply curve of the firm, depending on the time period in question. If we aggregate the MC curves for each and every firm (summing horizontally), we derive the industry MC curve. Since by aggregating the MC curves of each firm we are aggregating their supply curves, we also derive the industry supply curve. Figure 6.4 outlines this procedure in a simplified situation in which three firms constitute the industry.

The industry supply curve is therefore the sum of the individual firm MC curves in a competitive industry.

We have already defined the short run as that period of time in which at least one factor of production is fixed. Therefore no new firms can enter the market/industry, being unable to acquire all the factors of production needed to supply the product over this time period.

Normal profit

Before we discuss super- and sub-normal profits, we need to define **normal profit**.

Key definition

Normal profit

This is the level of profit that is just enough to persuade the firm to stay in the industry in the long run, but not high enough to attract new firms. It can, therefore, be considered as a 'cost' to the firm in that this minimum acceptable rate of profit must be met if the firm is to stay in the industry in the long run.

As we shall see, in the short-run time period the market (industry) and the firm may earn either above normal (*super-normal*) or below normal (*sub-normal*) profits. Figure 6.5(a) indicates the former and Figure 6.5(b) the latter.

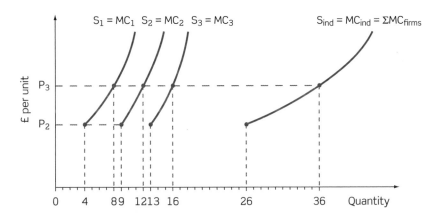

Figure 6.4 The industry supply curve is the industry MC curve, which in turn is the sum of the firm's MC curves.

Source: Griffiths, A. and Wall, S. (2011) *Economics for Business and Management* (3rd ed.) © 2011 Pearson Education. Reproduced with permission.

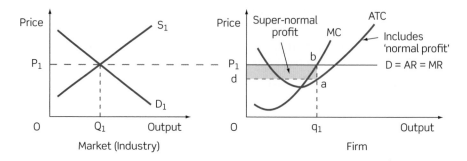

(a) Making super-normal profit (abP$_1$d)

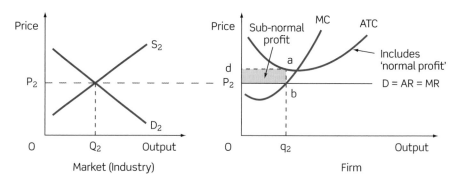

(b) Making sub-normal profit (abP$_2$d)

Figure 6.5 Short-run equilibrium.

Source: Griffiths, A. and Wall, S. (2011) *Economics for Business and Management* (3rd ed.) © 2011 Pearson Education. Reproduced with permission.

Making super-normal profit

In Figure 6.5(a) the profit-maximising firm equates MC with MR, produces output q_1, earns total revenue (price × quantity) of Oq_1bP_1, incurs total cost of Oq_1ad and therefore makes a super-normal profit of abP_1d. In the short run no new firms can enter and this excess profit can be retained.

Test yourself

Q1. Use Figure 6.5(b) to explain what is happening.

Making sub-normal profit

In the short run, no existing firms exit the industry (unless they are not even covering their variable costs – **see page 103**) and so these losses will remain.

In summary, in the short-run profit-maximising equilibrium,

$$P = AR = MR = MC$$

Equilibrium for industry and firm: long run

✳ Assessment advice

Remember, in the long run *all* factors of production can be varied, so new firms can be established and can enter an industry, if it is sufficiently attractive, and existing firms will be able to acquire all the factors of production needed to expand their output.

It will be helpful to see how we move from our short-run equilibrium positions of super-normal and sub-normal profits, respectively, to the long-run equilibrium where only normal profits are earned.

Eliminating short-run super-normal profits

If a large number of new (small) firms are attracted into the industry by super-normal profits, this will have an effect on the (long-run) industry supply curve, shifting it to the right in Figure 6.6(a), with the industry price falling from P_1 to P^* as industry supply increases from S_1 to S^*. New firms will continue to enter the industry until any super-normal profit is competed away, i.e. only normal profit is earned.

Long-run equilibrium will only be achieved when the profit-maximising firm (MC = MR) is just earning normal profit (ATC = AR), i.e. when the following condition holds true:

$$P = AR = MR = MC = ATC$$

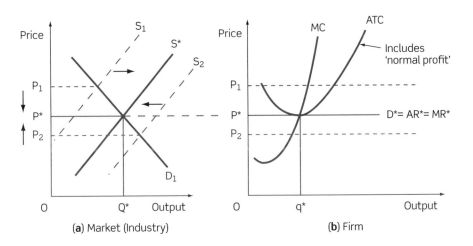

(a) Market (Industry) (b) Firm

Figure 6.6 Long-run equilibrium for a profit-maximising firm in perfect competition (P^*q^*): normal profit earned.

Source: Griffiths, A. and Wall, S. (2011) *Economics for Business and Management* (3rd ed.) © 2011 Pearson Education. Reproduced with permission.

This can only occur (see Figure 6.6(b)) when the price-taking firm faces a perfectly elastic demand curve that just touches (is a tangent to) the bottom of its ATC curve. Here, and here only, is the above condition satisfied (remember MC intersects ATC from below at the lowest point of ATC). The profit-maximising firm (MC = MR) is now earning only normal profit (ATC = AR), and no further incentive exists for new firms to enter the industry. We are in *long-run equilibrium*.

Eliminating short-run sub-normal profits

Test yourself

Q2. Use Figure 6.6 to explain how long-run equilibrium is achieved when the starting point is the sub-normal profits of Figure 6.5(b).

Q3. State the long-run equilibrium condition for perfect competition.

Perfect competition and efficiency

Perfect competition is seen as resulting in resources being allocated in ways that achieve both **productive efficiency** and **allocative efficiency**.

Key definitions

Productive efficiency
Productive efficiency means producing the output for which average total cost is a minimum.

Allocative efficiency
Allocative efficiency means allocating outputs so no one can be made better off without someone else being made worse off. This is sometimes referred to as a 'Pareto optimum' resource allocation, named after the Italian economist Vilfredo Pareto.

- *Productive efficiency.* To achieve productive efficiency (or cost efficiency) a firm must use its resources so as to produce at the lowest possible cost per unit of output. Therefore, productive efficiency is achieved at the lowest point on a firm's long-run average total cost curve. In other words, costs per unit of production in the long run are as low as technically possible. Productive efficiency is achieved by the firm in Figure 6.6(b) at output q* (and price P*).

- *Allocative efficiency.* To achieve allocative efficiency, *it should not be possible* to make someone better off by a reallocation of resources without, at the same time, making someone worse off. If you could make someone better off and no one worse off, then you should obviously reallocate resources. To achieve this situation (called a 'Pareto optimum' resource allocation), one key condition is that price should equal marginal cost. In other words, consumers should pay a price for the last unit of output that just covers the extra cost of producing that last unit of output. Allocative efficiency is achieved by the firm in Figure 6.6(b) at price P* (and output q*).

 Assessment advice

Being aware of these two different types of efficiency will help you to compare the outcomes of different types of market structure and gain extra marks.

In other words, the long-run equilibrium of the firm (and of the market/ industry) under perfect competition results in both productive and allocative efficiency. This is why the perfectly competitive market structure is often thought to be 'ideal' in terms of resource allocation.

Pure monopoly

In this section we move the analysis to the opposite end of the spectrum from perfect competition and look at what happens to price and output decisions in a *pure monopoly* market structure. This occurs in the extreme case when there is a *single* seller of the product, with no close substitute available, so that the firm is, in effect, the industry.

Barriers to entry and equilibrium for pure monopoly

Any monopoly situation, 'pure' or otherwise, can only exist in the long run because of barriers to new firm entry. These barriers can take various forms:

- *Substantial scale economies*, so that large firms have a significant cost advantage over smaller new entrants. In the extreme case the *minimum efficient size* (MES) of production **(see page 99)** may be so large that the industry can only sustain one technically (productively) efficient firm. This is the 'natural monopoly' argument, which we return to below **(page 161)**.
- *Control over scarce resources needed for production*, such as raw materials, key components, skilled labour, etc.
- *Possession of patents or copyrights* for products or for processes of production.
- *Awarding of franchises* giving firms the exclusive rights to sell a particular good or service in a specified location.

- *Government regulations*, such as those creating the nationalised industries or other public sector bodies.

Monopoly and price setting

Unlike perfect competition, the monopolist has the market power to set prices, rather than merely to accept the market price as a given (i.e. to be the 'price taking' firm of perfect competition). The 'Examples & evidence' here reviews the ability of Royal Mail to set prices for the delivery of letters, for which it has an effective pure monopoly via legislation.

Examples & evidence

Royal Mail, pricing and letters

In April 2012, Royal Mail used its monopoly power to sharply increase the price of both first- and second-class letters. The revenue and volume results over the following six-month period to the end of September 2012 are shown in Table 6.1 and compared with the previous six-month period (October 2011 to March 2012).

Table 6.1 Royal Mail letters: outcomes over two six-month periods, 2011–2012.

Price of 1st class stamp 2011 46p Price of 1st class stamp 2012 60p
Price of 2nd class stamp 2011 36p Price of 2nd class stamp 2012 50p
Total letter volume −9% over the two periods Total letter revenue +2% over the two periods

The 9% fall in total letter volume following these price increases was around 4% more than the projected fall of 5% expected over this period from the already well-established trend of a loss of letter post volume to Internet-driven substitutes for letters (email, texts, etc.). However, while the higher prices led to a loss of volume, this was more than compensated in revenue terms, with total letter revenue actually rising by 2% over these successive six-month periods.

Royal Mail also increased the price of its parcel deliveries in April 2012 by an average of 16% across the various parcel sizes. However, the volume of its parcel deliveries actually increased by 5.6% over the following six months, with revenues from parcel deliveries rising by as much as 13%. The rapid growth of parcel deliveries is seen as being linked to the rapid growth in B2C (business-to-customer) business for Royal Mail, fuelled by the success of Amazon and other e-commerce firms using Royal Mail parcel deliveries.

Questions

1. What barriers to entry apply to Royal Mail's business activities?

2. Can you use the earlier ideas of price elasticity of demand **(see Chapter 2)** to explain the results in Table 6.1?

3. What limitations are there to Royal Mail's monopoly power in terms of price setting?

Short- and long-run equilibrium

Because of these barriers to entry, any super-normal profits earned in the short run can be retained in the long run. Figure 6.7 outlines the equilibrium situation for a pure monopoly setting a single price.

It follows that under 'pure monopoly' the downward-sloping demand curve (AR) of the *industry* is now the downward-sloping demand curve of the *firm*. This means **(see Chapter 5, page 118)** that there will be a marginal revenue (MR) curve lying inside the downward-sloping demand curve (AR), as in Figure 6.7.

In Figure 6.7 the profit-maximising monopolist equates MC with MR, giving output Q_M and price P_M in equilibrium. Under 'pure monopoly', strict barriers to entry allow the super-normal profit (P_MVCW) to be retained in the long run, so this is both a short-run and a long-run equilibrium.

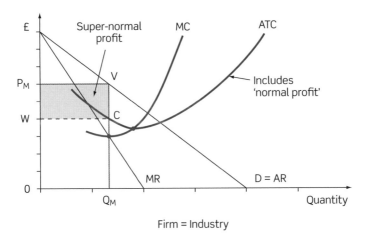

Figure 6.7 Price (P_M) and output (Q_M) for the 'pure monopoly'.

Source: Griffiths, A. and Wall, S. (2011) *Economics for Business and Management* (3rd ed.) © 2011 Pearson Education. Reproduced with permission.

Efficiency and pure monopoly

Notice here how, unlike perfect competition, monopoly fails to achieve either productive or allocative efficiency.

- Output (Q_M) is lower than that at which ATC is a minimum, so no 'productive efficiency'.
- Price (P_M) is higher than marginal cost (MC), so no 'allocative efficiency'.

'Classical' case against monopoly

The so-called 'classical' case against monopoly is that price is higher and quantity lower than under perfect competition. We now evaluate this case, for simplicity keeping our assumption of a pure monopoly.

Under perfect competition, price is determined for the industry (and for the firm) by the intersection of demand and supply, at P_C in Figure 6.8. We have already seen **(page 151)** that the supply curve, S, of the perfectly competitive industry is also the marginal cost (MC) curve of the industry.

Suppose now that the industry is taken over by a single firm (pure monopoly), and that both costs and demand are initially unchanged. It follows that the marginal cost curve remains in the same position; also that the demand curve for the perfectly competitive industry now becomes the demand (and AR) curve for the monopolist. The marginal revenue (MR) curve must then lie inside the negatively sloped AR curve.

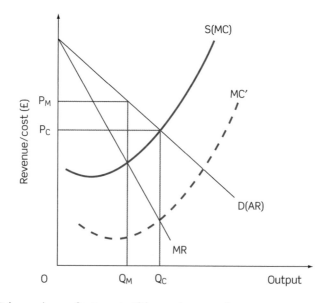

Figure 6.8 Price under perfect competition and monopoly.
Source: Griffiths, A. and Wall, S. (2011) *Economics for Business and Management* (3rd ed.) © 2011 Pearson Education. Reproduced with permission.

The profit-maximising price for the monopolist is p_M, corresponding to output Q_M where MC = MR. Price is higher under monopoly than under perfect competition ($P_M > P_C$) and quantity is lower ($Q_M < Q_C$). This is the so-called 'classical' case against monopoly.

This criticism of monopoly is additional to the fact that, as we noted from Figure 6.7, output is *not* at minimum average total cost, and price does *not* equal marginal cost, breaking the respective conditions for productive and allocative efficiency (productive and allocative inefficiency).

However, these criticisms of monopoly may not be as strong as they first appear:

- We have already seen that the increased size which underpins monopoly power may yield *economies of scale*, both technical and non-technical **(see Chapter 4, pages 95–102)**.

- Where these economies of scale are sufficiently large, it may even be that the 'classical' case against monopoly fails to hold true, with the firm now able to move to a lower short-run average cost curve and with it a lower marginal cost curve.

- In a switch from a competitive market to a monopoly, firms will now have incentives to promote and brand their own products, perhaps shifting their own and therefore the industry demand curve to the right.

- In Figure 6.8, if economies of scale were sufficiently large to lower the MC curve to MC', then the profit-maximising monopoly price P_M and quantity Q_M would be *identical* to those achieved under perfect competition.

- If economies of scale were even greater, lowering the MC curve *below* MC', then the monopoly price (P_M) would be below that of perfect competition and the monopoly output (Q_M) would be higher than that of perfect competition.

The key question is therefore how substantial are the economies of scale for the monopoly industry, and it is this *empirical* question which will determine whether or not the 'classical' case against monopoly still holds true.

Test yourself

Q4. Why might the demand curve be different for the monopoly than from the perfectly competitive industry?

Q5. What might this mean for the 'classical case' against monopoly?

Throughout this discussion of monopoly we have simplified the analysis by contrasting 'pure monopoly' with perfect competition. In fact, industries in which more than one-third of the output is in the hands of a single seller or group of linked sellers can technically be called 'monopoly' in the UK. However, such 'general' monopoly situations are in practice difficult to distinguish from the oligopoly form of market structure **which we consider in the next chapter**.

Welfare losses under monopoly

✴ Assessment advice

Other criticisms of monopoly make use of the ideas of consumer surplus and producer surplus **introduced in Chapters 2 and 4**. These ideas can be used to help identify the 'welfare loss' from monopoly as compared with perfect competition.

The traditional or classical case against monopoly is that price is higher and quantity lower than under perfect competition, but we can also show the net welfare impacts that might result from the presence of monopoly power.

- In Figure 6.9 (which for illustrative purposes assumes constant costs), the perfectly competitive price and output would be OP_c/OQ_c, yielding total consumer surplus of areas 1 + 2 + 3, with total cost of production given by areas 4 + 5.

- With entry barriers and identical demand/cost conditions, the profit-maximising monopoly price and output would be OP_M/OQ_M. Consumer surplus is now only area 1 (units Q_M to Q_c are no longer produced), area 2 switches from consumer surplus to producer surplus and area 3 is lost.

- This loss of area 3 resulting from monopoly is often referred to as a welfare loss or **deadweight loss**.

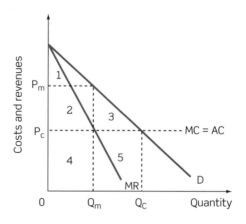

Figure 6.9 Reduction in economic welfare due to monopolisation.

- The loss of output indicated by area 5 might also be seen as a potential welfare loss of monopoly, as the resources released may not be used elsewhere (e.g. unemployment).

- The transfer of area 2 from consumer surplus to producer surplus is more difficult to assess in terms of welfare. It certainly represents a reallocation from consumer surplus to abnormal profit for the monopolist.

> ### Key definition
>
> **Deadweight loss**
>
> This is the loss of economic welfare (consumer surplus + producer surplus) as a result of a market imperfection.

'Natural' monopoly argument

Figure 6.10 provides a useful illustration of the natural monopoly argument which suggests that the minimum efficient size (MES) is so large that only one efficient firm producing at minimum long-run average cost (LRAC) can be sustained by that particular industry.

The falling long-run average total cost (LRAC) curve indicates that economies of scale occur as output rises. When there is only one firm operating in the market, the industry's and the firm's demand curve are the same. Here output can occur between points 1 and 2 profitably. Suppose a second firm enters the market and the industry demand is now divided between the two firms (in this case each firm has 50% of the market). Each firm now faces the same individual demand curve, i.e. D_2 in Figure 6.10. In this situation long-run average costs (LRAC) are greater than revenue at all levels of output. Consequently, one firm must leave the market, leaving a single (natural) monopoly.

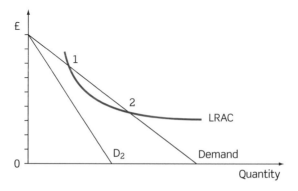

Figure 6.10 'Natural monopoly' situation.
Source: Griffiths, A. and Wall, S. (2011) *Economics for Business and Management* (3rd ed.) © 2011 Pearson Education. Reproduced with permission.

Assessment advice

Look back **to Chapter 4** for useful empirical evidence on economies of scale. The 'natural monopoly' argument can be used to support monopoly in certain circumstances and to counter the 'classical' case against monopoly.

The semiconductor industry and the manufacture of microchips is often used as an example of an industry in which technology is shifting it ever closer towards a natural monopoly.

Examples & evidence

FAB plants and natural monopoly

Technical change has been rapid in the global semiconductor business. In recent years large integrated FAB plants costing $3bn or more have been built to incorporate new developments in chemical processes and material technologies. They can produce over three times as many chips from each wafer of silicon and indeed from lower-cost alternatives to silicon itself. As a result the average chip costs from these huge FAB plants are 40% less than for chips produced by their smaller counterparts, providing these FAB plants are used to at least 90% of capacity. Analysts see no more than 10 such giant plants being required worldwide to meet current global demand for microchips, which means that the minimum efficient size (MES) for each FAB plant is larger than the national demand for microchips of all but a few countries!

Questions

1. How does this Examples & evidence support the 'natural monopoly' argument?
2. How would international trade issues be relevant to any conclusions?

Contestable markets

The theory of **contestable markets** indicates how the principles we have discussed for perfect competition and its 'efficiency' advantages over (pure) monopoly might generally apply to markets which are not, strictly, perfectly competitive. The emphasis here is on the *threat* of new entrants resulting in existing firms in non-perfectly competitive markets acting *as if* they were in a **perfectly competitive market**.

The idea of contestable markets broadens the application of competitive behaviour beyond the strict conditions needed for perfect competition. In other words, instead of regarding competitive behaviour as existing only in the perfectly competitive market structure, it could be exhibited in any market structure that was contestable. Generally speaking, the fewer the barriers to entry into a market, the more contestable is that market. In this sense, some monopoly and oligopoly markets could be regarded as contestable.

The absence of entry barriers increases the *threat* of new firms entering the market. It is this threat which is assumed to check any tendency by incumbent (existing) firms to raise prices substantially above average costs and thereby earn super-normal profit.

Key definitions

Contestable market

This is a market in which the threat of new firm entry causes incumbents to act as though such potential competition actually existed.

Perfectly contestable market

This is a market where there is free and costless entry and exit.

Sunk costs

These are costs that cannot be reversed when exiting the industry.

Perfectly contestable markets

It may be useful to illustrate this approach by considering the extreme case of perfect contestability. In a **perfectly contestable market** there are no barriers to entry, so that incumbent firms are constrained to keep prices at levels which, in relation to costs, earn only normal profits. Incumbents in perfectly contestable markets therefore earn no super-normal profits, are cost-efficient, and cannot cross-subsidise between products or in any way set prices below costs in order to deter new entrants.

At least three conditions must be fulfilled for a market to be perfectly contestable:

1 *An absence of sunk costs.* **Sunk costs** are the costs of acquiring an asset (tangible or intangible) which cannot be recouped by selling the asset or redeploying it in another market should the firm exit the industry. The presence of sunk costs, by increasing the costs of exiting the industry, can be assumed to make incumbent firms more determined to avoid being

forced to exit the industry and therefore more aggressive towards new entrants. They might then seek to resist new entrants by adopting a variety of strategies which essentially constitute a barrier to entry.

2 *The potential entrant must be at no disadvantage compared with incumbents as regards production technology or perceived product quality.* Any lack of access to equivalent production technology utilised by incumbents might prevent new entrants competing on the same cost base or quality of product base. This would inhibit the threat of potential new entrants, thereby permitting incumbents to earn and retain super-normal profits. Similarly, perceptions of consumers (via branding, etc.) as to the superiority of incumbent product quality would also inhibit the threat of new entrants and permit incumbents to earn and retain super-normal profits.

3 *The entrant must be able to engage in 'hit and run' tactics,* i.e. to enter a market, make a profit and exit before incumbents can adjust their prices downwards. Put another way, existing suppliers can only change their prices with time-lags whereas consumers respond immediately to any lower prices offered by new entrants.

Under these conditions there is a total absence of barriers to entry, and exit from the market is costless. Such a perfectly contestable market will ensure that incumbents are unable to earn super-normal profits in the long run, and that price will equate with long-run average total cost (including normal profit).

Test yourself

Q6. Suppose incumbents in a perfectly contestable market charge a price *above* long-run average cost. Explain the mechanism by which a perfectly competitive market will ensure that prices fall to equate with long-run average cost.

Imperfectly contestable markets

Although such perfect contestability is an ideal rarely, if ever, achieved, it sets the context for competitive behaviour in all types of market structure. Even highly monopolistic or oligopolistic markets could, in principle, experience a high degree of contestability, thereby achieving a competitive-type market solution with price close to long-run average costs and profits close to normal. The policy implication of such an approach is to encourage the removal of entry barriers and the lowering of exit costs in all types of market structure in order to increase the degree of contestability.

Cost contestability versus price contestability

A rather weaker, but more pragmatic, approach to contestability focuses on cost rather than price contestability. Here the suggestion is that the threat of entry may be more likely to induce incumbents to be *cost-efficient* than to set prices equal to long-run average costs. By 'cost-efficient' is meant the delivery of a given level of output at the lowest cost technically feasible. As we shall see later **(Chapter 9)**, the perspective of 'cost contestability' is a widely used argument in support of deregulation, i.e. the opening up of specified markets to potential new entrants as a means of securing efficiency gains via cost cutting by incumbents.

Chapter summary – pulling it all together

By the end of this chapter you should be able to:

	Confident ✓	Not confident?
Explain why perfect competition is often re-garded as the 'ideal' form of market structure in terms of resource allocation		Revise pages 148–155
Examine the barriers which deter new firm entry and generate 'market power' for existing firms		Revise pages 155–156
Evaluate the basis for the so-called 'classical' case against monopoly, namely higher industry prices and lower industry output than would exist under competitive market structures, and other criticisms of welfare loss under monopoly		Revise pages 156–161
Explain the 'natural monopoly' argument in which only one firm is seen as being the most efficient outcome		Revise pages 161–162
Explain how 'contestable market' analysis can still be used to predict competitive outcomes in industries which are anything but competitive!		Revise pages 162–165

Now try the **assessment question** at the start of this chapter, using the answer guidelines below.

Answer guidelines

✳ Assessment question

Consider the suggestion that monopoly will invariably operate to the disadvantage of consumers.

Approaching the question

A useful starting point is to define the two types of market structure, perfect competition and monopoly. You might alert the assessor to the fact that you are aware of the *actual* definition of monopoly in the UK (one-third of output in the hands of a single firm or group of linked firms) but that you will use pure monopoly (a single firm has the whole output) to simplify the analysis.

Important points to include

- A monopoly is often accused of using its market power to the disadvantage of consumers by keeping prices higher and output lower than would be the case in a perfectly competitive market. This is the so-called 'classical' case against monopoly.

- You can use Figure 6.6(a) to explain that in a perfectly competitive market, price and output are determined at the point where the demand curve cuts the marginal cost curve (i.e. the supply curve) for the industry.

- You can then use Figure 6.6(b) to explain that the long-run equilibrium price and output for a perfectly competitive industry will achieve both productive and allocative efficiency.

- *Productive efficiency*: price = minimum average cost (including normal profit) in the long run.

- *Allocative efficiency*: price = marginal cost.

- You can use Figure 6.8 to explain that for a (pure) monopoly the profit maximising price will be higher and output will be lower if the competitive industry is taken over by a single firm and cost and revenue conditions are unchanged.

- However, you can begin to challenge these assumptions about costs and revenue being unchanged by a pure monopolist taking over a competitive industry.

- You can use Figure 6.8 to explain that if the monopolist is able to lower costs significantly as it reaps the benefits of economies of scale, the marginal cost curve for the monopolist will be *lower* than in the competitive market, i.e. the MC curve will have shifted down and to the right. If the economies of scale are sufficiently large, this may even result in a profit maximising equilibrium in which price is lower and output higher than in the competitive market situation.

- You could present empirical evidence **(e.g. see Chapter 4)** on potential economies of scale at larger size for particular industries. If the economies of scale are sufficiently large for these industries, then the classical case may not hold.

- You could also examine how promotion and marketing activities by the monopoly might shift the demand curve to the right, again challenging the classical case against monopoly.

- You could refer to the 'natural monopoly' argument and use Figure 6.10 to support monopoly when economies of scale are substantial.

Make your answer stand out

The highest marks will be awarded to students who support their argument with diagrams which are clearly drawn, fully labelled and referred to in their answer to explain key points. If you can use case study evidence or data to support the existence of scale economies in various industries, this will also make your answer stand out. You could also go a little beyond simply exploring the classical case against monopoly, such as using consumer surplus and producer surplus in Figure 6.9 to examine the argument that monopoly power reduces consumer welfare.

Read to impress

Books

Griffiths, A. and Wall, S. (2011) *Economics for Business and Management*, 3rd edition, Chapter 6, Pearson Education.

Parkin, M., Powell, M. and Matthews, K. (2012) *Economics*, 8th edition, Chapters 11 and 12, Addison Wesley.

Sloman, J. and Garratt, D. (2010) *Essentials of Economics*, 5th edition, Chapters 4 and 5, FT/Prentice Hall.

Sloman, J., Wride, A. and Garratt, D. (2012) *Economics*, 8th edition, Pearson Education.

Journals and periodicals

The following are useful sources of articles and data on many aspects relevant to this and other topics:

Business Review, Philip Allan (quarterly)
Economic Review, Philip Allan (quarterly)
Economics Today, Anforme (quarterly)
Harvard Business Review (monthly)
The Economist (weekly)

Newspapers

Newspapers are important sources of up-to-date information, examples and data. Below are some of the main UK newspaper sources, many of which have websites with search facilities to identify specific topics and articles:

The Guardian
The Times
The Financial Times
The Independent
The Telegraph

Companion website

Go to the companion website at **www.pearsoned.co.uk/econexpress** to find revision support online for this topic area.

Notes

Notes

7

Oligopoly and monopolistic competition

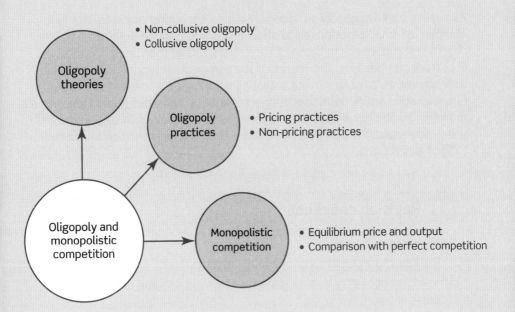

- Non-collusive oligopoly
- Collusive oligopoly

Oligopoly theories

Oligopoly practices
- Pricing practices
- Non-pricing practices

Oligopoly and monopolistic competition

Monopolistic competition
- Equilibrium price and output
- Comparison with perfect competition

A printable version of this topic map is available from **www.pearsoned.co.uk/econexpress**

Introduction

Perfect competition and pure monopoly **(reviewed in Chapter 6)** are the 'extreme' forms of market structure. In practice most industries and sectors lie somewhere in between, as when a few large firms dominate an industry (oligopoly) or a large number of smaller firms produce similar but not identical products (monopolistic competition).

In many markets there is intense rivalry between several large firms rather than dominance by one firm (pure monopoly). For example, when Googling 'car insurance' in the UK over the period December 2011 to May 2012, the '% click share' was as follows: Money Supermarket (17%), Tesco Bank (14%), Compare the market – the Meerkat advertising campaigners (12%), Co-operative Bank (11%), Confused (9%). In other words, the top five providers of car insurance advice over that period accounted for 63% of the total market share in the UK. Dominance of a market by a few large firms which compete actively against each other with branded products is widespread in the UK and internationally.

As well as these oligopoly situations, we also encounter markets with large numbers of small providers each offering a product (good or service) which differs in some way from those of their rivals, rather than being identical as in perfect competition. This monopolistic competition type of market is also widespread, as in many service activities with large numbers of solicitors, financial advisors, general practitioners, dentists, hairdressers and garages all providing similar but differentiated services to consumers. In fact, in the UK sole traders and firms employing no more than one person account for over 77% of all UK firms.

 Revision checklist

What you need to know:

- ❏ The key characteristics of oligopoly markets.
- ❏ How oligopolies try to anticipate rival firm actions and reactions (non-collusion).
- ❏ How oligopolies use formal and informal arrangements to reduce uncertainty (collusion).
- ❏ Price and non-price strategies widely used in practice by oligopolies.
- ❏ The key characteristics of monopolistically competitive markets.
- ❏ Comparison of equilibrium outcomes in monopolistic competition and perfect competition.

Assessment advice

Structure your answer

Oligopoly questions will usually involve an explanation of how large firms seek to deal with the potential actions and reactions of their rivals. Remember to distinguish between approaches used by oligopoly firms to anticipate the actions and reactions of rivals without any formal arrangements between them (*non-collusive oligopoly*) and approaches which depend on formal or informal arrangements (*collusive oligopoly*). Kinked demand theory and game theory are examples of non-collusive oligopoly, while the use of formal arrangements such as cartels and informal arrangements such as price leadership are examples of collusive oligopoly.

Use diagrams and tables

Diagrams can be effective in examining both non-collusive oligopoly theories (e.g. Figure 7.1 for kinked demand theory and Figure 7.2 for the Cournot model) and collusive oligopoly theories (e.g. Figure 7.5 for cartels and Figure 7.6 for dominant firm price leadership). Diagrams can also be used to examine price discrimination (Figures 7.7 and 7.8). Tables can be helpful in gaining higher marks such as the pay-off matrices shown in Tables 7.1 and 7.2 which can be used to explain how firms can evaluate the likely outcomes of their actions and rival reactions using game theory. Diagrams are also important for comparing and contrasting the equilibrium outcomes in monopolistically competitive markets with those in perfectly competitive markets (e.g. Figure 7.10).

Use empirical evidence

Higher marks can also be gained by providing case study examples and evidence of actual oligopoly markets and monopolistically competitive markets.

 Assessment question

Explain the approaches and strategies available to firms in oligopoly markets to reduce the uncertainties from their recognised interdependence with other large firms.

Oligopoly theories

Oligopoly refers to a situation in which a few large firms dominate the market. This type of market structure is common in most developed economies. For example, the three largest companies in the respective industries in the UK account for 91% of total tobacco sales, 78% of chocolate confectionery sales, 75% of electrical goods and 65% of coffee sales (see Table 7.1). The importance of these large firms is evidenced by the fact that large UK firms employing over 500 people account for less than 0.1% of all firms in number but contribute over 47% of all UK employment.

Table 7.1 Company shares of the UK market by sector/product, 2009–10.

Sector/product group	Percentage share of the UK market	
	Three largest companies	Five largest companies
Tobacco	91	98
Chocolate confectionery	78	87
Electrical retailers	75	82
Tour operators	68	75
Coffee shops	65	74
DIY	57	63
White goods	57	78
Motor insurance	51	63
Bottled water	48	58
Women's fragrances	48	71
Vacuum cleaners	45	57
Branded watches	28	38
Footwear retailing	22	26

Source: adapted from Mintel Reports (various) and other sources

Crucially, these few firms recognise their rivalry and *interdependence*, fully aware that any action on their part is likely to result in counter-actions by their rivals. Firms will therefore be drawn into devising strategies and counter-strategies taking into account their rivals' expected actions and reactions.

Another feature of oligopoly markets is *product differentiation*. There are often many brands of a particular product, with extensive advertising by rival firms emphasising the difference between their product and that of their rivals, whether real or imagined.

Next, we discuss oligopoly under the broad headings of **non-collusive oligopoly** and **collusive oligopoly**.

Key definitions

Non-collusive oligopoly

In non-collusive oligopoly, firms compete against each other using strategies and counter-strategies, and do not seek to make agreements, whether formal or informal, to 'fix' the market outcome.

Collusive oligopoly

In collusive oligopoly, firms seek various arrangements between themselves in an attempt to remove some of the market uncertainty they face.

Non-collusive oligopoly

First we consider situations in which each firm decides upon its strategy without any formal or even informal arrangement with its rivals.

Kinked demand curve

In an attempt to explain why prices often remain stable in oligopoly markets, even when costs rise, the so-called theory of the *kinked demand curve* was developed. To illustrate this theory, which resulted from the work of Hall and Hitch in the UK and Sweezy in the USA, we take an oligopoly market which sells similar but not identical products, i.e. there is some measure of product differentiation. If one firm raises its price, it will then lose some, though not all, of its customers to rivals. Similarly, if the firm reduces its price, it will attract some, though not all, of its rivals' customers. How many customers are lost or gained will depend partly on whether or not the rivals follow the initial price change.

Extensive interviews with managers of firms in oligopoly markets led Hall and Hitch to conclude that most firms have learnt a common lesson from past experience of how rivals react.

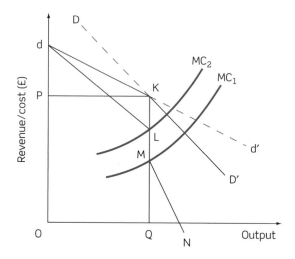

Note: d – d' = Demand curve when rivals *do not* follow price changes
D – D' = Demand curve when rivals *do* follow price changes
dKD' = Kinked demand curve
dLMN = Associated marginal revenue curve

Figure 7.1 Kinked demand curve and price stability.
Source: Griffiths, A. and Wall, S. (2011) *Economics for Business and Management* (3rd ed.) © 2011 Pearson Education. Reproduced with permission.

- If the firm were to *raise* its price above the current level (P in Figure 7.1), its rivals *would not follow*, content to let the firm lose sales to them. The firm will then expect its demand curve to be relatively elastic (dK) for price rises.
- However, if the firm were to *reduce* its price, rivals would follow to protect their market share, so that the firm gains few extra sales. The firm will then expect its demand curve to be relatively inelastic (KD') for price reductions.

Overall, the firm will believe that its demand curve is kinked at the current price P, as in Figure 7.1.

Associated with each demand (AR) curve in Figure 7.1 will be an associated marginal revenue (MR) curve which lies inside it.

- For price rises *above* P, dL is the relevant marginal revenue curve.
- For price reductions *below* P, MN is the relevant marginal revenue curve.

✳ Assessment advice

You can use Figure 7.1 to show that there is a *vertical discontinuity*, LM, in the overall marginal revenue curve dLMN. You can then use this discontinuity to explain price stickiness. For example, the marginal cost curve could vary between MC_1 and MC_2 without causing the firm to alter its profit-maximising price P (or its output Q).

In the kinked demand model the firm assumes that rivals will react to its own strategies, and uses past experience to assess the form that reaction might take. In this case the firm assumes that price increases will largely be ignored but price decreases will tend to be matched.

Examples & evidence

Kinked demand

A number of industries have exhibited price stability, despite rising costs. The UK confectionery industry, at present dominated by Mars, Nestlé and Cadbury Schweppes, is a good example of this tendency. For example, non-price competition has often taken the form of product weight: when Mars raised the weight of its Mars bars by 10%, Cadbury retaliated by raising the weight of its Fruit and Nut by 14% and Nestlé increased the chocolate content of KitKat by 5%. In all of these cases the firms accepted rises in their costs, i.e. more ingredients per bar, *without changing price*.

Similarly, when KP foods introduced its new crisp-like snack called 'Frisp' and spent £4.4m on marketing it in the first three months alone, Golden Wonder increased the packet size of all its crisps and snacks from 28 grams to 30 grams *without raising prices*. In terms of our kinked oligopoly model, the companies noted above preferred to accept the higher costs of non-price competition (which can be illustrated by the upward shift in the MC curve), rather than engage in price warfare. The reason for this is that companies sometimes believe they have a better idea of the costs and benefits involved in *non-price competition* as compared with the unknown risks of getting involved in a damaging price war. When a company becomes involved in price competition, gains and losses are more difficult to assess because they depend on the *reactions* of competitors to the initial company's pricing strategy.

Question

1. Can you identify any other examples of this tendency towards non-price competition?

Problems with kinked demand theory

- The theory does not explain how oligopolists actually *set* an initial price, but merely why a price, once set, might be stable. Kinked demand is *not* a theory of price determination.
- The observed stickiness of prices may have little to do with the rival-firm reaction patterns of kinked demand theory. It is, for instance, administratively expensive to change prices too often.

- The assertion, implicit in kinked demand theory, that prices are more 'sticky' under oligopoly than under other market forms, has not received strong support from empirical studies. For instance, Stigler, in a sample of 100 firms across 21 industries in the USA, had concluded as early as the 1940s that oligopoly prices hardly merited the description 'sticky'. Domberger, in a survey of 21 UK industries, found that the *more* oligopolistic the market, the more variable was price (Domberger, S., 1980, 'Mergers, market structure and the rate of price adjustment', in Cowling, K. *et al.* (eds) *Mergers and Economic Performance*, Cambridge University Press, Chapter 13).

- The precise nature of any kink in the demand curve may depend on the economic conditions prevailing at the time. For example, a study of 73 small owner-managed firms in Scotland found that price increases were more likely to be followed during booms, whilst price falls were more likely to be followed during times of recession (Bhaskar, V. *et al.*, 1991, 'Testing a model of the kinked demand curve', *Journal of Industrial Economics*, 39(3): 241–254).

Test yourself

Q1. What are the assumptions of kinked demand theory?

Q2. Explain the predictions of kinked demand theory.

Q3. Outline the problems facing kinked demand theory.

Cournot and Bertrand have also developed theories that make assumptions about how rivals will act and react.

Cournot: rivals produce a given quantity

In Cournot's model the assumption is that the rival will set a given output and keep to it. This is illustrated in Figure 7.2 which uses a duopoly (two-firm) model of oligopoly and shows output for Firm A, with the total market demand curve shown as D_M. If Firm A believes that its rival, Firm B, will produce Q_{B1} units, then Firm A will perceive its own demand curve (D_{A1}) to be Q_{B1} units less than total market demand. In other words, the horizontal gap between D_M and D_{A1} is Q_{B1} units. Given its perceived demand curve of D_{A1}, its marginal revenue curve will be MR_{A1} and the profit-maximising output will be Q_{A1} where $MR_{A1} = MC_A$. The profit-maximising price will be P_{A1}.

Bertrand: rivals set a given price

In Bertrand's model the assumption is that the rival will set a given price and keep to it. Again using the simplifying assumption of a duopoly, Bertrand showed that the outcome of his oligopoly model (no matter what the number of firms) would be continuous price cutting by the rivals until all supernormal profit has been competed away. The reasoning is that if Firm A assumes that its rival, Firm B, will hold price constant, then Firm A will have an incentive to

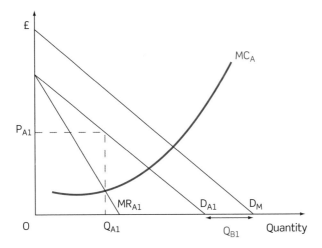

Figure 7.2 Cournot model of duopoly: profit-maximising position for Firm A.

undercut this price by a small amount and therefore secure a significant share of the market. Firm B will itself be free to respond by cutting its market price, with the 'price warfare' ceasing only when price is reduced to such a level that each firm merely covers its average cost (including normal profit). If any one firm is less cost-efficient than the other firm or firms, then it will be forced out of the market before the equilibrium is reached.

Instead of using past experience to assess future reactions by rivals, the firm itself could try to identify the *best possible moves* the opposition could make to each of its own strategies. The firm could then plan counter-measures if the rival reacts in these predicted ways. This is the essence of **game theory** in which we need to distinguish between **zero sum** and **non-zero sum** games, and between **maxi-min** and **mini-max** decision rules.

Key definitions

Game theory

This term refers to various theories which analyse oligopoly situations as though they were 'games' in which 'players' can adopt various strategies and counter-strategies in order to improve their position.

Zero sum

In a zero sum game, any gain by one player must be matched by an equivalent loss by one or more other players. A market share game is zero sum, since only 100% is available to all players.

Non-zero sum

In a non-zero sum game, gains and losses need not cancel out across all players.

Maxi-min

This decision rule says that the best of the worst-possible outcomes from any strategy is selected.

Mini-max

This decision rule says that the worst of the best-possible outcomes from any strategy is selected.

We can illustrate the application of game theory to business situations taking a zero-sum (market share) game involving two firms (duopoly). By its very nature, a market share game must be 'zero sum', in that any gain by one 'player' must be offset exactly by the loss of the other(s).

Examples & evidence

Zero sum market share game

We use a duopoly (two-firm) situation to illustrate a zero sum game with a maxi-min decision rule. Suppose Firm A is considering choosing one of two possible policies in order to raise its market share, a 20% price cut or a 10% increase in advertising expenditure. Whatever initial policy Firm A adopts, it anticipates that its rival, Firm B, will react by using either a price cut or extra advertising to defend its market share.

Firm A now evaluates the market share it can expect for each initial policy decision and each possible reaction by B. The outcomes expected by A are summarised in the pay-off matrix of Table 7.2.

Table 7.2 Firm A's pay-off matrix.

		Firm B's strategies	
		Price cut	Extra advertising
Firm A's strategies	**Price cut**	60*#	70#
	Extra advertising	50*	55

* 'Worst' outcome for A of each A strategy
# 'Worst' outcome for B of each B strategy

- If A cuts price, and B responds with a price cut, A receives 60% of the market. However, if B responds with extra advertising, A receives 70% of the market. The 'worst' outcome for A (60% of the market) will occur if B responds with a price cut.
- If A uses extra advertising, then the 'worst' outcome for A (50% of the market) will again occur if B responds with a price cut.

We will assume that both players adopt a *maxi-min* decision rule, always selecting that policy which results in the best of the worst-possible outcomes.

- Firm A will select the price-cut policy since this gives it 60% market share rather than 50%, i.e. the best of these 'worst-possible' outcomes.
- If firm B adopts the same *maxi-min* decision rule as A, and has made the same evaluation of outcomes as A, it also will adopt a price-cut strategy. For instance, if B adopts a price-cut policy, its 'worst' outcome would occur if A responds with a price cut – B then gets 40% of the market (100% minus 60%), rather than 50% if A responds with extra advertising. If B adopts extra advertising, its 'worst' outcome would again occur if A responds with a price cut – B then receives 30% rather than 45%.
- The best of the 'worst-possible' outcomes for B occurs if B adopts a price cut, which gives it 40% of the market rather than 30%.

In this particular game we have a *stable equilibrium*, without any resort to collusion. Both firms initially cut price, then accept the respective market shares which fulfil their maxi-min targets, i.e. 60% to A, 40% to B.

Question

1. Can you suggest possible reasons why there might be no stable equilibrium for this game?

Alternative decision rules

The problem with game theory is that it can equally predict unstable solutions. An unstable solution might follow if each firm, faced with the pay-off matrix of Table 7.2, adopts an entirely different decision rule.

A mini-max approach is arguably a more optimistic but riskier approach to the game. You assume your rival does not react in the worst way possible to each decision you make, but in the best way for you. You then introduce a note of caution by selecting the 'worst' of these 'best possible' outcomes.

Test yourself

Q4. What would happen in Table 7.2 if A adopts a maxi-min decision rule and B a mini-max decision rule?

Alternative outcomes/pay-off matrices

An unstable solution might also follow if each firm evaluates the pay-off matrix differently from the other. Even if they then adopt the same approach to the game, one firm at least will be 'disappointed', possibly provoking action and counter-action.

If we could tell before the event which oligopoly situations would be stable, and which unstable, then the many possible outcomes of game theory would be considerably narrowed. At present this is beyond the state of the art. However, game theory has been useful in making more explicit the interdependence of oligopoly situations.

Alternative types of game

We can equally apply our terms and definitions to a *non-zero sum* game, namely a profits game, as in the 'Examples & evidence' here.

Key definitions

Game theory: types of strategy and equilibrium

Dominant strategy

The dominant strategy applies where a firm is able to identify *one* policy option as being best for it, regardless of the reactions of any rivals.

Nash equilibrium

This term refers to a situation where each firm is doing the best that it can in terms of its own objectives, taking into account the strategies chosen by the other firms in the market.

Prisoner's dilemma

This term refers to a situation where firms attempt independently to choose the best strategy for themselves, but end up worse off than if they had cooperated with others.

Examples & evidence

Non-zero sum profit game

Alpha and Beta are two rival firms and each must choose whether to charge relatively high or relatively low prices for their products. Market research suggests the pay-off matrix (profits) shown in Table 7.3. For simplicity we assume that both firms evaluate the pay-off matrix as shown in this table.

Table 7.3 Pay-off matrix showing profits in £ millions for Alpha and Beta.

		Beta's strategies	
		Low price	High price
Alpha's strategies	**Low price**	(a) Alpha 200, Beta 200	(c) Alpha 40, Beta 260
	High price	(b) Alpha 260, Beta 140	(d) Alpha 100, Beta 100

Pay-off matrices invariably have some outcomes that are worse than others. The maxi-min decision rule is to adopt the policy option that gives the 'best of the worst' of these outcomes.

- *Alpha adopts a maxi-min decision rule.* Alpha looks at its policy outcomes and then asks 'what is the worst that can happen?'
  - For Alpha's low price policy, the worst that could happen would be for Beta to charge a high price and reduce Alpha's profits to £40m (cell c).
  - For Alpha's high price policy, the worst that could happen would be for Beta to charge a high price, giving Alpha £100m profit (cell d).
  - The best of these 'worst-possible outcomes' is £100m, thus Alpha's maxi-min strategy would be to charge the higher price.
- *Beta adopts a maxi-min decision rule.* Beta looks at its policy outcomes and then asks 'what is the worst that can happen'?
  - Beta's low price policy gives £140m (cell b) as the worst-possible outcome.
  - Beta's high price policy gives £100m (cell d) as the worst-possible outcome.
  - The best of these 'worst-possible outcomes' is £140m, thus Beta's maxi-min policy would be to charge a low price.

Questions

1. Look back at the game theory definitions, then review the equilibrium for the non-zero sum profit game. Explain whether or not the equilibrium for this game meets the following criteria:

   (a) Is it stable?

   (b) Is it a *Nash equilibrium*?

   (c) Is it one in which Beta has a *dominant strategy*?

2. What would happen if Beta adopted a mini-max decision rule but Alpha stayed with its maxi-min decision rule?

✳ Assessment advice

If you want to deepen your analysis of game theory even further, you can explore various other types of game. These include one-shot games, repeated games with potential for 'cheating' and 'tit-for-tat' strategies, sequential games with potential for 'first mover advantages' and so on. See 'Read to impress' at the end of this chapter.

Collusive oligopoly

Another way of handling uncertainty in markets which are interdependent is by some form of *central coordination*; in other words, 'collusion'. The methods that are used to promote collusion may be formal, such as by making explicit agreements of one kind or another between the parties or even 'acting as one' as in a cartel. The methods may also be informal, as in the case of tacit understandings involved in various types of price leadership.

At least two features of collusive oligopoly are worth emphasising:

1 The objectives that are sought through collusion.
2 The methods that are used to promote collusion – whether formal, as in a cartel, or informal, via tacit agreement.

Objectives of collusion
Joint profit maximisation

The firms may seek to coordinate their price, output and other policies to achieve maximum profits for the industry as a whole. In the extreme case the firms may act together as a monopoly, aggregating their marginal costs and equating these with marginal revenue for the whole market. If achieved, the

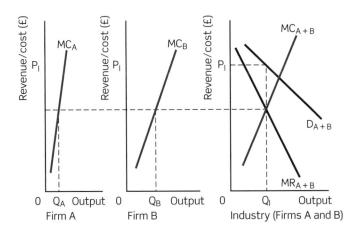

Figure 7.3 Joint profit maximisation in duopoly.
Source: Griffiths, A. and Wall, S. (2012) *Applied Economics* (12th ed.) © 2012 Pearson Education.
Reproduced with permission.

result would be to maximise joint profits, with a unique industry price and output $(P_I Q_I)$, as in Figure 7.3.

A major problem is, of course, how to achieve the close coordination required. We consider this further below, but we might note from Figure 7.3 that coordination is required both to *establish* the profit-maximising solution for the industry $P_I Q_I$ and to *enforce* it once established. For instance, some agreement must be reached on sharing the output Q_I between the colluding firms. One solution is to equate marginal revenue for whole output with marginal cost in each separate market, with Firm A producing Q_A and Firm B producing Q_B. Whatever the agreement, it must remain in force – since if any firm produces above its quota, this will raise industry output, depress price and move the industry away from the joint profit-maximising solution.

Deterrence of new entrants – limit-pricing

Firms may seek to coordinate policies, to maximise not so much short-run profit but rather some longer-run notion of profit **(see Chapter 5)**. A major threat to long-run profit is the potential entrance of new firms into the industry. Economists such as Andrews and Bain have therefore suggested that oligopolistic firms may collude with the objectives of setting price below the level which maximises joint profits, in order to deter new entrants. The 'limit price' can be defined as the highest price which the established firms believe they can charge without inducing entry. Its precise value will depend upon the nature and extent of the 'barriers to entry' for any particular industry. The greater the barriers to entry, the higher the 'limit price' will be.

- Substantial economies of scale are a 'barrier to entry', in that a new firm will usually be smaller than established firms, and will therefore be at a cost disadvantage.

- Product differentiation itself, reinforced by extensive advertising, is also a barrier – since product loyalty, once captured, is difficult and expensive for new entrants to dislodge.
- Other barriers might include legally enforced patents to new technologies in the hands of established firms, and even inelastic market demands. This latter is a barrier in that the less elastic the market demand for the product, the greater will be the price fall from any extra supply contributed by new entrants.

The principle of 'limit-pricing' can be illustrated from Figure 7.4. Let us make the analysis easier by supposing that each established firm has an identical average total cost (ATC) curve, and sells an identical output, Q_F, at the joint profit-maximising price P* set for the industry. Suppose a new firm, with an identical cost profile, is considering entering the industry, and is capable of selling E units in the first instance. Despite the initial cost disadvantage, the new firm believes it can survive. One way of preventing the survival of the new firm, perhaps even deterring its entry, would be for the colluding established firms to reduce the industry price to P_L. Although this would reduce their own excess profits in the short run (by VW per unit) the new entrant would make a loss selling E at price P_L, since price would be less than average cost at that output. It would have needed to produce as much as output S *immediately* at the price P_L, even to have just covered its average costs.

Methods of collusion

Both formal and informal methods of collusion can be used.

Formal collusion: cartels

Cartels involve establishing and maintaining some kind of organisation which seeks to direct the policy of its members to reach some agreed end. For example, OPEC (Oil Producing and Exporting Countries) seeks to control the output of its member countries in order to keep the oil price above a target level previously agreed.

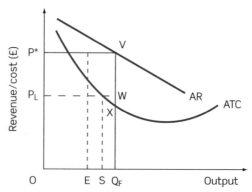

Figure 7.4 Limit pricing as a barrier to entry.

Source: Griffiths, A. and Wall, S. (2011) *Economics for Business and Management* (3rd ed.) © 2011 Pearson Education. Reproduced with permission.

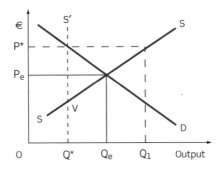

Figure 7.5 Operation of a cartel seeking minimum price P*.

Source: Griffiths, A. and Wall, S. (2011) *Economics for Business and Management* (3rd ed.) © 2011 Pearson Education. Reproduced with permission.

The operation of a cartel can be illustrated in terms of Figure 7.5. If no agreement is reached among suppliers, the suggestion in Figure 7.5 is that an equilibrium price P_e and quantity Q_e will result from the market. However, suppose the producers establish an organisation which seeks to prevent prices falling below P*. In effect the cartel must prevent output rising above Q*. It can do this by capping output at Q*, causing the original supply curve SS to take the shape SVS' in Figure 7.5.

An obvious problem is that at price P* the producers would (in the absence of the cartel) have supplied quantity Q_1, giving *excess supply* $Q^* - Q_1$.

Test yourself

Q5. Can you suggest how the use of quotas might help resolve this 'problem'?

The governments of most advanced industrialised nations subscribe to the view that formal (or informal) agreements to restrict output are harmful and therefore have passed legislation making cartels illegal. However, certain international cartels have not been prohibited, covering commodities such as oil, tin and coffee and indeed services such as air transport and telecommunications.

Examples & evidence

The OPEC cartel and oil prices

Around one-third of the total supply of crude oil is in the hands of a small group of 12 well-organised oil producing and exporting countries (OPEC) – Saudi Arabia, Ecuador, Angola, Algeria, Iraq, Iran, Qatar, Libya, Kuwait, United Arab Emirates, Nigeria and Venezuela. These countries meet regularly to decide on the total supply they should collectively produce, seeking to limit the total supply in order to keep the world price of crude oil at a 'reasonable' level. Having fixed the total supply, OPEC then allocates a *quota* to each member state which specifies their maximum oil production in that year.

When OPEC increases or decreases the agreed total supply of oil, this clearly has a major impact on the oil price. It was the sharp cuts in OPEC oil production that resulted in the major world 'oil crises' of 1967 and 1973, with rapid rises in the oil price leading to global recession. However, another unpredictable variable has been added to oil supply in recent years, namely the growing contribution of *non-OPEC* oil-producing countries. For example, Russia and the US are outside OPEC but each produces almost as much oil as the world's largest oil producer, Saudi Arabia, and many new oil resources in the former Soviet Republics such as Azerbaijan and Kazakhstan are now on stream. The top 10 producers and consumers of oil are listed in Table 7.4, with the OPEC and non-OPEC producers identified.

Table 7.4 Top 10 oil producers and consumers.

Top 10 oil producers (million barrels per day)		Top 10 oil consumers (million barrels per day)	
Saudi Arabia (OPEC)	10.8	USA	19.5
Russia (non OPEC)	9.8	China	8.9
USA (non OPEC)	8.5	Japan	4.8
Iran (OPEC)	4.1	Russia	2.8
China (non OPEC)	3.8	Germany	2.7
Mexico (non OPEC)	3.7	India	2.6
Canada (non OPEC)	3.4	Canada	2.5
United Arab Emirates (OPEC)	3.2	Brazil	2.4
Venezuela (OPEC)	3.0	South Korea	2.3
Norway (non OPEC)	2.6	Saudi Arabia	2.2

Source: adapted from CIA (2010), *The Factbook*.

It is not only actual events but *possible future events* that can influence the price of oil. For example, in the months before the second Iraq War in 2003, it was claimed that there was a 'war risk premium' of $5 a barrel built into the then current price, and Wall Street analysts suggested that uncertainties created by events in Iraq, Iran and Venezuela have added a $10–$20 risk premium to the price of oil.

Questions

OPEC has tried to restrict the total supply of crude oil from its member countries to keep the world price at a 'reasonable' level. Suppose it now aims for a higher world price per barrel.

1. How might it achieve this new target?
2. What problems might OPEC encounter in trying to achieve this higher oil price?

Informal collusion: price leadership

Certain forms of informal (tacit) collusion are also illegal in many countries. However, other forms are legal, including various types of 'price leadership'. In these situations one or more firms become recognised as the main price-setters for the industry and the other firms tend to act as followers.

Three different types of price leadership are often identified, namely dominant, barometric and collusive.

- *Dominant firm price leadership.* This is when the firm that is widely regarded as dominating the industry or market is acknowledged by others as the price leader. Ford has frequently acted as the dominant price leader in the motor vehicle industry by being first to announce price increases for various models of car.
- *Barometric price leadership.* In some cases the price leader is a small firm that is recognised by others to have a close knowledge of prevailing market conditions. The firm acts as a 'barometer' to others of changing market conditions, and its price changes are closely followed.
- *Collusive price leadership.* This is a more complicated form of price leadership; essentially it is an informal cartel in which members arrange to introduce price changes almost simultaneously. Such 'parallel' price changes have been noticed in the wholesale petrol market from time to time. In practice it is often difficult to distinguish collusive price leadership from types in which firms follow price leaders very quickly. Collusive price leadership is actually illegal in many countries.

✴ Assessment advice

The more advanced material below will be useful if you wish to develop your analysis of price leadership in a particular question, using the cost and revenue curves encountered in earlier chapters to explore dominant firm price leadership. This might include giving greater depth to the informal collusion part of an answer on oligopoly. However, this material is quite advanced, so you can pass over it for now if you wish and come back to it later should you decide to prepare for this type of question.

Dominant firm as price leader

Frequently the price leader is the dominant firm: controlling a major share of the industry output, it is regarded by other firms as the *price setter*. It sets the price that meets its primary objective, say maximising profits, and then allows smaller firms in the industry to sell all they wish at that price.

We can use Figure 7.6 to indicate the price-setting problem faced by the dominant firm. We can effectively regard the smaller firms as price takers, so that the short-run supply curve for each of these smaller firms is its marginal cost curve above minimum average variable cost **(see pages 102–104)**. For the aggregate of these smaller firms in the industry (i.e. all but the dominant firm) the supply curve will then be the horizontal sum of these individual marginal cost curves (i.e. MC_S). The industry (or market) demand curve is $D_1D'_1$. The dominant firm is seen here as behaving like a monopolist and equating its marginal revenue (MR_{DF}) to its marginal cost (MC_{DF}) in order to establish its profit-maximising price OP.

To explain this it will help to use Figure 7.6 to demonstrate how the dominant firm demand curve (and therefore its marginal revenue curve) is established. Note that the demand curve for the dominant firm ($D_{DF} D'_{DF}$) can be regarded here as a residual after the smaller firms have supplied (MC_S) all they wish to at a given price. So at price OV and below, when the smaller firms wish to supply zero, all the industry demand is available to the dominant firm (i.e. segment $D'_{DF}D'_1$). At the other extreme, for price OD_{DF} and above, when the smaller firms wish to supply all that the industry requires, none of the industry demand is available to the dominant firm. For intermediate prices between OV and OD_{DF} the residual demand available to the dominant firm is given by $OD_{DF}D'_{DF}$.

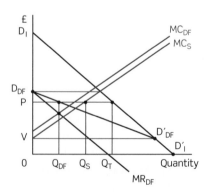

```
D₁D'₁  = industry demand curve
MC_S   = marginal cost/supply curve of the
          aggregate of smaller firms
MC_DF  = marginal cost curve of the dominant firm
D_DFD'_DFD'₁ = dominant firm demand curve
MR_DF  = dominant firm marginal revenue curve
```

Figure 7.6 Price leadership by a dominant firm (DF).

Source: Griffiths, A. and Wall, S. (2012) *Intermediate Microeconomics* (2nd ed.) © 2000 Pearson Education. Reproduced with permission.

In other words, between these (extreme) prices the quantity demanded from the dominant firm is the quantity demanded in the whole industry minus that quantity supplied by the (aggregate of) smaller firms. For example, at price OP the quantity demanded from the dominant firm is $OQ_T - OQ_S = OQ_{DF}$. The dominant firm's demand curve is then given by segments $D_{DF}D'_{DF}D'_1$ in Figure 7.6.

Having derived the (residual) dominant firm demand curve, we can construct the associated marginal revenue curve (MR_{DF}) in the usual way. The profit-maximising dominant firm now equates MR_{DF} with MC_{DF} (shown here as greater than MC_S), giving output Q_{DF}. The profit-maximising dominant firm then sets price at OP. Note that only by setting price along the segment of its demand curve $D_{DF}D'_{DF}$ is the dominant firm acting in a way different from that of a monopolist.

At price OP the dominant firm supplies OQ_{DF} and the aggregate of smaller firms supplies OQ_S. It follows that OP is a market-clearing price, with industry/total supply matching industry/total demand at that price. This must be so since, by construction, $OQ_{DF} + OQ_S = OQ_T$, the total quantity demanded at price OP.

Oligopoly practices

Here we review a number of practices which are often associated with oligopoly market structures.

Pricing practices

Oligopoly firms have market power and a range of pricing practices are often used.

- *Penetration pricing*, where price for a new product may even be set below average cost in order to capture market share. The expectation is that prices can be raised and profit margins restored later in the growth/maturity stages, helped by the fact that average costs may themselves be falling in those stages via the various economies of scale.
- *'Price-skimming'*, where a high price is set for a new product in the *introduction early growth* stages which 'skims off' a small but lucrative part of the market. Producers of fashion products, which have a short life and high innovative value as long as only a few people own them, often adopt a skimming strategy. Companies such as IBM, Polaroid and Bosch have operated such price-skimming systems over time. Bosch used a successful skimming policy, supported by patents, in its launch of fuel injection and antilock braking systems.
- *Prestige pricing*, where higher prices are associated with higher quality ('Veblen effect').
- *Loss leader (bait) pricing*, where a limited number of products are priced at or below cost to entice customers who may then pay full price on other purchases (e.g. for selected products in supermarkets).

- *Clearance pricing*, where rock-bottom prices are charged to clear stock and make resources available for alternative uses.
- *Parallel pricing*, where several firms change prices in the same direction and by broadly the same amount.
- *Product line pricing*, where the pricing of one item is related to that of complementary items, with a view to maximising the return on the whole product line. For example, the price of a 'core' product might be set at a low level to encourage sales and then the 'accessories' priced at high levels.

 Assessment advice

These pricing practices can equally be applied to monopoly market structures. They become feasible whenever producers have the market power to actually set prices, rather than merely having to respond to prices set by others. It will be useful to combine the pricing practices of monopolies **(Chapter 6, page 156)** with those above to have a fuller picture of the range of pricing initiatives available to firms with market power to set prices.

Examples & evidence

Pricing strategies

Penetration pricing and Freeview

Freeview, the successor to ITV Digital, was the first to provide 'free' access to 25 channels for the cost of a once-only purchase of a £100 set-top decoder, rather than expensive and recurrent subscription charges. Over 500,000 decoders were sold in the first three months of operation in 2003.

Price-skimming in soap-capsules

Both Unilever and Procter & Gamble launched liquid soap-capsules in 2001, i.e. capsules of pre-measured doses of liquid detergent which could be placed into washing machines, to save people the bother of working out how much soap to use per wash. As a 'premium priced' product, the capsules were seen by the two companies as offering good price-skimming opportunities.

Premium pricing and shampoo

Shampoo was once considered one market, but new product development, branding and packaging have segmented this in many ways. Shampoo products may be seen to be segmented into medicated hair products (Head & Shoulders), two-in-one (Wash & Go), children's shampoo (L'Oréal

Kids), 'balanced' shampoos (Organics, Fructis) and environmentally sensitive shampoos (The Body Shop range). Such strategies permit manufacturers such as Unilever and Procter & Gamble to place a premium price on many of their shampoo products. These forms of lifestyle segmentation are now used by many firms in preference to the social class distinctions of the previous four decades.

Prestige pricing, 'Veblen effect' and higher education

Here price is itself associated with *quality* by users of the product. In situations where the information available to users is imperfect, price is often used as a proxy variable for quality. Student and parent assessment of educational courses characterised by differential top-up fees is an obvious candidate for such a 'Veblen effect', reinforced by the fact that the 'older' universities (widely perceived by the general public to be of the highest quality) will be seen to charge the full £9,000 annual tuition fee for most of their courses.

A major cross-country study into higher education by IDP Education Australia in association with the British Council strongly supported the existence of this 'Veblen effect' as regards international student demand for higher education. Senior researcher Anthony Bohm commented: 'Students cannot make an informed choice about the exact quality of comparable products, so they use price as a proxy for understanding the value they will get out of an international programme.'

Question

1. Can you provide any other examples for these four pricing strategies?

Price discrimination

A strategy often associated with oligopoly (though equally available to monopoly) is that of *price discrimination*. So far we have assumed that firms charge only one price for their product. In practice, firms may charge different prices for an *identical* product – which is what 'price discrimination' refers to. Examples might include:

- manufacturers selling an identical product at different prices in different geographical locations (e.g. different regions of a country, different national markets, etc.);
- electricity, gas and rail companies charging higher prices at peak hours than at off-peak hours for the same service;
- cinemas, theatres and transport companies cutting prices for both younger and older customers;

- student discounts for rail travel, restaurant meals and holidays;
- hotels offering cheap weekend breaks and winter discounts.

Examples & evidence

Price discrimination in pharmaceuticals

In April 2001 the Office of Fair Trading (OFT) in the UK imposed a penalty on Napp Pharmaceuticals Holdings Ltd, a Cambridge-based pharmaceutical company, for abuse of its dominant position in the market for a drug called MST, a slow-release morphine product used to treat severe pain in cancer patients. The company controlled 94% of the overall sales of the drug, which was sold to two distinct markets – the community segment and the hospital segment. The community segment involved MST sold to pharmacies which, in turn, supplied them to patients through GP prescriptions, while the hospital segment involved sales of MST direct to hospitals.

The OFT Report commented that GPs were strongly influenced by the reputation of the product and were reluctant to experiment with new products of which they had no direct experience. In addition, for GPs, cost seemed to be 'rarely considered in terminal care pain relief'. On the other hand, hospital doctors were found to be more willing to accept 'intra-molecular substitution' – that is, they were willing to use any brand of a single molecular product to treat their patients. The OFT Report found that the price which Napp charged for its 5 mg tablets of MST to the *community market* was 70% higher than its price to the *hospital market* – where prices were set at below average variable cost (AVC). The OFT found that Napp had engaged in anti-competitive activity and proposed that the company should immediately reduce the price of MST tablets to the community sector. It was estimated that this would save the NHS around £2m annually.

Questions

1. What indicators are there that Napp had monopoly power in the market for MST?
2. Identify the factors which would ensure that Napp could apply price discrimination policies in this market.
3. How was Napp keeping other rivals out of the market?

Reasons for price discrimination

A key reason for price discrimination is to increase revenue and profit (revenue minus cost) for the firm. Suppose that if, instead of charging the single, uniform price OP in Figure 7.7 (a), the firm were to charge what each consumer is *willing to pay*, as indicated by the demand curve.

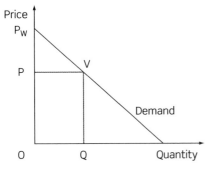
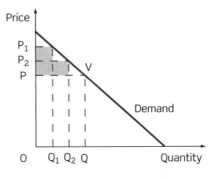

(a) First-degree price discrimination   **(b)** Second-degree price discrimination

Figure 7.7 First- and second-degree price discrimination.

Source: Griffiths, A. and Wall, S. (2011) *Economics for Business and Management* (3rd ed.) © 2011 Pearson Education. Reproduced with permission.

It follows that an additional PP_wV of revenue will result. Total revenue would be OP_wVQ compared with $OPVQ$ with a single, uniform price OP. This type of price discrimination is capturing all the consumer surplus that occurs at price OP and converting it into revenue for the producer. It is sometimes called 'first degree' price discrimination. In fact, three types of price discrimination are often identified in the literature:

- *First-degree price discrimination*, where, as in Figure 7.7(a), the firm charges a different price to every consumer, reflecting each consumer's willingness to pay.
- *Second-degree price discrimination*, where different prices are charged for different quantities or 'blocks' of the same product. So, for example, in Figure 7.7(b) the quantity OQ is split into three equal-sized blocks (O–Q_1, Q_1–Q_2 and Q_2–Q) and a different price is charged for each block (P_1, P_2 and P respectively). The idea is that while consumers cannot, in practice, be identified in terms of individual willingness to pay, different prices might be charged to groups of consumers. Again, the extra total revenue (shaded area) is greater than would have occurred with a single uniform price ($OPVQ$).
- *Third-degree price discrimination*, where the market is separated into two or more groups of consumers, with a different price charged to each group. We now discuss this in more detail.

Third-degree price discrimination

 Assessment advice

Providing a detailed analysis of third-degree price discrimination will demonstrate a fuller understanding of price-setting behaviour.

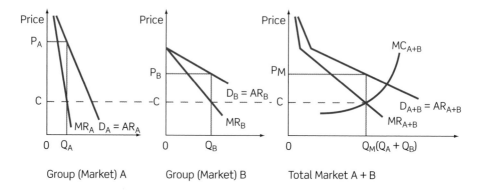

Figure 7.8 Third-degree price discrimination: charging different prices to different groups of customers.

Source: Griffiths, A. and Wall, S. (2011) *Economics for Business and Management* (3rd ed.) © 2011 Pearson Education. Reproduced with permission.

For third-degree price discrimination to be undertaken it must be both possible and profitable to segment the market into two or more groups of consumers, with a different price charged to each group.

- *To be possible*, the firm must be able to prevent consumers moving from the higher-priced market segment to the lower-priced market segment. In other words, there must be 'barriers' separating the respective market segments. Such barriers could include geographical distance (domestic/overseas markets), time (peak/off-peak), personal identification (young/old), etc.
- *To be profitable*, the price elasticity of demand must be different in each separate market segment.

Figure 7.8 outlines the situation of third-degree price discrimination.

In Figure 7.8 we assume that the large oligopoly firm produces in one location and sells its output to two separate markets, A and B, with different price elasticities of demand in each market. Market B has a much higher price elasticity of demand than Market A. The corresponding *total market* marginal and average revenue curves are obtained by summing horizontally the *individual market* marginal and average revenue curves.

With production in a single location there is one MC curve, giving the overall profit-maximising output of Q_M, which might be sold at a single price P_M. However, total profit can, in this situation, be raised by selling this output at a different price to each group (market).

The profit-maximising condition is that MC for the whole output must equal MR in each separate market:

i.e. $MC_{A+B} = MR_A = MR_B$

In Figure 7.8 total output Q_M will be allocated so that Q_A goes to group (market) A and Q_B to group (market) B, resulting in the respective prices P_A and P_B.

Any other allocation of total output Q_M must reduce total revenue and therefore, with unchanged costs, reduce total profit. We can illustrate this by considering a single unit reallocation from market A to market B. The addition to total revenue (MR_B) of this unit when sold in market B is less than C, whereas the loss to total revenue (MR_A) of not selling this unit in market A is C. The overall change in total revenue from this unit reallocation is clearly negative, which, with total costs unchanged, must reduce total profit.

As we can see from Figure 7.8, the implication of third-degree price discrimination is a higher price in the market with lowest price elasticity of demand ($P_A > P_B$).

 Assessment advice

Remember that the other pricing practices considered earlier **(pages 191–192)** can also be used in monopoly-type questions.

Non-pricing practices

Rivalry between oligopoly firms is often expressed in terms of non-price competitions, with advertising and branding, as well as service quality, often being used in an attempt to gain market share.

Advertising

Data on advertising provide a useful, if indirect, method for gauging both the rise of oligopoly markets and the tendency towards product differentiation. Advertising is essentially aimed at binding consumers to particular brands for reasons other than price. Estimates in the USA of branded, processed foods put their prices almost 9% higher than those of 'private label' equivalents – similar products packaged under the retailer's own name – due solely to more extensive media advertising.

Companies advertise their branded products intensively in order to 'bind' the consumer to the product for reasons other than price. Where successful, such advertising may help in two ways (see Figure 7.9):

1 It may *shift* the demand curve outwards from D to D_1, raising market share.
2 It may simultaneously cause the demand curve to pivot from D_1 to D_2 and become steeper. Demand then becomes less price elastic, creating new opportunities for raising both price and revenue.

The examples here emphasise the importance of cultural awareness in advertising.

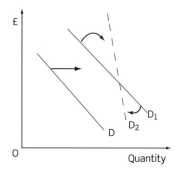

Figure 7.9 Impacts of advertising.

Examples & evidence

Advertising and culture

Many pan-European advertising campaigns have failed to deliver because of lack of research into how cultural differences may affect the viewer's response to the advertising. For example, an advert for slimming pills showing an overweight person on the left, pointing to slimming pills in the middle, pointing to a slim person on the right is appropriate if the advert runs in a country where the population reads from left to right. However, if the advert were to go out in Japan (where the population read from right to left), this would translate as: eat slimming pills to gain weight!

It is worth remembering that different cultures have different types of humour. Something that may appear humorous to a UK audience may not necessarily have the same effect in Germany. Also, special attention needs to be paid to the use of celebrities in advertising. First, for the purpose of a pan-European campaign, the celebrity should be known throughout Europe. Second, they should carry a positive reputation, encouraging people to buy the product. Third, ideally there should be a certain amount of synergy between the celebrity and the product, e.g. David Beckham advertising Adidas sportswear. David Beckham is certainly well known throughout Europe, and also in the USA since his 2007 move to LA Galaxy from Real Madrid.

Question

1. Can you suggest any other examples of the advertising approach being influenced by national cultural characteristics?

Monopolistic competition

This type of market structure is sometimes called 'imperfect competition'.

- It contains elements of a competitive market structure in that it assumes both a large number of small firms in the industry, and freedom of entry into, and exit from, the industry.
- It contains elements of an 'imperfect' market structure in that it assumes that each small firm supplies a product which is not homogeneous but is differentiated in some way from that of its rivals. Put another way, the product of each small firm is a close but not perfect substitute for the product of other small firms in the industry.

Product differentiation and demand

There are many Chinese takeaway restaurants in most cities and towns. The menus are very similar but each one arguably cooks or presents its food in ways which differ from its rivals. Similarly, wine producers in France often differentiate their wines from domestic and foreign rivals by designating the region of France in which the grapes were grown.

Downward-sloping demand curve

Because the product is differentiated from that of its rivals, the firm's demand curve will no longer be the perfectly elastic (horizontal) demand curve of perfect competition. In fact, it will be the downward (negatively) sloping demand curve shown in Figure 7.10 (a).

- If the firm lowers the price of its (differentiated) product it will capture some, but not all, consumers from other firms.
- If the firm raises its price it will lose some, but not all, of its consumers to rival firms.

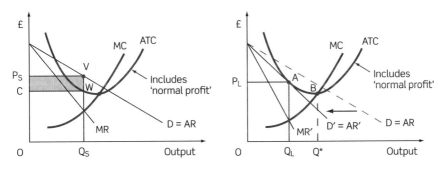

(a) Short-run equilibrium: super-normal profit (P$_S$VWC)

(b) Long-run equilibrium: normal profit

Figure 7.10 Short-run and long-run equilibrium under monopolistic competition.

Source: Griffiths, A. and Wall, S. (2011) *Economics for Business and Management* (3rd ed.) © 2011 Pearson Education. Reproduced with permission.

Loyalty to the differentiated products of the respective firms means that price, while important, is not the sole influence on consumer choice. Hence we have a negatively sloped demand curve for the firm's products. Of course, the greater the loyalty to the firm's differentiated product, the greater the price rise needed to induce consumers to switch from the product to that of a rival, and similarly the greater the price cut needed to attract (loyal) consumers attached to its rival firm's products. It follows that the greater the product differentiation and consumer loyalty to the product, the *less price elastic* the demand curve for a particular firm will be, and of course the greater the monopoly power over price available to the firm.

Equilibrium price and output

Short-run equilibrium

In Figure 7.10(a) the profit-maximising firm (MC = MR) will, in the short run, produce output Q_S and sell this at price P_S, yielding super-normal profit P_SVWC. This excess profit will, given freedom of entry into the market, attract new entrants.

Unlike perfect competition, the new entrants do not increase the overall market supply of a single, homogeneous product. Rather, the new entrants will partly erode the consumer demand for an existing firm's (differentiated) product, i.e. the new entrants will capture some of the customers of the existing firm by offering a still wider variety of differentiated products. We show this by a leftward shift (decrease) in the existing firm's demand curve in Figure 7.10(a).

Long-run equilibrium

Only when profit is reduced to normal for firms already in the market will the attraction for new entrants be removed, i.e. when ATC = AR, with normal profit included in ATC. In other words, the demand (AR) curve for the existing firm will shift leftwards until it just touches the ATC curve. This long-run equilibrium occurs in Figure 7.10(b) with demand curve D', at price P_L and output Q_L.

- If the demand curve is still to the right of D' in Figure 7.10(b), then super-normal profits will still be made and new entry will continue.
- If the demand curve has shifted to the left of D', then sub-normal profits will be made and some firms will leave the industry (bankruptcy) and the demand curve will shift back to the right.
- Only at D', when normal profits are earned, will there be no long-run tendency for firms to enter or leave the industry.

In this analysis, the firm will produce an output of Q_L and charge a price of P_L, making normal profit – there is no further entry of firms into the industry. The firm will operate where the average cost is tangential to the demand curve (point A) but technically the firm is able to operate at point B with an output of Q^*. In other words, the firm has a capacity to produce more at a lower average cost. Consequently, a criticism of monopolistic competition is that each firm is serving a market that is too small and has the capacity to serve more customers. The firm in monopolistic competition therefore operates with *excess capacity* in the long run, equivalent to the difference between Q_L and Q^* in Figure 7.10(b). The excess capacity leads to higher average costs than would exist if output were expanded, and to higher consumer prices.

Comparison with perfect competition

We might usefully summarise the 'efficiency' aspects of long-run equilibrium for monopolistic competition:

- *Normal profits.* Only normal profits are earned in the long run, as with perfect competition.
- *Higher price, lower output.* Price is higher and output lower than would be the case in the long run for perfect competition (which would be at the price and output corresponding to point B).
- *Productive efficiency.* ATC (at A) is higher than the minimum level technically achievable (B), so productive efficiency is *not* achieved.
- *Excess capacity.* In Figure 7.10(b) output is Q_L but for minimum ATC output should be higher at Q^*. This shortfall in actual output (Q_L) below the productively (technically) efficient output (Q^*) is often called excess capacity.
- *Allocative efficiency.* Price is higher than marginal cost, so allocative efficiency is *not* achieved.

Chapter summary – pulling it all together

By the end of this chapter you should be able to:

	Confident ✓	Not confident?
Outline the key characteristics of oligopoly markets		Revise pages 174–175
Assess how oligopolies try to anticipate rival firm actions and reactions (non-collusion)		Revise pages 175–184
Explain how oligopolies use formal and informal arrangements to reduce uncertainty (collusion)		Revise pages 184–191
Review price and non-price strategies widely used in practice by oligopolies		Revise pages 191–198

	Confident ✓	Not confident?
Outline the key characteristics of monopolistically competitive markets		Revise pages 199–200
Compare equilibrium outcomes in monopolistic competition and perfect competition		Revise pages 200–201

Now try the **assessment question** at the start of this chapter, using the answer guidelines below.

Answer guidelines

✳ Assessment question

Explain the approaches and strategies available to firms in oligopoly markets to reduce the uncertainties from their recognised interdependence with other large firms.

Approaching the question

- Defining key terms used in the question is always a useful beginning, here making clear that the term 'oligopoly' involves 'recognised interdependence' between rivals in a market dominated by the few. Examples of industries and sectors with high concentration ratios might be presented.
- You could also briefly outline the structure you intend to follow, such as examining approaches and strategies in the following situations:

  1 Non-collusive oligopoly (which you define)

  2 Collusive oligopoly (which you define).

Important points to include

- *Non-collusive oligopoly strategies.* These can include attempts to anticipate the actions and reactions of rivals without any formal or informal arrangements with them.

  1 The *kinked demand model* assumes rivals react to your price cuts but not your price rises (e.g. Figure 7.1).

2   The *Cournot model* assumes rivals set output levels and don't change (e.g. Figure 7.2).

3   The *Bertrand model* assumes rivals set prices and don't change.

4   *Game theory models* seek to evaluate the potential reactions of rivals to your strategies and the implications for market share, profit, etc., using a pay-off matrix. You could use tables (pay-off matrices) to review different types of game (zero sum, non-zero sum) and different types of decision rule (maxi-min, mini-max).

- *Collusive oligopoly strategies.* These can include attempts to seek various arrangements between the oligopoly firms in an attempt to remove some of the uncertainty they face. These arrangements might be formal or informal.

1   *Formal arrangements*, e.g. cartel (Figure 7.5)

2   *Informal arrangements*, e.g. limit pricing (Figure 7.4) and price leadership (Figure 7.6).

Make your answer stand out

The presentation and use of the diagrams already mentioned will give greater depth to your answer. So too will your use of tables such as pay-off matrices to illustrate game playing. Case study examples and evidence will demonstrate your ability to apply theory to contemporary events.

Read to impress

You can further explore the various types of game (e.g. one-stop, repeated and sequential) and various types of strategies (e.g. tit-for-tat, first mover) in more specialised sources for oligopoly. These include:

Books

Binmark, K. (2007) *Game Theory: A Very Short Introduction*, Oxford University Press.

Griffiths, A. and Wall, S. (2012) *Applied Economics*, Chapter 6, Pearson Education.

Griffiths, A. and Wall, S. (2011) *Economics for Business and Management*, 3rd edition, Chapter 6, Pearson Education.

Parkin, M., Powell, M. and Matthews, K. (2012) *Economics*, 8th edition, Chapter 14, Addison Wesley.

Sloman, J. and Garratt, D. (2010) *Essentials of Economics*, 5th edition, FT/Prentice Hall.

Sloman, J., Wride, A. and Garratt, D. (2012) *Economics*, 8th edition, Chapter 2, Pearson Education.

Journals and periodicals

The following are useful sources of articles and data on many aspects relevant to this and other topics:

Business Review, Philip Allan (quarterly)
Economic Review, Philip Allan (quarterly)
Economics Today, Anforme (quarterly)
Harvard Business Review (monthly)
The Economist (weekly)

Newspapers

Newspapers are important sources of up-to-date information, examples and data. Below are some of the main UK newspaper sources, many of which have websites with search facilities to identify specific topics and articles:

The Guardian
The Times
The Financial Times
The Independent
The Telegraph

Companion website

Go to the companion website at **www.pearsoned.co.uk/econexpress** to find revision support online for this topic area.

Notes

Notes

8

Labour and other factor markets

Topic map

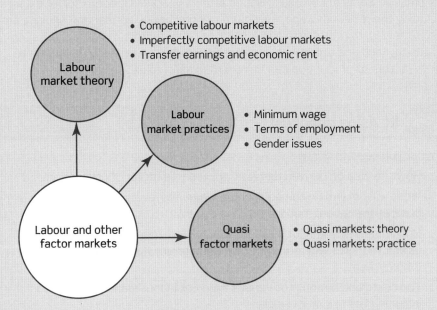

- Competitive labour markets
- Imperfectly competitive labour markets
- Transfer earnings and economic rent

Labour market theory

Labour market practices
- Minimum wage
- Terms of employment
- Gender issues

Labour and other factor markets

Quasi factor markets
- Quasi markets: theory
- Quasi markets: practice

A printable version of this topic map is available from **www.pearsoned.co.uk/econexpress**

Introduction

The proportion of the annual revenue of a football club in the English Premier League going to its players rose dramatically from 48% in 1997 to over 70% in 2013, an increase of 22% in just 16 years. In fact, since 1992, while the average salary of employees in the UK had risen by 186% (i.e. almost trebled) in money terms, the average salary of a Premier League footballer had risen by an astonishing 1,500%.

What factors are involved in determining employee pay in football and other labour markets? In this chapter we consider how the price and output of the various factors of production are determined, giving particular attention to the labour market. We begin by discussing the idea that the return to all factors of production is 'derived' from the demand for the product or service they help produce. Attention then switches exclusively to labour as a factor of production and to those elements influencing the wage rate and the level of employment for various occupations. We review the wage/employment outcome for competitive labour markets and for those in which 'imperfections' such as monopoly power (trade unions) or monopsony power (employer groupings) are present. Some of the policy issues affecting work in modern societies, including the minimum wage, maximum working hours, gender and ageism, are also reviewed, together with the returns to other factors of production, such as capital, land and enterprise, and the circumstances in which payments to some factors of production can be regarded as 'surplus'.

 Revision checklist

What you need to know:

- ❏ How the idea of 'derived demand' applies to a factor of production.
- ❏ What will determine the equilibrium wage and level of employment in a competitive labour market.
- ❏ How imperfections such as 'monopoly' and 'monopsony' in labour markets will influence the equilibrium wage and level of employment.
- ❏ The costs and benefits of various types of labour market regulation, including the minimum wage.
- ❏ The circumstances in which returns to a factor of production will include an element of surplus payment ('economic rent').
- ❏ The role of 'quasi' factor markets in resource allocations.

Assessment advice

Structure your argument

It will help if you define any terms used in the question and clearly structure your approach. For example, you might start by examining the returns to the factor of production (usually labour) under a competitive factor market before introducing various types of 'imperfection'. These could, for the labour market, include elements of monopoly (e.g. trade unions) and monopsony (e.g. employer associations). The outcomes from the competitive factor market could then be compared and contrasted with outcomes from factor markets with various types of 'imperfection'.

Use diagrams

There are key diagrams you can use to illustrate your arguments and gain higher marks. For example, Figure 8.1 can be used to establish the equilibrium wage and employment in a competitive labour market; Figure 8.3(a) can then be used to show the impact of monopoly (seller power, e.g. trade unions) in the labour market on wages and employment; and Figure 8.3(b) can be used to show the impact of monopsony (buyer power, e.g. employer associations) in the labour market on wages and employment. These diagrams can be used to demonstrate the impacts of various types of labour market 'imperfections' and to explain why the wages in some occupations differ substantially from those in others.

Use consistent terminology

Make sure you understand terminology such as 'marginal physical productivity' and 'marginal revenue productivity' when discussing factor markets. Also use terms such as monopoly and monopsony in appropriate ways when applied to factor markets.

Use empirical evidence

Data on wage differences between occupations such as those in Tables 8.1 and 8.2 will help to further strengthen your arguments, as will data on differences in gender earnings, etc.

 Assessment question

How would you explain the difference in earnings between consultants and healthcare workers in a hospital?

Labour market theory

A conventional listing of factors of production often includes land, labour and capital, though some might include enterprise or 'entrepreneurship' as a factor in its own right.

 Assessment advice

Most assessment questions involve the labour market and ask you to explore reasons why wages and/or levels of employment differ between occupations or how gender, age or other characteristics can affect labour market outcomes.

Factors of production are not demanded for purposes of ownership, as is arguably the case with consumer goods, but rather because of the stream of services they provide. For example, in the case of labour, workers are demanded for their mental and physical contribution to the production process. We therefore say that the demand for a factor of production is a *derived demand* rather than a direct demand. It is derived from the demand for the product, whether a good or a service, which the factor helps to produce.

Competitive labour markets

 Assessment advice

It is often useful to begin your analysis by assuming a competitive labour market with the (unrealistic) assumption of perfect competition in both product and labour markets before relaxing these assumptions later.

Marginal productivity theory and derived demand

The *marginal productivity theory* of wages is often used to explain the demand for a particular occupation and therefore the wage it can command in the marketplace. According to this theory, firms will continue to employ labour until the employment of the marginal worker adds as much to revenue as it does to costs. The 'law of variable proportions' applies in the short run **(see Chapter 4, page 88)** and predicts that when labour is the variable factor being applied to some fixed factor (such as land or capital), the **marginal physical product of labour** at first rises but subsequently falls as the employment of workers increases. The **marginal revenue product of labour** is then derived from the marginal physical product of labour.

Key definitions

Marginal physical product of labour (MPP$_L$)

This is the additional (physical) output contributed by the last person employed.

Marginal revenue product of labour (MRP$_L$)

This is the addition to total revenue contributed by the last person employed. In a perfectly competitive product market, MRP$_L$ is found by multiplying MPP$_L$ by the price of the product:

MRP$_L$ = MPP$_L$ × product price

Productivity comparisons

Of course, the importance of productivity performance is widely recognised by individual firms and countries.

Examples & evidence

Labour productivity

Table 8.1 provides useful data on the labour productivity performance during 1999–2011 of some major countries, using index numbers with base 2008 = 100.

Table 8.1 Labour productivity in selected countries (2008 = 100).

Country	1999	2003	2007	2011
UK	83	92	98	96
Germany	87	92	98	99
US	89	94	99	106
France	91	94	98	100
Spain	99	101	101	108

Source: Adapted from Fleming, S. (2012).

Questions

1. Why is the table relevant to wage determination?
2. Which countries would appear to be the most competitive in terms of the labour market?
3. Can you explain why the US and Spain have high unemploymnet and fast productivity growth?

Under marginal productivity theory, the profit-maximising firm will continue to employ workers until the last person employed adds exactly the same value to revenue as he or she adds to costs, i.e. until MRP_L from employment = MC_L of employment:

> $MRP_L = MC_L$ for profit maximisation

MRP_L as the firm's demand curve for labour

In a competitive labour market the firm can hire as many workers as it wants at the going wage (see Figure 8.1). It follows that the supply of labour (S_L) to each firm would be perfectly elastic at the going wage rate (W_1), so that the wage rate is itself both the average and the marginal cost of labour.

The profit-maximising firm would then hire people until MRP_L equalled MC_L, i.e. L_1 persons in Figure 8.1.

- If *more than* L_1 people were hired, then the extra revenue from hiring an extra person would be less than the extra cost. Profit will rise by hiring fewer people.
- If *fewer than* L_1 people were hired, then the extra revenue from hiring an extra person would be greater than the extra cost. Profit will rise by hiring more people.

Under these conditions the MRP_L curve becomes the demand curve for labour (D_L), since at any given wage rate the profit-maximising firm will employ labour until MRP_L equals that wage rate. For example, if the wage rate falls to W_2 in Figure 8.1 then demand for labour expands to L_2.

Market (industry) demand for labour

If we know the number of workers of a certain type (occupation) that each *firm* in an industry demands at any given wage rate, then we can derive the overall *market* (industry) demand for that occupation by adding together all the individual firms' demand curves. Because each individual firm's demand

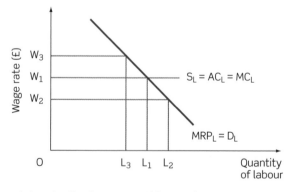

Figure 8.1 Wage determination in a competitive market.

Source: Griffiths, A. and Wall, S. (2011) *Economics for Business and Management* (3rd ed.) © 2011 Pearson Education. Reproduced with permission.

for a type of labour will vary inversely with the wage rate, the overall market demand for that type of labour will also vary inversely with the wage rate. In other words, market demand for any type of labour (occupation) will expand as the wage rate falls (see Figure 8.1).

Elasticity of demand for labour

It is clearly useful to know how responsive the demand for labour will be to a change in its price (e.g. wage rate). Clearly the demand for labour will vary *inversely* with the wage rate, with the demand for labour expanding as the wage rate falls. However, as with price elasticity of demand, we usually ignore the sign. The range of numerical possibilities and terminology are in fact the same as given earlier **(Table 2.1 of Chapter 2, pages 30-31)** for price elasticity of demand.

$$\text{Elasticity of demand for labour} = \frac{\% \text{ change in quantity of labour demanded}}{\% \text{ change in price of labour}}$$

Influences on the elasticity of demand for labour

We can say that the elasticity of demand for labour will depend upon the following:

- *The price elasticity of demand (PED) for the product produced by labour.* If PED for the product is relatively inelastic, then elasticity of demand for labour will tend to be relatively inelastic, with a given percentage rise in the price of labour resulting in a smaller percentage fall in the demand for labour. The reasoning is that employers will be able to pass on the higher wage costs as higher product prices in the knowledge that consumer demand will be little affected.

- *The proportion of the total costs of production accounted for by labour.* Where this is relatively small, the demand for labour will tend to be relatively inelastic. Even a large percentage rise in the price of labour will have little effect on the price of the product and therefore on the demand for labour.

- *The ease with which other factors of production can be substituted for labour.* Where it is difficult to substitute capital equipment or other factors of production for the now more expensive labour input, then elasticity of demand for labour will tend to be relatively inelastic, with any given percentage rise in the price of labour having little effect on the demand for labour in the production process.

Test yourself

Q1. Outline the situations which will tend to make the demand for a particular type of labour (occupation) relatively elastic.

Elasticity of supply for labour

We have seen that the equilibrium price (wage rate) and quantity of labour employed depend on both demand and supply conditions. The supply of labour to any particular industry or occupation will vary *directly* with the wage rate. At higher wage rates more workers make themselves available for employment in this particular industry or occupation and vice versa. At the higher wage, extra workers are attracted to this occupation, since they now earn more than in the next best paid alternative employment.

Again, it will be useful to know how responsive the supply of labour will be to a change in its price (e.g. wage rate). The (price) elasticity of supply for labour can be expressed as follows:

$$\text{Elasticity of supply for labour} = \frac{\% \text{ change in quantity of labour supplied}}{\% \text{ change in price of labour}}$$

Influences on the elasticity of supply for labour

We can say that the elasticity of supply for labour will depend upon the following:

- *The degree to which labour is mobile, both geographically and occupationally.* The less mobile a particular type of labour (e.g. occupation) is between geographical regions and occupations, then the less responsive (less elastic) will be its supply to a change in the wage rate.

- *The time period in question.* The supply of labour to all industries or occupations will tend to be less responsive (less elastic) in the short run than in the long run since it may take time for labour to acquire the new skills and experience required for many occupations. This is especially true where the nature of the work is highly skilled and requires considerable training. In this case the supply of labour to the occupation will not rise substantially, at least initially, as wage rates increase, as for example with doctors and barristers.

We now seek to apply what we have learnt to the key question of why some occupations achieve higher levels of earnings and higher rates of employment than others. That differences in occupational earnings exist and are actually widening is evident from recent data, such as in Table 8.2 in the 'Examples & evidence' here.

Examples & evidence

Occupational earnings

From Table 8.2 it can be seen that managers and senior officials earn 47% above the average for all occupations and enjoy higher earnings than those in professional occupations (e.g. scientists, engineers,

Table 8.2 Relative earnings by occupational groups, 2011.

Occupational group	Median gross weekly wage (all occupations = 100)
Managers and senior officials	147
Professional occupations	142
Associate professional and technical occupations	113
Skilled trades occupations	93
Process, plant and machine operatives	85
Administrative and secretarial occupations	76
Personal service occupations	67
Elementary occupations	66
Sales and customer service occupations	61
All occupations	**100**

Source: Adapted from ONS (2012), *Annual Survey of Hours and Earnings 2011*.

teachers, accountants, etc.). Associate professionals and technical occupations (technicians, therapists, prison officers, etc.) earn, on average, 13% above the median earnings for the whole country. It is also true to say that many occupations classed as 'manual' (e.g. process, plant and machine operatives) earn more than 'non-manual' workers, such as those in sales or personal services. Indeed, a more detailed analysis also reveals that certain manual occupations, such as construction operatives, vehicle assemblers, stevedores and heavy goods vehicle drivers, earn the equivalent or more than further education teachers or healthcare managers. Although the picture is complicated, it can be seen that substantial inequality of occupational earnings is clearly present in UK society.

Question

1. Can you think of reasons for these differences in average annual earnings across the various occupational groups?

We first approach the 'Examples & evidence' question assuming no imperfections in the labour market before relaxing this assumption and examining the labour market as it really is in practice.

Competitive labour markets

In competitive labour markets, wage rates are determined by the forces of supply and demand for labour. In these circumstances, different wage rates between occupations will reflect differences in the respective conditions of supply and demand, as in the two hypothetical labour markets shown in Figure 8.2.

In Figure 8.2(a) the higher wage rate (W_1) in one of these competitive labour markets is due to the fact that, at any given wage rate, demand for labour is greater (D_1D_1) and supply of labour is lower (S_1S_1) in this market than in the other competitive labour market. This wage difference can be maintained over time if the labour markets are separate, i.e. with little or no mobility between the two occupations (e.g. surgeons and nurses).

However, if workers can easily move between the two occupations, as in Figure 8.2(b), then any initial wage difference is unlikely to be maintained over time (e.g. bus and lorry drivers).

Test yourself

Q2. Use Figure 8.2(a) to explain the circumstances under which the wage rate for the occupation described by the DD and SS curves respectively might rise *above* W.

Q3. How might the level of employment be affected at this now higher wage?

Q4. Use Figure 8.2(b) to explain why the initially higher wage (W_1) for bus drivers may not last.

Given a competitive labour market and a particular set of supply and demand conditions for labour, we can now make a number of assertions:

- Only one wage rate is sustainable (i.e. in equilibrium), namely that which equates supply of labour with demand for labour.
- Wages in a particular industry or occupation can only change if there is a change in the conditions of supply or in the conditions of demand, or in both.

Of course, in reality the labour market may not be competitive at all. After reviewing the issue of executive pay in this 'Examples & evidence', we consider the impacts of different types of 'market failure' in labour markets.

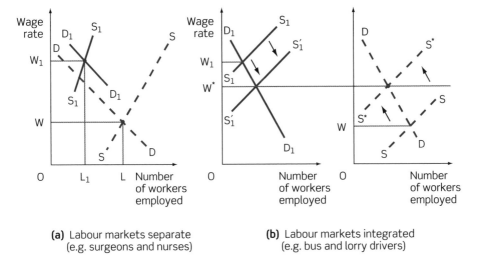

(a) Labour markets separate
(e.g. surgeons and nurses)

(b) Labour markets integrated
(e.g. bus and lorry drivers)

Figure 8.2 Equilibrium wage rates and levels of employment in two competitive labour markets.

Source: Griffiths, A. and Wall, S. (2011) *Economics for Business and Management* (3rd ed.) © 2011 Pearson Education. Reproduced with permission.

Examples & evidence

Executive pay and wage inequality

Two-thirds of the UK workforce in 2012 was earning less than the average wage as a result of excessive pay deals for executives and directors. Pay researchers at Incomes Data Services (IDS) say that wage inequality is rising because top pay is increasing faster than pay for the rest of the workforce.

In Europe 84% of companies place decisions about executive pay in the hands of their compensation or remuneration committees, according to a survey by consultants Hewitt, Bacon and Woodrow. So ultimately it is remuneration committees that are as responsible as anyone when executive pay appears to bear little relationship to corporate performance. Pension and Investment Research Consultants (PIRC), the UK corporate governance watchdog, regularly reports that the pay of executive directors at FTSE 100 companies has spiralled high above inflation.

This rapid rise in executive pay, when the companies themselves have been performing modestly at best, has created widespread criticism from shareholders and others. *Stock options* have been a particular source of criticism – the practice whereby senior executives have been given the 'option' of buying company shares at a heavily discounted price (i.e. lower than the market price) and then selling them at a profit should they succeed

Table 8.3 Compensation in the FTSE 100.

Year	Average CEO earnings (£)	Average employee earnings (£)	Multiple
1998	1,012,380	21,540	47
1999	1,235,401	20,939	59
2000	1,684,900	24,070	70
2001	1,812,750	24,170	75
2002	2,587,474	24,182	107
2003	2,773,904	24,767	112
2004	3,121,435	25,955	119
2005	3,312,285	27,254	121
2006	3,339,421	30,828	107
2007	3,935,820	25,677	151
2008	3,950,642	30,994	128
2009	3,710,440	32,521	115
2010	3,740,628	32,019	117
2011	3,820,501	32,320	118

Source: FT (various).

in raising the share price above an agreed target. Often, exercising these options has given far more income to executives than their basic salaries.

Table 8.3 shows the average CEO compensation across the FTSE 100 companies over the period 1998–2011, the average employee earnings across those companies, and the multiple between the two. Clearly the general trend has been one whereby the multiple is rising, though with some reduction in the recessionary period 2007–2011. However, there has been a major change from a situation where the average CEO salary of FTSE 100 companies was 47 times the average employee salary in 1998 to one in which it was 118 times that salary in 2011.

In the US some 60% of total CEO compensation is in the form of incentive plans (stock options, etc.) with only 23% of such compensation derived from basic salary and a further 17% from cash bonuses. The situation is, however, reversed in Japan, with only 17% of CEO compensation being awarded via incentive plans, 71% consisting of basic salary and 12% being made up of cash bonuses. EU countries tend to be somewhere in between these two extremes, with the UK having 22% of total CEO compensation via incentive plans, 40% from basic salary and 38% from cash bonuses.

Questions

1. Can you explain how two-thirds of UK workers can be on less than average pay?
2. What factors have contributed to these findings?
3. What policy implications are suggested for reducing such wage and income inequality?

Imperfectly competitive labour markets

We turn first to the presence of **monopoly** and **monopsony** conditions in the supply of labour.

Key definitions

Monopoly

Monopoly in product markets refers to situations where a firm is responsible for at least one third of the output of a product or group of linked products. Monopoly in labour markets refers to situations where sellers of labour have market power, e.g. trade unions.

Monopsony

Monopsony in labour markets refers to situations where buyers of labour have market power, e.g. employer associations.

Monopoly in labour markets: trade unions

If the labour force is now unionised, the *supply* of labour to the firm (or industry) may be restricted. However, even though unions bring an element of *monopoly* into labour supply, theory suggests that they can influence only price or quantity, but not both. For example, in Figure 8.3(a):

- The union may seek wage rate W_3, but must accept in return lower employment at L_3.
- The union may seek a level of employment L_2, but must then accept a lower wage rate at W_2.

- Except (see below) where unions are able to force employers off their demand curve for labour (MRP_L), unions can raise wages only at the 'cost' of reduced employment.

A given rise in wages will reduce employment by less, under the following circumstances:

- the less elastic final demand is for the product;
- the less easy it is to substitute other factors for the workers in question;
- the lower the proportion of labour costs to total costs of production.

All of these circumstances, as we have already noted, will make the demand curve for labour, MRP_L, less elastic (i.e. steeper).

 Assessment advice

Figures 8.3(a) and (b) are an excellent way of showing the impacts of monopoly and monopsony labour market imperfections on the wage and employment outcome.

Unions and bargaining power

Unions may seek to force employers *off* their demand curve for labour so that they make less than maximum profits. It may then be possible for wages to rise from W_1 to W_3 with no loss of employment, i.e. point A in Figure 8.3(a). How effective unions will be in such strategies will depend upon the extent of their 'bargaining power'. Chamberlain defines union bargaining power as:

$$\text{Union bargaining power} = \frac{\text{Management costs of disagreeing (to union terms)}}{\text{Management costs of agreeing (to union terms)}}$$

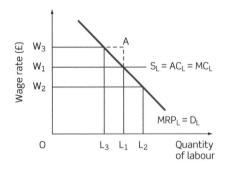

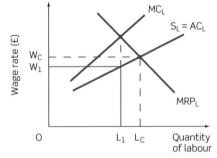

(a) Monopoly power: Trade unions force employers off their demand curve (i.e. point A)

(b) Monopsony power: Employer associations exert power in the hiring of labour

Figure 8.3 Imperfections in the labour market.

Source: Griffiths, A. and Wall, S. (2011) *Economics for Business and Management* (3rd ed.) © 2011 Pearson Education. Reproduced with permission.

Although the ratio cannot be measured, as it relies on subjective assessments, it is a useful analytical tool. If unions are to exert effective influence on management, the ratio must exceed unity. That is to say, it must be more costly for management to disagree (e.g. loss of profits or loss of market share as a result of industrial action) than to agree (e.g. higher labour costs and higher employment levels) to the union's terms.

- The higher the ratio, the more likely it is that management will agree to the union's terms. The 'management costs of disagreeing' to union terms are likely to be greater, the higher the proportion of total workers in a union.
- For the UK as a whole this 'union density' has fallen dramatically in recent times and with it, arguably, the 'bargaining power' of unions. For example, union density in the UK reached a peak of 55% in 1979 but is only about 26% in 2013.

Monopsony in labour markets: employer associations

It may, however, be the case that market power lies not with the 'suppliers' of labour (e.g. the trade unions) but with the 'buyers' of labour. In this case we use the term *monopsony* to refer to market power in the hands of those who demand labour.

Employer associations are groups of employers who come together to create an element of monopoly on the *demand* side of the labour market (i.e. monopsony). These associations bring together the employers of labour in order to exert greater influence in collective bargaining. Standard theory suggests that monopsony in the labour market will, by itself, reduce both wages and employment in the labour market.

In Figure 8.3(b), under competitive labour market conditions the equilibrium would occur where the supply of labour ($S_L = AC_L$) equalled the demand for labour (MRP_L), giving wage W_c and employment L_c. If monopsony occurs, so that employers bid the wage rate up against themselves, then it can be shown that the MC_L curve will lie *above* the $S_L = AC_L$ curve. For example, if by hiring the fourth worker, the wage (= AC_L) of all three existing workers is bid up from £5 to £6, then the AC_L for the fourth worker is £6 but the MC_L for the fourth worker is higher at £9 (£24 − £15). The profit-maximising employer will want to equate the extra revenue contributed by the last worker employed (MRP_L) to the extra cost of employing the last worker (MC_L). In Figure 8.3(b) this occurs with L_1 workers employed.

Note, however, that the employer only has to offer a wage of W_1 in order to get L_1 workers to supply themselves to the labour market. The wage W_1 is *below* the competitive wage W_c, and the level of employment L_1 is *below* the competitive level of employment L_c. This is the standard case against monopsony in a labour market, namely lower wages and lower employment than in a competitive labour market.

Transfer earnings and economic rent

These ideas apply to any factor of production:

> ### Key definitions
>
> **Transfer earnings**
>
> Transfer earnings are defined as the payments that are absolutely necessary to keep a factor of production in its present use.
>
> **Economic rent**
>
> Economic rent is any extra (surplus) payment to the factor over and above its transfer earnings.
>
> **Quasi rent**
>
> Quasi rent applies where factors of production earn economic rent in the *short run* which is eliminated in the *long run*.

The term '**economic rent**' is used here to mean a surplus payment to *any* factor over and above its next best paid alternative (**transfer earnings**). For example, if Wayne Rooney (factor – labour) currently receives £100,000 a week as a footballer but could earn £40,000 a week in his next best paid alternative employment as, say, a celebrity on television, then we might regard £60,000 per week as *economic rent* and £40,000 per week as *transfer earnings*. If he were to receive less than £40,000 per week as a footballer, he might be expected to 'transfer' to his next best paid alternative employment.

We can use the earlier demand and supply diagrams **(Chapter 1)** to illustrate these ideas further.

In Figure 8.4(a) SS and DD represent the relevant supply and demand curves for any factor of production. In this market the equilibrium price is P. However, all but the last unit employed would have been prepared to accept a *lower price* than P to offer themselves to this factor market. In fact, the very first unit would have been supplied at a price approximately equal to S. All units except the last unit supplied therefore receive an amount *in excess* of their supply price or transfer earnings. Because of this, the area PRS is referred to as *economic rent* (surplus) and the area OSRQ is referred to as *transfer earnings*.

To earn relatively high rewards it is necessary to possess those abilities which are in scarce supply and are demanded by others and for which people are prepared to pay. It is, therefore, both supply and demand that account for the relatively large earnings of pop singers, film stars and some individuals from the sporting and entertainment worlds. Figure 8.4(b) is used to illustrate this

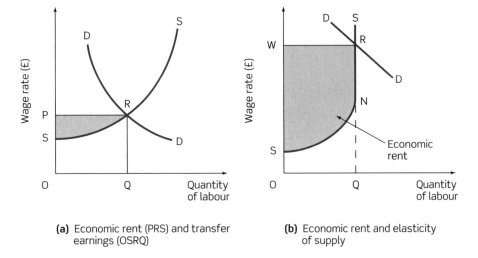

(a) Economic rent (PRS) and transfer earnings (OSRQ)

(b) Economic rent and elasticity of supply

Figure 8.4 Economic rent and transfer earnings.

Source: Griffiths, A. and Wall, S. (2011) *Economics for Business and Management* (3rd ed.) © 2011 Pearson Education. Reproduced with permission.

point. Above some relatively low rate of pay, the supply of this individual's services becomes totally inelastic (at N). The actual rate of pay is determined by the intersection of supply and demand at W. Because of the inelastic supply and high level of demand, the bulk of this person's earnings consists of economic rent, equal to WRNS.

It is clear that any factor of production can earn economic rent and that the main determinant of such rent involves both the supply and demand curves for the factor of production.

Should economic rent be taxed?

It is often suggested that economic rent should be taxed. The reasoning behind this is that since economic rent is a surplus rather than a cost of supply, a tax on economic rent will be borne entirely by the factor of production receiving economic rent. This will leave the supply of that factor, and therefore the output it produces, unchanged.

The case for taxing economic rent is therefore a powerful one. However, there are major difficulties with implementing such a tax. In the first place, it is extremely difficult to identify economic rent. If a tax exceeds the value of the surplus, then the supply of the factor of production will be reduced and its price, along with the price of whatever it produces, will be increased. Another problem is that not all economic rent that is earned is true economic rent; it might simply be **quasi rent**, a term used to refer to income that is entirely a surplus in the short run, but part of which is transfer earning in the long run. Taxing this will reduce the long-run supply of the factor of production.

Test yourself

Q5. Look at the following table for a monopsony labour market.

Wage rate(AC$_L$)(£)	Number of workers supplied (per day)	Total cost of labour (£)	Marginal cost of labour (MC$_L$)(£)
50	1		
60	2		
70	3		
80	4		
90	5		
100	6		
110	7		
120	8		

(a) Complete the table.

(b) Draw the labour supply (AC$_L$) curve.

(c) Draw the marginal cost of labour (MC$_L$) curve.

(d) What do you notice?

(e) How will your answer to (d) influence the equilibrium level of wages and employment under monopsony? Draw a sketch diagram to illustrate your answer.

Q2. Assume that a trade union is important in a particular labour market.

(a) Draw a sketch diagram and use it to show how the union might be able to raise wages *without* reducing employment.

(b) What will determine the ability of the union to achieve the outcome in (a)?

Labour market practices

We first consider the introduction of the National Minimum Wage in the UK, before moving to a variety of other important labour market regulations.

Minimum wage

Many countries have some form of minimum wage. In the UK the Low Pay Commission for the first time recommended the introduction of a National Minimum Wage (NMW) in October 2000.

Figure 8.5(a) illustrates the problem of setting too high a minimum wage. If the NMW is set *above* the competitive wage (W_c) for any labour market, there will be an excess supply of labour of L' – L*, with more people supplying themselves to work in this labour market than there are jobs available. In Figure 8.5(a) the actual level of employment falls from L_c to L*.

However, there have been a number of studies suggesting that in the USA a higher minimum wage has actually increased *both* wages and employment, although it has been noted that many of the US studies have involved labour markets (e.g. the fast food sector) which are dominated by a few large employers of labour, i.e. *monopsonistic* labour markets.

In fact, our earlier analysis of monopsony might have led us to expect this. For example, in Figure 8.5(b), if the initial monopsony equilibrium was wage W_1 and employment L_1, then setting a minimum wage of W* would result in a rise in both wages (from W_1 to W*) and employment (from L_1 to L*). It will be helpful to explain this outcome using Figure 8.5(b).

Since no labour is supplied *below* the minimum wage W*, then W*NS$_L$ becomes the effective labour supply curve. Along the horizontal segment W*N, we then have W* = AC$_L$ = MC$_L$ (as in Figure 8.1). The profit-maximising situation is at point M on the MRP$_L$ curve, where the marginal cost of hiring the last person (MC$_L$) exactly equals the extra revenue resulting from employing that last person (MRP$_L$). So imposing a minimum wage on a labour market that is already imperfect (here monopsony) can increase both wages and levels of employment.

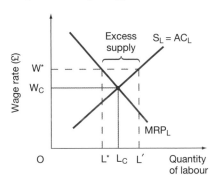

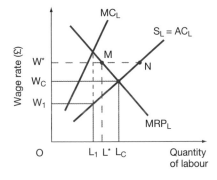

(a) Minimum wage (W*) set above the competitive market wage (W$_C$)

(b) Minimum wage (W*) raising both wages and employment under monopsony

Figure 8.5 Impacts of a minimum wage.

Source: Griffiths, A. and Wall, S. (2011) *Economics for Business and Management* (3rd ed.) © 2011 Pearson Education. Reproduced with permission.

Terms of employment

Apart from the National Minimum Wage, a number of other changes have been made in recent years to the regulations governing the UK labour market. These regulations have involved particular aspects of labour market activity.

Examples & evidence

Regulation and employment

It is often suggested that reducing employment protection in the UK and elsewhere will lead to more jobs and faster economic growth. The data in Table 8.4 suggest that any such hypothesis is, at best, simplistic! The OECD's employment protection index measures the procedures and costs involved in dismissing individuals or groups of workers and the procedures involved in hiring workers on fixed-term or temporary work agency contracts. On this index, which is presented in column 1 of Table 8.4 for 21 countries, the UK ranks third, behind only Canada (second) and the US (first) for the states with the *lowest employment protection*. Italy is 14th, Portugal 18th, Greece 19th and France 20th.

Importantly, there is only a very weak statistical correlation between the degree of employment protection and the increase in unemployment since the onset of recession from January 2008 through to the end of 2011. Germany and the Netherlands have much higher levels of employment protection than the UK, but a much smaller rise in unemployment. There is no evidence there to support this hypothesis.

Table 8.4 Employment protection and unemployment.

Country	OECD employment protection index	% change in the unemployment rate since January 2008
US	0.85	3.3
Canada	1.02	1.7
UK	1.09	3.3
Australia	1.38	1.0

Country	OECD employment protection index	% change in the unemployment rate since January 2008
Ireland	1.39	9.6
Japan	1.73	0.7
Denmark	1.91	4.4
Sweden	2.06	1.5
South Korea	2.13	0
Netherlands	2.23	1.7
Finland	2.29	1.2
Austria	2.41	0
Poland	2.41	2.1
Italy	2.58	2.4
Belgium	2.61	0.1
Germany	2.63	−2.6
Norway	2.65	0.9
Portugal	2.84	5.2
Greece	2.97	13.1
France	3.00	2.3
Spain	3.11	13.9

Source: OECD, adapted from The Independent, 27 February 2012, p. 49.

Question

1. Can you identify any other patterns from the data in the table?

Union-related conditions

We use the UK labour market to illustrate the impacts of union-related conditions.

Closed shops

This is a situation where employees obtain or retain a job only if they become a member of a specified trade union. This practice was progressively weakened by legislation in the 1980s and 1990s making unions liable to legal action from both employees and management if they tried to enforce the closed shop.

Strikes and other industrial action

- *Secondary action.* An important provision in the *Employment Act 1982* restricted 'lawful trade disputes' to those between workers and their own employer, making 'secondary action' unlawful, i.e. action against an employer who is not part of a dispute.

- *Picketing.* This is where striking workers approach non-strikers as they enter their place of work. Picketing is now restricted in law to the 'place of work' of the union members, often even excluding another plant of the same employer. If illegal picketing occurs, unions are now liable to pay damages in civil actions brought against them by employers.

- *Secret ballots.* Official industrial action, i.e. that approved by the union leadership, must be sanctioned by a secret ballot of the membership. The ballot must be held no more than four weeks before the event, and a majority of union members must be in favour of the action. If the action takes place without majority consent, then the union loses any legal immunity for organising industrial action that it may have enjoyed in the past. These provisions were strengthened by the *Employment Act 1988* which gave the individual union member the right not to be called out on strike without a properly held secret ballot and the right not to be disciplined by his or her union for refusing to strike or for crossing a picket line.

- *Unofficial action.* The *Employment Act 1990* and *Trade Union and Labour Relations Act 1992* took the control of union behaviour even further by requiring that the union leadership must take positive steps to repudiate 'unofficial action', i.e. actions undertaken by union members without union consent (that is, of the executive committee or president or general secretary). For instance, the union must do its best to give written notice to all members participating in the unofficial action that it does not receive the union's support. Failure by the union to take such steps could mean loss of immunity for the union, even though the action is unofficial.

- *Postal ballots.* The *Trade Union Reform and Employment Rights Act 1993* passed two main provisions relating to the organisation of industrial action. First, ballots held in support of action should be fully postal and subject to independent scrutiny, effectively restricting the ability of the 'rank-and-file' to initiate action. Second, unions are to be required to give seven days' written notice before industrial action can be taken. This gives a longer waiting period which may help in settling any dispute.

Employer-related conditions

We use the EU labour market to illustrate the impacts of employer-related conditions.

Social Chapter

The 'Social Chapter' was the name given to the bringing together in the 1992 *Maastricht Treaty* of many work-related provisions contained in earlier EU treaties. It was made clear in the Maastricht Treaty that these provisions would be further developed by a series of 'Directives' and other EU regulations. The idea was to provide minimum agreed working conditions for all employees in EU firms, creating a 'level playing field' when those firms compete in the Single European Market. It was expected that these minimum working conditions might then be improved throughout the EU over time.

EU Directives

After initially 'opting out' of the Social Chapter, the new Labour government agreed to join it shortly after its election in 1997, though reserving the right to delay implementation of certain specified Directives.

Over 30 Directives have so far been adopted by the EU, including the following.

- *Parental Leave Directive.* Women, regardless of length of service, are to have 14 weeks' *maternity leave* during which their jobs will be protected and firms will have to find replacements. Various rights to take time off after the birth or adoption of a child have now been extended to fathers. Prior to this Directive there was a requirement for length of service with the employer of two years for full-timers and five years for part-timers. Women with over 26 weeks' service have the right to *maternity pay*.

- *Working Hours Directive.* A maximum of 48 hours is imposed on the working week (with exceptions for hospital doctors and for workers with 'autonomous decision making powers' such as managers). Other requirements include a four-week paid annual holiday, and an eight-hour limitation on shifts.

- *Part-time Workers Directive.* This extends equal rights and pro-rata benefits to part-time staff.

- *European Works Council Directive.* Companies employing over 1,000 workers, with at least 150 in two or more member states, are required to install a *transnational worker council* with information and consultation rights over the introduction of new production processes, mergers and plant closures.

- *Information and Consultation Directive.* In 2002 these rights were extended to any establishments in EU states with at least 50 employees. These now have the right to information and consultation on the performance of the business and on decisions relevant to employment, particularly where jobs are threatened.

- *Young Workers Directive.* There is a ban on work for those under 15. For those who are 17 or under and in education, work must be for less than three hours a day; if out of education, the limit is eight hours a day; five weeks' paid holiday is also required and there is a ban on night work.

Gender issues

It will be useful at this stage to review another issue often raised in labour market discussions, namely gender discrimination. In the UK in 2011, the gap between the *hourly pay* of men and women narrowed to its smallest yet, with women's hourly pay at 83% of that for men. However, the gender gap for *annual earnings* was wider, with the average annual salary of women in 2011 around 73% of that for men.

That such a gender gap still exists would disappoint those who framed two key Acts of Parliament seeking to reduce gender inequalities in the UK.

- *Equal Pay Act* (1970): women performing similar tasks to men, or performing work of equal value to that of men, must be treated equally to men.

- *Sex Discrimination Act* (1975): men and women should have equal opportunities.

Examples & evidence

Women close the gender gap

The World Economic Forum published its *Global Gender Report* in late 2012. It ranked 111 countries in terms of the extent to which they had closed their gender gaps over the period 2006–2012. Iceland, Finland, Norway and Sweden were the top four, all closing their overall gender gaps by more than 80% since 2006. Britain came 18th, down two places from the previous year. The report stated that 88% of the countries had improved their performance in terms of closing the 2006 overall gender gap, while 12% had widening gaps.

Table 8.5 presents the overall women:men gender gap, as an average over various sub-components such as 'Economic participation and opportunity', 'Educational attainment', 'Health and survival' and 'Political empowerment'.

Table 8.5 Measuring the overall gender gap.

Country	Index (overall female:male gender gap)	Ranking
Iceland	0.8640	1
Germany	0.7629	13
UK	0.7433	18
US	0.7373	22
France	0.6984	57
Russia	0.6980	59
Brazil	0.6909	62
China	0.6853	69
Italy	0.6729	80
Japan	0.6530	101
India	0.6442	105

Source: Adapted from *World Economic Forum* (2012), *Global Gender Report*.

Question

1. Can you identify any other patterns from the data in the table?

Possible reasons for lower female earnings

Of course, for any particular task, to the extent that men and women pre-sent *different characteristics* to the labour market, some of the observed pay differentials might be justified, i.e. not be caused by discrimination as such.

- *Less continuous employment* is more likely to be the experience of women than of men, given child-bearing and rearing responsibilities. For example, some 28% of women graduates leave the labour force for family reasons within five years of joining it.

- Continuous employment is associated with an earnings premium of around 3% per year for both men and women in the UK.
- Continuous employment implies being more up-to-date with changing technologies and work practices, thereby raising marginal productivity.
- Continuous employment implies greater opportunities to receive in-firm education and training, acquiring skills which raise marginal productivity.

- *Less geographical mobility* for women when partners' or husbands' jobs take priority. Where this is the case, an oversupply of women in a given geographical location may depress female wages.
- *Less unionisation of women workers*, especially for the higher proportion of part-time employment, reduces female bargaining power. Statistically, union membership is associated with an hourly wage some 7% higher than for non-unionised labour.
- *Less unsocial working hours* for women than for men, with such unsocial hours receiving, on average, an extra 11% in earnings per hour in the UK.

Where these different labour market characteristics are presented by women, it might be argued that at least some of the gender pay gap actually observed may be 'justified' rather than 'discriminatory'.

Other gender inequalities

The so-called 'glass ceiling' for women is still with us in the UK, despite more females working than ever before.

Quasi factor markets

The provision of many government and welfare services is increasingly being undertaken by what might be called *quasi-markets* or *internal markets*, instead of being directly controlled by a government department, as previously. In many cases the state ceases to provide the services in question, relying instead on independent institutions to compete against each other to win contracts to supply such services. As well as competition on the supply side there is usually a purchasing aspect on the demand side of the quasi-markets, often state funded.

 Assessment advice

Internal or 'quasi' markets are increasing in importance as governments try to open up markets dominated by the public sector to private competition.

Quasi markets: theory

There are a number of aspects on both the supply and demand sides of these internal or quasi markets which are untypical of any market – hence the term 'quasi'.

- On the supply side there is a wider variety of types of service provider than is usual in a market, for example private 'for profit' organisations, private 'not for profit' organisations (e.g. voluntary bodies and charities), various public organisations, etc. There is therefore a greater than usual diversity of ownership structures and organisational objectives than is typical of more conventional markets.

- On the demand side, consumer purchasing power is often expressed in terms of vouchers, or budgets allocated for specific purposes, rather than in terms of cash changing hands. In addition, instead of market preferences being expressed by the consumer directly, as in normal markets, the consumers' preferences are often expressed indirectly by an agent or intermediary (e.g. a GP, health authority or care manager).

Advocates of these emerging quasi markets argue that they promote greater efficiency in supply, respond more rapidly to consumer preferences and are more accountable to those who fund their operation.

Critics argue that the market conditions necessary for such favourable outcomes do not exist in most welfare sectors. As a consequence, movements towards quasi-market provision will increase administrative and other transaction costs and lead to greater inequalities among recipients of such services.

Quasi markets and resource allocation

Economic theory suggests a number of conditions which must be met if the more favourable outcomes claimed for quasi markets are to occur.

1. *The market structure must be competitive in both supply and demand, with many providers and many purchasers.* If markets are to operate 'efficiently', in terms of price, output and quality, dissatisfied purchasers must be able to seek alternative sources of supply (i.e. there must be an absence of monopoly in supply). Similarly, suppliers must not be dependent on a few, powerful purchasers, otherwise price can be kept artificially low and many potentially efficient suppliers can be driven out of business (i.e. there must be an absence of monopsony in demand).
2. *Accurate, easily accessible information as to the cost and quality of provision must be available to both suppliers and purchasers.* Otherwise suppliers will be unable to cost and price their activities appropriately and purchasers will be unable to monitor the price and quality of the services they receive. 'Market failure' in respect of this condition could, for example,

lead to suppliers reducing costs by lowering the quality of services without purchasers being aware of the fact.

3 *Profit must be a significant factor in motivating suppliers.* Price is a key 'signal' in markets, and if suppliers do not respond to the signal of higher prices and profits by increasing supply, because profit is not a motivating factor, then resource allocation will be impaired. It follows that an over-representation of voluntary and charitable bodies in provision, pursuing various 'praiseworthy' aims, may lead to unpredictable and arguably 'inefficient' responses by suppliers to market signals.

4 *There must be few opportunities in the market for 'adverse selection' or its opposite, 'cream skimming'.* Both are the consequence of a lack of symmetry in the information available to sellers and buyers and may inhibit the existence of a market. In the case of 'adverse selection', purchasers who know themselves to be 'bad risks', but who are not known to be so by providers, may be over-represented in the market. This will reduce profitability for providers and may even cause the welfare provision to cease as suppliers make excessive losses. On the other hand, 'cream skimming' can impair market efficiency by permitting providers to use information available only to themselves to select purchasers who are 'good risks', thereby raising profits. In this case welfare services may fail to reach those who most require them.

Quasi markets: practice

It will be useful to illustrate here the application of these key principles involving quasi markets in a particular context, that of healthcare.

Quasi market in healthcare

In the UK the 'internal' market and associated 'rules' which have developed within the National Health Service (NHS) provide a useful illustration of the institutional, as opposed to the neoclassical, approach to markets.

Creating an internal (quasi) market in the National Health Service (NHS)

The contemporary structure and developments in the healthcare sector are continually changing but embody the key elements below. The mandate of the NHS is to provide healthcare services according to need, free at the point of delivery. It was, and continues to be, financed from central government tax revenues via the Consolidated Fund. Some 80% of funding comes from these tax revenues, with another 14% from a proportion of the National Insurance contributions of employers and employees, and only about 4% of NHS receipts being currently funded from charges for prescriptions, dental services, etc. The consequence for resource allocation of providing healthcare services essentially free at the point of delivery can be discussed using Figure 8.6.

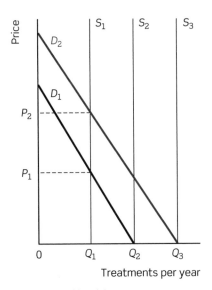

Figure 8.6 Demand for and supply of healthcare.

Source: Griffiths, A. and Wall, S. (2012) *Applied Economics* (12th ed.) © 2012 Pearson Education. Reproduced with permission.

We assume demand for healthcare services to be downward sloping with respect to price, i.e. people demand fewer treatments per time period if price rises. If a market were established with demand D_1 and a short-run supply S_1 (here perfectly inelastic supply), then a price P_1 would be established with an equilibrium number of treatments demanded and supplied per year of Q_1. If demand now increases to D_2, then *price adjusts* in the market, rising to P_2 to allocate the unchanged Q_1.

However, the NHS does not operate by price adjustment but by *quantity adjustment* (since service is free at the point of treatment); with the initial demand D_1, at a zero price $0Q_2$ treatments are demanded. This requires the supply curve of treatments to shift rightwards to S_2 if the NHS is to satisfy this demand. If demand now rises to D_2, supply must further increase to S_3, since no price adjustment is permitted, otherwise $Q_3 - Q_2$ patients would be untreated, leading to a rise in waiting lists. It is clear that by relying mainly on quantity adjustment, the NHS must either allocate more resources to health-care in the face of increased demand or accept a rise in waiting lists.

NHS and quasi (internal) markets

In April 1991 the then Conservative government introduced major changes into the UK healthcare market. The responsibility for *purchasing* healthcare was to be separated from the responsibility for *providing* it.

These objectives were to be accomplished by the implementation of a number of key measures.

1 Increased delegation of responsibilities from central to local levels, for example the delegation of functions from Regions to Districts, and from Districts to individual hospitals.

2 Certain of the larger hospitals were invited to apply to become NHS Hospital Trusts. Trust status would permit the hospital increased freedom of action in terms of local pay settlements, easier access to borrowing, more choice in deciding upon output mix (e.g. types of speciality) and new opportunities to retain profit.

3 All hospitals in the future were to be free to offer their services, at agreed prices, to any District Health Authority in the UK, and to the private sector. Previously hospitals within a given area normally treated only patients originating from within that area.

4 A facility was to be provided for the larger general practices to hold and operate their own budgets, for the purchase of services directly from hospitals and to cover drug prescribing costs. This meant the creation of a new category of General Practitioner Fund Holders (GPFH). For smaller practices the General Practitioners (GPs) could *combine* to form various types of commissioning groups, purchasing on behalf of individual GPs within such groups.

However, the efficiency benefits claimed for this internal (quasi) market in healthcare depend upon the 'signals' or incentives given to both providers and purchasers and the nature of their likely response to such signals. We now consider this in more detail: first, the incentives to purchasers; and second, the incentives to providers.

Issues for the internal markets

A number of other problems were seen, by critics, as likely to prevent the new internal market from making a significant contribution to the improvement of healthcare.

Asymmetry of information

When the provider and purchaser were one and the same, as with the DHAs before 1991, the quality of healthcare provision could be monitored through internal channels. However, they became separated after the creation of the internal market in 1991, the problem then being that while the providers may be aware of any diminution in quality of service, the purchasers may not. This *asymmetry of information* between seller and buyer is a classic instance of 'market failure' which may lead to an inefficient allocation of resources, with purchasers paying more than the competitive price for any given quality of service.

High transaction costs

The main means by which purchasers seek to gain assurances as to the price and quality of provision is by the issuing of contracts, which may of necessity be rather detailed. Drawing up such contracts takes time and money, as does the whole tendering process between rival providers and the eventual requirements for issuing and processing invoices and other documents between contracting parties. These *transaction costs* may absorb some or all of any efficiency gains via the internal market. Before the creation of the internal market some 5% of total healthcare spending in the UK involved administrative costs; there were fears that the internal market might raise this figure nearer to the 20% of total healthcare spending involving the various transaction costs commonly experienced in the US.

Non-contestable markets

To avoid excessive transaction costs, there may be the incentive for individual providers and purchasers to develop *long-term relationships* in response to the creation of an internal market. The billing and invoicing system of the respective parties might then be simplified and made compatible, as might other aspects of provision. Familiarity and convenience may then serve to make it difficult for *potential new entrants* to secure existing contracts when these are due for renewal. This lack of opportunity for new entrants may permit existing providers in the internal market to be less efficient than is technically feasible, as a result of the long-term relationships established between providers and purchasers. In other words these long-term relationships may make the internal healthcare market less contestable (by new entrants) than hitherto.

Monopoly provision

Some districts and regions within the internal market may be too small, in themselves, to support more than one (or perhaps even one) 'efficient' service provider. This may be the case where significant economies of scale are available in respect of various types of treatment, giving large hospitals a cost advantage. Significant travel costs (transport, time and convenience) may then deter patients (or their agents) from undermining the higher cost provision in these local monopoly cases by seeking treatment in other regions and districts.

Chapter summary – pulling it all together

By the end of this chapter you should be able to:

	Confident ✓	Not confident?
Demonstrate how the idea of 'derived demand' applies to a factor of production		Revise pages 210–216
Assess what will determine the equilibrium wage and level of employment in a competitive labour market		Revise pages 216–219

	Confident ✓	Not confident?
Explain how imperfections such as 'monopoly' and 'monopsony' in labour markets will influence the equilibrium wage and level of employment		Revise pages 219–221
Evaluate the costs and benefits of various types of labour market regulation, including the minimum wage		Revise pages 224–232
Examine the circumstances in which returns to a factor of production will include an element of surplus payment ('economic rent')		Revise pages 222–224
Review the role of 'quasi' factor markets in resource allocations		Revise pages 232–237

Now try the **assessment question** at the start of this chapter, using the answer guidelines below.

Answer guidelines

✳ Assessment question

How would you explain the difference in earnings between consultants and healthcare workers in a hospital?

Approaching the question

A useful approach would be to start by reviewing whether a competitive labour market for both occupations would be likely to lead to differences in earnings. In other words, are demand and supply conditions likely to lead to higher earnings for hospital consultants compared with healthcare workers? You could then introduce 'imperfections' into the respective labour markets in terms of monopoly (seller power for labour) and monopsony (buyer power of labour). You could discuss whether these imperfections would be likely to widen or narrow any differences in earnings that might be expected if the labour markets had been competitive.

Important points to include

The difference in the earnings of consultants and healthcare workers in a hospital is due to many factors which can be linked to demand and supply in labour markets (Figure 8.2).

- First, the high qualifications and long training needed to become a consultant yields high levels of skills which are highly valued in the marketplace (high marginal revenue product). As a result, the demand curve for consultants is likely to be further to the right than for healthcare workers.

- Second, there are far fewer consultants than healthcare workers, so that the more limited supply also helps increase the earnings of consultants in relation to healthcare workers.

- Any such differences in earnings between these occupations are likely to persist over time. For example, the supply of consultants is difficult to increase due to the long training times and the restricted number of training places available. Further, there is very little possibility of mobility between the two groups, i.e. very little chance of healthcare workers becoming consultants, so that the high earnings of consultants are 'protected' by entry barriers.

- You could then introduce potential 'imperfections' in the relative labour markets.

- The influence of monopoly (seller power of employee groupings) is likely to be greater for consultants with their long-established professional bodies compared with healthcare workers with various and fragmented trade unions covering a wide range of occupational types. Figure 8.3(a) can be used to show how consultants would be able to use their bargaining power to raise wages (earnings) with no loss of employment.

- The influence of monopsony (buyer power of employers) is likely to be greater over healthcare workers than over consultants. Employer associations (including government bodies) representing hospitals often coordinate their wage bargaining approach and are likely to be more powerful vis-à-vis healthcare unions and individuals. Figure 8.3(b) can be used to show how monopsony power can depress the earnings or wages of healthcare employees in particular.

Make your answer stand out

A clear structure, with earnings differences between the two occupations linked to demand (MRP$_L$) and supply factors, and to market imperfections such as monopoly and monopsony in factor markets, will bring high marks, especially if well drawn, fully labelled diagrams are used to support your arguments. Some knowledge of the consultant and healthcare occupations and labour markets will also help your answer to stand out.

Read to impress

Books

Griffiths, A. and Wall, S. (2011) *Economics for Business and Management*, 3rd edition, Chapter 7, Pearson Education.

Parkin, M., Powell, M. and Matthews, K. (2012) *Economics*, 8th edition, Chapter 17, Addison Wesley.

Sloman, J., Wride, A. and Garratt, D. (2012) *Economics*, 8th edition, Chapter 9, FT/Prentice Hall.

Journals and periodicals

The following are useful sources of articles and data on many aspects relevant to this and other topics:

Business Review, Philip Allan (quarterly)
Economic Review, Philip Allan (quarterly)
Economics Today, Anforme (quarterly)
Harvard Business Review (monthly)
The Economist (weekly)

Newspapers

Newspapers are important sources of up-to-date information, examples and data. Below are some of the main UK newspaper sources, many of which have websites with search facilities to identify specific topics and articles:

The Guardian
The Times
The Financial Times
The Independent
The Telegraph

Companion website

Go to the companion website at **www.pearsoned.co.uk/econexpress** to find revision support online for this topic area.

Notes

Notes

9 Market failure, regulation and deregulation

Topic map

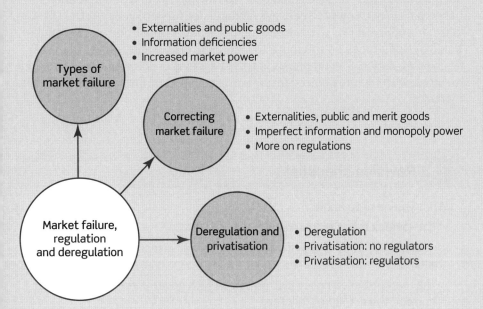

- Externalities and public goods
- Information deficiencies
- Increased market power

Types of market failure

Correcting market failure
- Externalities, public and merit goods
- Imperfect information and monopoly power
- More on regulations

Market failure, regulation and deregulation

Deregulation and privatisation
- Deregulation
- Privatisation: no regulators
- Privatisation: regulators

A printable version of this topic map is available from **www.pearsoned.co.uk/econexpress**

Introduction

If you ever wondered about how important regulations can be, consider the impacts of the new fuel economy regulations announced in the USA in 2012. While the average family vehicle in the US currently achieves 29 miles to the US gallon, by 2017 all new cars must achieve 36.6 miles per gallon, rising to 54.5 miles per gallon by 2025. These are the toughest emission standards in the world. Some analysts see the US benefiting from these regulations as they will ensure that major investments in fuel efficiency technologies will be undertaken by US car producers, giving them a competitive edge. Others argue that the extra R&D and other expenditures needed to achieve these fuel efficiency targets will add $1,000 to the average cost of US cars by 2017, pricing many consumers out of the market.

This chapter reviews the suggestion that 'market failures' of various kinds will require government intervention in the form of various taxes, subsidies and regulations if they are to be 'corrected'. Various types of intervention are reviewed, some involving the use of market-based policy instruments such as taxes and subsidies, and others involving the use of non-market-based policy instruments such as standards for fuel efficiency in the US. The counter-argument is also reviewed, namely that privatisation and deregulation may sometimes be the route to increased efficiencies rather than still further regulation. The emphasis in this chapter is on intervention in *product* markets, with the previous chapter having touched on intervention in *factor* markets.

 ### Revision checklist

What you need to know:
- ❏ The various types of 'market failure'.
- ❏ How the different types of 'market failure' will affect resource allocation.
- ❏ The market-based policy instruments which governments might use to 'correct' these market failures.
- ❏ The non-market-based policy instruments which governments might use to 'correct' these market failures.
- ❏ How to examine the case for and against privatisation and deregulation.

Assessment advice

Clear structure

It will help to identify the various types of market failure. Four types are widely recognised, namely externalities, imperfect information, monopoly (market power) and public goods. For each of these types of market failure you can then identify:

- impacts on resource allocation;
- policies that might be used to 'correct' these market failures.

Use diagrams

Figure 9.1 is a vital diagram which can be used to explore different types of market failure, especially externalities and imperfect information. Figure 9.2 is very relevant for explaining pure public goods and mixed public goods types of externality. Other key diagrams include Figure 9.5 to help investigate the impacts of regulation (and deregulation) on economic welfare, using ideas of consumer and producer surplus.

Use empirical evidence

The first 'Examples & evidence' provides important evidence on the empirical case for intervention or non-intervention in the context of climate change. Figure 9.4 suggest a linkage between over-regulation and a tendency to inefficiency and even corruption.

 Assessment question

Under what circumstances might you support government intervention in the economy?

Types of market failure

Strictly speaking, any departure from the conditions necessary for perfectly competitive *product* markets or perfectly competitive *factor* markets can be regarded as 'market failure'. However, four broad types of market failure are often identified, namely externalities, imperfect information, monopoly power and 'public good' types of market failure.

Assessment advice

Questions are often set involving market failure and the policies to correct them. Being able to identify the various 'types' and appropriate policies for each type will score higher marks.

Externalities and public goods

We first look at **externalities** in general and then at a particular type of externality, namely one involving 'public goods'.

Externalities

Key definition

Externalities

Externalities occur when economic decisions create costs or benefits for people other than the decision taker: these are called the *external costs* or *external benefits* of that decision.

- *External costs.* For example, a firm producing paint may discharge various chemicals into a nearby river, polluting the river, spoiling its use for leisure activities and damaging the health of those coming into contact with it. The true cost to society is then more than the (scarce) resources of labour and capital used up by the firm in producing paint. To these *private costs* of firm production, reflected by wages bills, raw material costs, lease of premises, interest payments, etc., we must add any *external costs* that do not appear in the firm's balance sheet but which have resource implications for society, if we are to assess the true *social costs* of production:

$$\text{Marginal social cost} = \text{Marginal private cost} + \text{Marginal external cost}$$
$$\text{MSC} = \text{MPC} + \text{MEC}$$

- *External benefits.* For example, a firm developing a successful drug to treat motor neurone disease may spend large amounts on research but will only be able to sell the drug to the relatively few people suffering from this severe affliction. The true benefit to society is arguably more than the (small) revenue stream to the firm selling the drug. To these *private revenues* from firm production we must add any *external benefits* that do not appear in the firm's balance sheet (such as the value to society of being able to improve the quality of life of those with the disease) if we are to assess the true *social benefits* of production:

Marginal social benefit = Marginal private benefit + Marginal external benefit
MSB   =   MPB   +   MEB

Externalities and resource allocation

It will be useful to consider how the presence of externalities may distort the signals conveyed by prices in a market economy and lead to a misallocation of resources. Here we use an example where marginal social cost is higher than marginal private cost (MSC > MPC) because of the presence of a marginal external cost (MEC > 0).

Negative externalities

We shall see that when negative externalities are present, the firm that seeks to maximise its *private surplus* (profit) will fail to act in the best interests of society. Put another way, when private surplus (profit) is a maximum, *social surplus* is not as high as it could be.

The profit-maximising firm in Figure 9.1 will produce output OQ_1 at price OP_1 since marginal private cost = marginal revenue (marginal private benefit) at this output. Total profit can be regarded as *total private surplus*, and this is a maximum, given by area JKL in the diagram. To produce one extra unit beyond OQ_1 would reduce total private surplus, as the extra unit would incur a loss (MPC > MR); to produce one fewer unit than OQ_1 would also reduce this total private surplus, since that extra unit would have yielded a profit (MR > MPC) had it been produced.

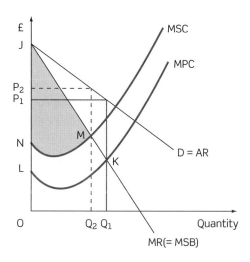

Note: MEC is the vertical difference (at each level of output) between MSC and MPC.

Figure 9.1 With negative externalities (MSC > MPC), the output Q_1 maximising private surplus (profit) differs from the output Q_2 maximising social surplus.

Source: Griffiths, A. and Wall, S. (2011) *Economics for Business and Management* (3rd ed.) © 2011 Pearson Education. Reproduced with permission.

Assessment advice

Figure 9.1 is very flexible and can be used to explain many aspects of the resource impacts of market failure and how to correct those failures.

Unfortunately this output Q_1 which maximises total private surplus (profit) is *not* the output that maximises *total social surplus*. This occurs where the marginal social benefit of production, MSB (here shown as being the same as MR), equals the marginal social cost of production, MSC. This occurs at output OQ_2 with total social surplus a maximum given by area JMN, using the same reasoning as before.

Test yourself

Q1. Explain in your own words why total social surplus is a maximum at output OQ_2.

Clearly, a situation in which output Q_1 and price P_1 result will, if uncorrected, be one in which prices are conveying inappropriate signals to producers. They are leading to profit maximisers producing too much of the product and selling it at too low a price, as compared with the needs of society as a whole.

Externalities of both a negative (adverse) and even a positive (beneficial) type can have major impacts on resource allocation if left uncorrected.

Positive externalities
You should be able to use Figure 9.1 to consider the implications of a *positive externality* (MSC < MPC) on firm output, as, for example, when a firm uses its scarce resources to support some type of environmental improvement. If marginal social costs (MSC) were now *below* marginal private costs in the diagram, then the target output for society would need to be raised above OQ_1 if social surplus is to be a maximum, and price would need to be reduced below OP_1. This time, price signals, if uncorrected, are leading to profit maximisers producing too little of the product and selling it at too high a price, as compared with the needs of society as a whole.

Public goods
The term 'public goods' is used to refer to goods (or services) which have particular characteristics of a type which makes it impractical for private markets to provide them. It follows that if they are to be provided, only the 'public' sector will be able to fund them out of general tax revenues, hence the name 'public good'.

Assessment advice

You can use Figure 9.2 **(page 254)** to introduce the idea of public goods as well as to discuss policies for 'correcting' a public good type of externality.

Pure public goods

Two particular characteristics must be present for what is called a 'pure' public good.

- *Non-excludable.* This refers to the difficulty of excluding those who do not wish to pay for the good (or service). For example, how could you charge individuals a price for police or army protection? If you tried to use a national referendum, only charging those who say 'yes' in the referendum to wanting a police or defence force, you will encounter the so-called 'free rider' problem. This refers to people who, while they do want this protection, may vote 'no', hoping that sufficient others vote 'yes' for them still to have the protection but not to have to pay for it themselves. The non-excludable condition prevents a free market developing, since it is difficult to make 'free riders' actually pay for the public good, which means that it can only be provided by the 'public' sector out of tax revenue.

- *Non-exhaustible.* This refers to the fact that the marginal cost of providing the 'pure' public good is essentially zero. To protect an extra person in the country using the police or army effectively costs nothing. If marginal cost is zero, then the price set under perfect competition should also be zero. But private markets guided by the profit motive are hardly in the business of charging zero prices! The non-exhaustible condition implies that any price that is charged should, for 'allocative efficiency', equal marginal cost and therefore be zero, which means that it can only be provided by the 'public' sector out of tax revenue.

Both conditions imply that when the market failure involves a 'pure public good', then it is best supplied by the public sector at zero price, using general tax revenue to fund provision.

Mixed (quasi) public goods

The suggestion here is that a broader category of products (goods or services) will have elements of these characteristics, while not fully meeting the criteria for a 'pure' public good. For example, many products may be *non-exhaustible* in the sense that (at least up to the congestion point) extra people can consume that product without detracting from existing consumers' ability to benefit from it, e.g. use of a motorway, a bridge or a scenic view. However, the *non-excludable* condition may not apply, since it may be possible to exclude consumers from that product, e.g. tolls on motorways and bridges, or fencing (with admission charges) around scenic views. So a private market could be established for such a *mixed* or *quasi public good*, with a non-zero price charged.

Information deficiencies

Firms may have information on their product which is not available to the purchasers. For example, a number of court cases brought by cancer sufferers have shown that cigarette companies knew from their own research about the dangers to health of smoking cigarettes decades ago but concealed this information from the general public. Similarly, recent court cases involving the mis-selling of pensions have shown that the companies involved withheld information from purchasers. Where one party has information not available to another party, this is often called 'information asymmetry'. This can again lead to a misallocation of resources.

We can again illustrate the effect of imperfect information using Figure 9.1. For example, smoking has been shown to damage the health of those who smoke (via increased risks of cancer, heart and lung diseases) and of those ('passive smokers') who inhale the air polluted by smokers. In other words, the marginal social cost of the cigarettes produced by a tobacco company is considerably higher than the marginal private costs of producing those cigarettes. We are in the *negative externality* situation of Figure 9.1, with the cigarette companies seeking to profit-maximise (MPC = MR) at output Q_1 but with society preferring output Q_2 (MSC = MSB) where *social surplus* is maximised at JMN.

Increased market power

Earlier chapters have shown how 'market power' in the form of monopoly can lead to higher prices and lower outputs than in a perfectly competitive market structure. This is the so-called 'classical case against monopoly'. The same situation can arise under an oligopoly market structure, where a few large firms dominate the market.

Nor is the problem of 'market power' leading to a misallocation of resources confined to product markets! We noted **(Chapter 8)** that when the trade unions have market power over the supply of labour (monopoly), wages can be higher and employment lower than might have been the case under competitive labour market conditions. Similarly, where the purchasers of labour have market power (monopsony), the wages can be lower and employment lower than under competitive labour market conditions.

Correcting market failure

Here we consider the various policy instruments that can be used by governments to correct the four types of 'market failure' we have identified. Such corrective policies can include a number of different policy instruments.

However, it will be useful to use the context of climate change to emphasise why government intervention to regulate markets is seen as important by many analysts.

Examples & evidence

Stern Report on climate change

The Stern Report on climate change was published in late 2006, and is widely regarded as the most authoritative of its kind. Key findings include the following.

- CO_2 in the atmosphere in about 1780, i.e. just before the Industrial Revolution, has been estimated at around 280 ppm (parts per million).
- CO_2 in 2006, however, had risen significantly to 382 ppm.
- Greenhouse gases (CO_2, methane, nitrous oxide, etc.) in 2006 were even higher at 430 ppm in CO_2 equivalents.

Two key scenarios were identified in the Stern Report:

Do nothing scenario

- Temperature rise of 2°C by 2050.
- Temperature rise of 5°C or more by 2100.
- The damage to the global economy of such climate change from the 'do nothing' scenario is an estimated reduction in global GDP per head (i.e. consumption per head) of between 5% and 20% over the next two centuries. This occurs via rising temperatures, droughts, floods, water shortages and extreme weather events.

Intervene scenario

- The Stern Report advocates measures to stabilise greenhouse gas emissions at 550 ppm CO_2 equivalents by 2050.
- This requires global emissions of CO_2 to peak in the next 10 to 20 years, then fall at a rate of at least 1% to 3% per year.
- By 2050 global emissions of CO_2 must be around 25% below current levels.
- Since global GDP in 2050 is expected to be around three times as high as it is today, the CO_2 emissions *per unit* of global GDP must be less than one-third of today's level (and sufficiently less to give the 25% reduction on today's levels).

- The Stern Report estimated the cost of stabilisation at 550 ppm CO_2 equivalents to be around 1% of current global GDP (i.e. around £200bn). This expenditure will be required *every year*, rising to £600bn per annum in 2050 if global GDP is three times as high as it is today.
- Stabilisation would limit temperature rises by 2050 to 2°C, but not prevent them. Otherwise temperature rises well in excess of 2°C are predicted – possibly as much as 5°C by 2100.
- Even limiting temperature rises to 2°C by 2050 will inflict substantial damage, especially in terms of flooding low-lying countries as the ice caps melt, but also via more extreme weather conditions in various parts of the world.

Questions

1. Why did the Stern Report not seek still tighter limits on the growth of CO_2 in the atmosphere?
2. What mechanisms or policies might be used to achieve the stabilisation path proposed in the Stern Report?

Government intervention to correct various 'market failures' can take many different forms. It can involve the application of maximum or minimum prices and the imposition of various types of standards, taxes, quotas, procedures, directives, etc., whether issued by national bodies (e.g. the UK government or its agencies) or international bodies (e.g. the EU Commission, the World Trade Organization, etc.).

Externalities, public and merit goods

It may be useful to illustrate the ways in which government intervention can improve resource allocation by first considering how the *negative externality* situation might be approached.

Correcting a negative externality

Again we can illustrate the situation using Figure 9.1. It shows that with the firm producing a *negative externality* (MSC > MPC) society's best interests are served with an output of OQ_2 (where MSC = MSB) which maximises *social surplus* at JMN. However, the profit-maximising firm is given inappropriate 'signals' in the market, so that it seeks an output of OQ_1 (where MPC = MR) which maximises its own *private surplus* at JKL. Sometimes those who impose external costs in this way can be controlled by regulation (e.g. pollution controls such as Clean Air Acts with fines for breaches of minimum standards) or can be given incentives to reduce pollution through the tax mechanism.

- *Regulations.* The government could impose a regulation setting a *maximum level of output* of OQ_2, so that the firm is prevented from producing the extra $Q_2 - Q_1$ output which would have raised profit still further.

 Assessment advice

We have already seen **(Chapter 1, page 17)** that the government can also use regulations to set a minimum price, as in the case of alcohol, or a maximum price.

- *Taxes.* The government can set a tax on the product to make the firm pay for the external cost it imposes on society. The 'ideal' tax would be one which exactly captures the marginal external cost at each level of output **(Pigouvian tax)**. This would now make the firm pay for its own internal costs and for the external costs it imposes. In other words, the tax policy is 'internalising the externality' so that the (previous) externality now shows up as a private cost on the firm's own balance sheet. In terms of Figure 9.1 the new MPC curve after this 'ideal' tax will be the same as the MSC curve. It follows that the profit-maximising firm will itself now want to produce output Q_2 at which the new MPC (= MSC) exactly equals MR, with both private surplus (profit) and social surplus maximised at JMN.

Key definition

Pigouvian tax
Pigouvian tax is a tax on each unit of output which is exactly equal to the marginal external cost.

Correcting a positive externality

On the other hand, firms creating positive externalities (MSB > MPB) may be rewarded by the receipt of *subsidies*. For instance, it can be argued that railways reduce road usage, creating external benefits by relieving urban congestion, pollution and traffic accidents. This is one aspect of the case for subsidising railways so that they can continue to offer some loss-making services.

Of course, the government may wish to intervene to correct market failures other than those involving externalities.

Test yourself

Q2. Draw a diagram and use it to explain how a positive externality might be 'corrected' by a government subsidy.

Correcting public and merit good situations

In recognition of the need to provide certain goods and services largely through the public sector, *general taxation* is used in the UK to support the provision of important services such as the police, the defence forces (army, navy, air force), health and social services, education, transport and so on. Some of these are 'mixed' (quasi) public goods rather than 'pure' public goods, which means that some private market provision may take place alongside the public sector provision.

Pure public goods

We noted earlier that products which satisfy the two key characteristics of being non-excludable and non-exhaustible are called 'pure' public goods. In this case we should have a situation similar to that shown in Figure 9.2(a), with two consumers for simplicity. Strictly speaking, the marginal social cost (MSC) of providing an extra unit of the pure public good to another consumer is zero. This follows from the non-exhaustible or non-rivalry characteristic: once provided for one person, someone else can also consume that unit at no extra cost and without reducing the first person's ability to consume that same unit. In this case we can regard the MSC curve as zero, coinciding with the horizontal axis, and can sum the respective demand curves vertically, since both consumers can consume each unit of output.

The socially optimum solution is where MSB = MSC, i.e. output Q_S in Figure 9.2(a). In this extreme case we can see that the appropriate target is the output level demanded at zero price. Clearly, private markets, driven by the profit motive, will have no incentive to be established under these conditions (zero price); hence the suggestion that these are public goods. Only if general tax receipts are used to fund such products will they be provided.

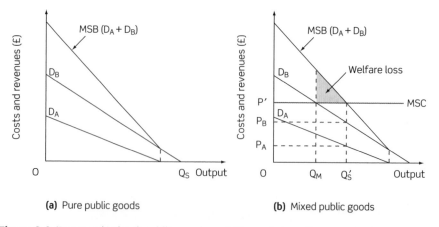

(a) Pure public goods   **(b)** Mixed public goods

Figure 9.2 'Pure' and 'mixed' public goods and the socially optimum output.
Source: Griffiths, A. and Wall, S. (2011) *Economics for Business and Management* (3rd ed.) © 2011 Pearson Education. Reproduced with permission.

Mixed (quasi) public goods

The suggestion here is that a broader category of products (goods or services) will have elements of these characteristics, while not fully meeting the criteria for a pure public good. For example, many products may be *exhaustible* in the sense that (at least up to the congestion point) extra people can consume that product without detracting from existing consumers' ability to benefit from it, e.g. use of a motorway, a bridge or a scenic view.

However, the *non-excludable* condition may not apply, since it may be possible to exclude consumers from that product: e.g. tolls on motorways and bridges, or fencing (with admission charges) around scenic views. So a market could be established for such a *mixed or quasi public good*, with a non-zero price charged. Moreover, at least beyond the congestion point, the marginal social cost of provision is also non-zero, since extra cars cause existing users to slow down on roads and bridges, and extra people hinder the enjoyment of the scenic view. As a result MSB = MSC above the horizontal axis, implying a non-zero price.

In Figure 9.2(b) the socially optimum output (MSB = MSC) occurs at Q_s' with market price P'. This price might be composed of two parts (where price discrimination is possible in the market) equivalent to the individual valuation of each consumer of output Q_s', namely P_A and P_B. Of course, there is the practical problem of identifying what sum of money each person is really willing to pay for this output. If consumers want the product but understate their true preferences in the hope that they can 'free ride', then this social optimum output Q_s' may not occur. For example, if only consumer B reveals his true preference or willingness to pay market price P' in Figure 9.2(b) (perhaps via response to a questionnaire) then the market solution might be output Q_M, with the shaded area corresponding to the welfare loss resulting from the free-rider problem.

Free-rider problem

This analysis highlights one of the problems with public goods: namely, that everyone has an incentive to rely on their neighbours to provide them, rather than provide them themselves. A shipping company may desire lighthouses to guide its ships, as may other shipping companies. Unfortunately, all may delay investment decisions, hoping that a rival builds the lighthouses, on which they can then 'free ride'. Eventually perhaps one company for whom the lighthouses have most value may relent and begin construction, but the level of provision may be less than optimal. This is because it is only the (vertical) sum of the marginal valuations of all consumers of the good that can help to determine the social optimum solution. If any consumer fails to express their true marginal valuation (i.e. attempts to free ride), then we have the suboptimal type of solution shown at Q_M in Figure 9.2(b).

Merit goods

This term refers to goods and services which tend to create positive externalities, i.e. benefiting society as well as the firms and individuals providing the good or service. Education is a well-used example of a merit good, since a better-educated population not only benefits the *individual* (via higher lifetime earnings) but also *society* as a whole. For example, labour productivity is likely to be higher for better-educated workers, raising income levels not only for the worker but for the firm (higher profits) and the government (higher tax revenue from higher employee incomes and higher corporate profits). In addition, a better-educated population raises levels of employment, saving the government expenditure on unemployment and other benefits. A better-educated workforce is also likely to be a healthier workforce, reducing spending on health and related services.

In all these ways, the positive externalities associated with 'merit goods' argues in favour of their receiving government support (e.g. *subsidies*) to encourage a higher output of these 'merit goods' than might otherwise occur. We are in a situation in which marginal social benefit (MSB) is greater than marginal private benefit (MR) in our earlier Figure 9.1.

Test yourself

Q3. Go back to Figure 9.1 and redraw the diagram for a merit good (MSB > MR).

Imperfect information and monopoly power

Correcting imperfect information

Regulations may force firms to give more information to consumers or to employees, or to shareholders. For example, regulations on the labelling of ingredients in foodstuffs help to increase consumer information. Other regulations may establish maximum levels for known toxins in various situations (e.g. CO_2 and other air pollutants near airports) or minimum standards to meet health and safety requirements at work (e.g. number and width of fire-exits in a building). Still other regulations require secret ballots before employees can be asked to take industrial action by unions or give rights to shareholders to vote on executive remuneration packages at Annual General Meetings.

Governments can be even more proactive in this area, such as, for example, in providing job centres to help those without jobs to be aware of vacancies or training opportunities. In all these cases the objective is to give more information to the various parties than would otherwise be available, thereby helping to reduce any 'information asymmetry' that might exist. The general approach is that better-informed decisions are likely to be in both the private and public interest.

Correcting monopoly power

We have already noted **(Chapter 4, pages 96–98)** some of the benefits from increased firm size, as with various technical and non-technical economies of scale. However, we have also noted the potential for increased size and greater market power in the case of monopoly and oligopoly market structures to be used to raise prices and lower outputs **(Chapter 6, pages 160–163)**. Governments are well aware of the tensions created by a desire on the one hand to support large, efficient firms, and on the other to protect consumers and employees from any abuse of such monopoly (or oligopoly) power.

To this end both the UK government and the EU have set certain rules and regulations to establish the institutions and procedures used for investigating proposed mergers and acquisitions, and the conditions under which approval is likely to be given or withheld.

✳ Assessment advice

You could use **Figure 6.8 (page 160)** to indicate the 'classical' case against monopoly of high price and lower output.

More on regulations

In seeking to 'correct' market failures we have seen that governments can use a wide variety of policy instruments, one of which is to use *regulations*. These usually involve rules setting minimum standards for products or processes.

The 'Examples & evidence' here is an example of the use of regulations, in this case in favour of a particular product.

Examples & evidence

Forced rhubarb gains protection

There were celebrations in the 'rhubarb triangle' in 2010 as Yorkshire Forced Rhubarb was recognised as a delicacy on a par with Parma ham and champagne by receiving EU protected origin status.

After six years the European Union gave the product, which is grown indoors and harvested by candlelight, protected origin status. This means that only plants grown by the traditional method in the triangle between Leeds, Bradford and Wakefield can be classed as *Yorkshire Forced Rhubarb*. There are just 12 producers left to enjoy the fruits of the decision. They produce pink-tinged plants – sweeter than most – in giant sheds using a process discovered almost 200 years ago.

The process was discovered by chance in the early nineteenth century at Chelsea Physic Garden in London, but it was Yorkshire that had the rich soil needed to grow the plant in the dark. By the turn of the century growers had made fortunes. Their businesses collapsed after the Second World War, however, with the arrival of the banana and other exotic refrigerated foods. The fruit has enjoyed a revival as celebrity chefs such as Rick Stein and Jamie Oliver added it to their menus. The rhubarb sells wholesale at between £3.75 and £6 a kilo depending on quantity – comparable with supermarket prices for the ordinary plant. That is still cheaper than in the seventeenth century, when rhubarb – greatly prized as a drug to cure stomach and liver ailments – sold for three times the price of opium.

Question

1. Can you identify any other examples of a specific product being granted EU 'protected origin' status?

Types of regulation

It is very difficult to classify all the different types of regulation or rules that can be imposed on firms by the UK government or by the EU. However, two broad types are often identified:

1 Regulations aimed at protecting the consumer from the consequences of market failure.
2 Regulations aimed at preventing the market failure from happening in the first place.

We might illustrate these two types using regulations imposed by the EU on business.

1 *Protection of the consumer against market failure.* In terms of the financial sector, the *Deposit Guarantee Directive* of the EU is of this first type. This protects customers of accredited EU banks by restoring at least 90% of any losses up to £12,000 which might result from the failure of a particular bank. In part this is a response to 'asymmetric information', since customers do not have the information to evaluate the creditworthiness of a particular bank, and might not be able to interpret that information even if it were available.
2 *Preventing market failure from occurring.* The *Capital Adequacy Directive* of the EU is of this second type. This seeks to prevent market failure (such as a bank collapse) by directly relating the value of the capital a bank must hold to the riskiness of its business. The idea here is that the greater the value of capital available to a bank, the larger the 'buffer stock' it has in place should it need to absorb any losses. Various elements of the Capital

Adequacy Directive force the banks to increase their capital base if the riskiness of their portfolio (indicated by various statistical measures) is deemed to have increased. In part this EU regulation is in response to the potential for negative externalities in this sector. One bank failure can invariably lead to a 'domino effect' and risk system collapse, with incalculable consequences for the banking system as a whole.

In these ways the regulatory system for EU financial markets is seeking to provide a framework within which greater competition between banks can occur, while at the same time addressing the fact that greater competition can increase the risks of bank failure. It is seeking both to protect consumers should any mishap occur and at the same time to prevent such a mishap actually occurring.

Whilst regulations are usually imposed to protect consumers or producers from one or more types of 'market failures', businesses often complain about the time they waste filling in forms and complying with a vast number of regulations, many of which they claim are unnecessary. A National Audit Office (NAO) report on 'Better Regulation' estimated that around £11,000 a year was spent on average by small companies in the UK in implementing new regulations.

Types of policy instrument

We have reviewed various types of policy instrument to 'correct' the various types of market failures:

- *Market-based policy instruments*, e.g. taxes and subsidies
- *Non-market-based policy instruments*, e.g. regulations and standards.

However, there is a third 'mixed' category which has elements of both of these types of policy instrument, namely tradeable permits, which we review in this 'Examples & evidence'.

Examples & evidence

EU emissions trading schemes

Another market-based solution to environmental problems could involve tradeable permits, and this mechanism is becoming widely used by governments, firms and individuals in attempting to reduce pollution. Here the polluter receives a permit to emit a specified amount of waste, whether carbon dioxide, sulphur dioxide or another pollutant. The total amount of pollutant allowed by permits issued must, of course, be within the currently accepted guidelines of 'safe' levels of emission for that pollutant. Within the overall limit of the permits issued, individual polluters can then buy and sell the permits between themselves. The distribution of pollution is then market directed even though the overall total is regulated, the expectation being that those firms which are already able to meet 'clean' standards will benefit by selling permits to those firms which currently find it too difficult or expensive to meet those standards.

Figure 9.3 provides an outline of how the tradeable permits system works. With this policy option the polluter is issued with a number of permits to emit a specified amount of pollution. The total number of permits in existence (Q_s) places a limit on the total amount of emissions allowed. Polluters can buy and sell the permits to each other, at a price agreed between the two polluters. In other words the permits are *transferable*.

The market for permits can be illustrated by use of Figure 9.3. In order to achieve an optimum level of pollution, the agency responsible for permits may issue Q_s permits. With demand for permits at D_1 the price will be set at P_1. If new polluters enter the market the demand for permits will increase, e.g. to D_2, and the equilibrium permit price will rise to P_2.

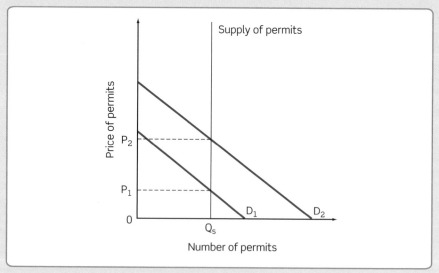

Figure 9.3 Determining the market price for permits.
Source: Griffiths, A. and Wall, S. (2011) *Economics for Business and Management* (3rd ed.) © 2011 Pearson Education. Reproduced with permission.

If, for any reason, the agency wishes to relax the standard set, then more permits will be issued and the supply curve for permits will shift to the right. Alternatively, the standard could be tightened by the agency purchasing permits on the open market from polluters, which would have the effect of shifting the supply curve to the left.

The EU's *Emissions Trading Scheme* (ETS) uses the idea of tradeable permits in seeking to reduce greenhouse gas emissions. It is being seen as a key economic instrument in a move to reduce such emissions. The ETS is intended to help the EU meet its commitments as part of the Kyoto Protocol. The EU undertook, as part of the Protocol, to reduce greenhouse gas emissions by 8% (from 1990 levels) by 2008–2012. The idea behind the ETS is to ensure that those companies within certain sectors that are responsible for greenhouse gas emissions keep within specific limits by either reducing their emissions or buying *allowances* from other organisations with lower emissions. The ETS is essentially aimed at placing a cap on total greenhouse gas emissions.

Question

1. Can you identify any advantages or disadvantages of the EU emissions trading scheme?

Deregulation and privatisation

Governments can intervene to correct 'market failures' by imposing rules and regulations. They can also intervene by *removing* rules and regulations, i.e. by using policies of deregulation. The next 'Examples & evidence' suggests that deregulation may even help reduce corruption and increase efficiency.

Examples & evidence

Regulation, corruption and efficiency

The International Finance Corporation (IFC) and the World Bank have, over the past decade, tried to assess the impact of regulations on business activity. The IFC has plotted its own measure of the regulatory burden on business (the 'Ease of Doing Business' index) against the Transparency International measure of corruption. The hypothesis both the IFC and the World Bank generally accept is that if the regulatory burden is excessive, then such onerous rules will tend to encourage corruption. Figure 9.4 broadly supports this hypothesis, with those countries having least regulation (a low 'Ease of Doing Business' ranking, 1 being best) having least corruption (again 1 being best), and vice versa.

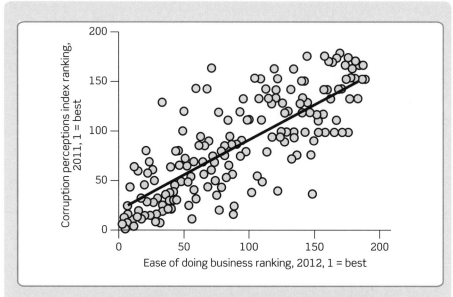

Figure 9.4 Ease of doing business and corruption-perception rankings.

However, this does not mean that no regulation will also breed least corruption – Somalia and other developing nation states have little regulation – but it does mean, according to the IFC, that countries with rules that are relatively few, are simple and are designed to make markets work better (i.e. to correct obvious 'market failures') generally do have less corruption. The top 20 countries (in terms of lowest indices on both axes) include Singapore, Hong Kong, the USA, Norway, Sweden, Denmark and the UK. However, the top 20 also include perhaps less obvious countries such as Malaysia and Thailand.

A positive sign of a general easing of regulations is that for all the countries in Figure 9.4, the average time it takes to start a business has fallen from 50 days in 2005 to only 30 days in 2012. In fact, two-thirds of all the countries in Figure 9.4 have seen a significant improvement in the 'Ease of Doing Business' measure since 2005. The World Bank reported in 2012 that better business conditions (lighter regulations) will significantly boost economic growth, employment and international trade. For example, it noted that simply reducing the time it takes to fill in the forms for shipping goods can itself result in a 1% rise in exports.

Source: Adapted from *The Economist*, 27 October–2 November 2012, p. 70.

Question

1. What does this study suggest about easing the regulatory burden (i.e. deregulation)?

Deregulation

Deregulation can be supported from a number of viewpoints:

- *Opening markets up to competition.* If removing regulations helps bring more competition into a market, then consumers arguably benefit from the extra choice and lower prices that usually result.
- *Removing unnecessary obstacles to business efficiency.* Firms, small, medium and large, regularly complain about the time and money 'wasted' having to comply (e.g. by form-filling) with what they regard as unnecessary bureaucratic regulations.
- *Raising economic welfare.* If regulations have themselves become so complex, time-consuming and expensive for businesses and employees to comply with, then there may be a case for removing at least some of them. 'Public interest theory' would propose removing regulations where it can be shown that 'economic welfare', defined as consumer surplus plus producer surplus, is increased by removing the regulations.

Deregulation and economic welfare

We can define *economic welfare* as consumer surplus plus producer surplus.

- The *consumer surplus* is the amount consumers are willing to pay over and above the amount they need to pay.
- The *producer surplus* is the amount producers receive over and above the amount they need for them to supply the product.

In Figure 9.5 we start with an initial demand curve DD and supply curve SS giving market equilibrium price P_1 and quantity Q_1.

Suppose that a *regulation* has been introduced whereby, in order to prevent price falling below P_2, the government has set a *quota* restricting output of the product to OQ_2. In terms of Figure 9.5, if the quota is set at Q_2, then the effective supply curve becomes S_vS', since no more than Q_2 can be supplied whatever the price.

The result is to raise the 'equilibrium' price to P_2 and reduce the 'equilibrium' quantity to Q_2.

- The quota regulation has resulted in a loss of economic welfare equivalent to the area B plus area C. The reduction in output from Q_1 to Q_2 means a loss of area B in consumer surplus and a loss of area C in producer surplus.
- However, the higher price results in a gain of area A in producer surplus which exactly offsets the loss of area A in consumer surplus.
- This means that the *net* welfare change is negative, i.e. there is a 'deadweight loss' of area B + area C.

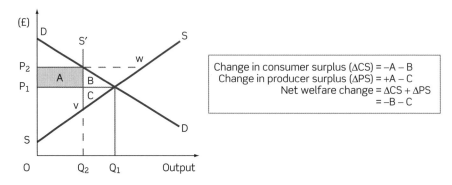

Figure 9.5 Welfare loss with a quota scheme OQ_2 raising price (P_2) above the market clearing level P_1.

Source: Griffiths, A. and Wall, S. (2011) *Economics for Business and Management* (3rd ed.) © 2011 Pearson Education. Reproduced with permission.

'Public interest theory' suggests that deregulation should occur whenever the net welfare change of removing regulations is deemed to be positive. In terms of Figure 9.5 it might be argued that removing the regulation whereby the government restricts output to keep price artificially high at P_2 will give a net welfare change which is *positive*, namely a net gain of area B + area C.

In other words, allowing the free market equilibrium price P_1 and quantity Q_1 to prevail restores the previous loss of economic welfare via regulation. Put another way, public interest theory is suggesting that deregulation should occur whenever the outcome is a net welfare gain, so that those who gain can, at least potentially, more than compensate those who lose.

Privatisation: no regulators

Privatisation is usually used to refer to a situation in which a good or service previously provided wholly or mainly by the public sector can now be provided by private-sector firms. In the UK some important nationalised industries such as coal, telecommunications, gas, water and railways were until recently run by public corporations, not private firms. In 1979, with the election of Margaret Thatcher, these *nationalised industries* were privatised, with shares (ownership) now offered in most cases to the general public.

Privatisation in the UK has reduced the number of nationalised industries to a mere handful of enterprises accounting for less than 2% of UK GDP, around 3% of UK investment and under 1.5% of UK employment. By contrast, in 1979 the then nationalised industries were a very significant part of the economy, producing 9% of GDP, being responsible for 11.5% of UK investment and employing 7.3% of all UK employees.

We might usefully consider the arguments for and against privatisation.

Case for privatisation

- *Greater efficiency.* The suggestion here is that breaking up the state monopoly and allowing private companies to provide the good or service makes resource allocation more efficient. Two main points are often made in this respect:
  - *Public choice theory.* This sees politicians and civil servants seeking to maximise their own interests (utility functions) in the nationalised industries. Politicians seek votes; civil servants support their departments which are lobbied by pressure groups, such as trade unions. As a result, objectives pursued in nationalised industries tend to be confused and inconsistent, resulting in inefficient management and operation of the industry.
  - *Property rights theory.* This emphasises the inability of the public to exercise control over nationalised industries. For example, the public (unlike private shareholders) have limited property rights over the company even though the public 'owns' them. In contrast, the private shareholders buying and selling shares and attending AGMs, and the threat of takeovers, all resulting from private share ownership, are thought to increase the 'efficiency' of corporate activity.
- *X-inefficiency* is the term often given to the result of these shortcomings; i.e. management failing to minimise cost in producing a given output – or failing to maximise output from a given set of resources.
- *Greater managerial freedom.* The nationalised industries, being dependent on the Treasury for finance, had long complained of insufficient funds for investment. When the industry is privatised these constraints no longer apply, and management can now seek to raise finance for investment from the capital market (e.g. share issues).
- *Wider share ownership.* In 1979, before the major privatisations took place, only 7% of UK adults owned shares. Today around 20% own shares, many having for the first time bought shares in some of the major privatisations. In this view, privatisation has helped create a 'property-owning democracy', resulting in more shareholders so more people sympathetic to a capitalist/market-based economy and a more committed and efficient workforce as a result of owning shares in the company.
- *More government revenue.* The privatisation programme since 1979 has raised well over £50bn in revenue for the Treasury.

Case against privatisation

- *It simply converts a state monopoly to a private monopoly.* The argument here is that economies of scale are so large for many of the industries and sectors privatised that it will only ever be efficient to have one, or at most a few, large firms in those sectors. We reviewed **(Chapter 6, page 163)** the *natural monopoly* argument which suggests that only a single efficient firm may be regarded as viable in that industry. This criticism of privatisation points to the fact that one merely exchanges a 'state monopoly' for a 'private monopoly' by privatisation, with few if any benefits of lower price and extra choice for consumers.

- *Need for industry regulation and extra bureaucracy.* Related to the previous point, governments have appointed industry regulators to protect the public from the market power of large private companies that have replaced the nationalised industries. So we have Ofgas, Ofwat, Oftel, Ofcom and many other regulators which try to limit price increases and impose conditions on the operations of the now large private companies in gas, water, telecommunications and many other industries. Firms in these industries often complain of their lack of freedom to manage, excessive 'red tape' and bureaucracy from these industry regulators.

- *Concentration of share ownership.* Whilst more individuals own shares, the larger shareholding institutions such as pension funds, insurance companies and unit trusts have increased their shareholdings and together own almost 60% of all shares in the UK. Only those shareholders who have a significant stake in the company can, in practice, influence company policy. Having some extra individuals with a few shares each does little to bring about a true 'property-owning democracy', in this view.

- *Loss of government revenue.* At the time of privatisation, the new shares were offered to the public at largely 'knock-down' prices to create public interest in the privatisation. This undervaluation of shares lost the Treasury considerable potential revenue at the time of these privatisations.

Privatisation: regulators

The privatisation of public utility companies with 'natural' monopolies creates the possibility that the companies might abuse their monopoly power. In these cases UK privatisations have offered reassurance to the public in the form of regulatory offices for each privatised utility, for example Oftel for telecommunications and Ofwat for the water industry.

Objectives of regulators

Regulators have two fundamental objectives:

1 They attempt to create the constraints and stimuli which companies would experience in a competitive market environment. For example, companies in competitive markets must bear in mind what their competitors are doing when setting their prices and are under competitive pressure to improve their service to consumers in order to gain or retain market share. Regulators can simulate the effects of a competitive market by setting price caps and performance standards.

2 Regulators have the longer-term objective of encouraging actual competition by easing the entry of new producers and by preventing privatised monopoly power maintaining barriers to entry.

An ideal is the creation of markets sufficiently competitive to make regulation unnecessary. The market for gas has moved substantially in this direction. British Gas, when first privatised, had an apparent classic natural monopoly in the supply of gas to industry, but by the end of 2007 their market share was below 30% for industrial users. Since 1998 the company has faced nationwide competition in the supply of gas to domestic consumers. Similarly, the regulator insisted on the introduction of competition into the supply of electricity to domestic consumers by 1998.

Problems facing regulators

Regulators have an unenviable role as they try to create the constraints and stimuli of a competitive market. Essentially they are arbitrating between the interests of consumers and producers.

- Other things being equal, attempts by regulators to achieve improvements in service levels will cause increases in costs and so lower profits, while price caps (see below) on services with price inelastic demand will also reduce profits by preventing the regulated industries raising prices and therefore revenue.
- The privatised company subject to a price cap may well look for ways of lowering costs to allow profits to be at least maintained, or perhaps raised. In most organisations there are economies to be gained by reducing staffing levels, and the utility companies have dramatically reduced their numbers of employees. Investment in new technology may also enable unit costs to be lowered so that profits are greater than they otherwise would have been.

Establishing a price cap

In deciding on a price cap the regulator has in mind some 'satisfactory' rate of profit on the value of assets employed. A key issue is then the valuation of the assets. If the basis of valuation is historical, using the market value at privatisation plus an estimate of investment since that date, then the company will face a stricter price cap than if current market valuations are used for assets. This is because historical valuations will usually be much smaller than the current valuations and so will justify much smaller total profits and therefore lower prices to achieve that profit.

Price caps are often associated with job losses. In an economy with less than full employment, it may then be argued that such cost savings in the privatised companies are only achieved at the expense of extra public expenditure on welfare benefit. However, a counter-argument is that lower public utility prices benefit all consumers, with lower costs of production across the economy stimulating output and creating employment.

Costs of regulation

While regulation should produce clear benefits for the consumers of each privatised company, there are inevitable costs involved in running regulatory offices and also costs for the regulated company which has to supply information and present its case to the regulator. It is likely that companies will go further than this and try to anticipate the regulator's activities, so incurring further costs.

Chapter summary – pulling it all together

By the end of this chapter you should be able to:

	Confident ✓	Not confident?
Review the various types of market failure and explain how the different types of market failure will affect resource allocation		Revise pages 245–250
Examine the policy instruments which governments might use to 'correct' these market failures		Revise pages 250–261
Assess the case for and against privatisation and deregulation		Revise pages 261–268

Now try the **assessment question** at the start of this chapter, using the answer guidelines below.

Answer guidelines

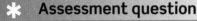 Assessment question

Under what circumstances might you support government intervention in the economy?

Approaching the question

A useful starting point is to identify and define the types of market failure. In each of the four cases of externalities, public goods, imperfect information and monopoly power, you can show how, if left uncorrected, there will be adverse effects on resource allocation. You can then examine the different types of policy instrument that can help 'correct' these market failures, including market-based policy instruments such as taxes and subsidies, non-market-based policy instruments such as regulations and standards, and 'mixed' policy instruments such as tradeable permits.

Important points to include

- You could mention externalities and show that as a result maximising private surplus (e.g. profits) no longer maximises social surplus. Figure 9.1 is useful here.

- Public goods and adverse impacts on resource allocation via non-excludable and non-exhaustible properties (Figure 9.2).

- Imperfect information and adverse impacts on resource allocation (again you can use Figure 9.1).

- Monopoly power and adverse impacts on resource allocation (e.g. the 'classical case' against monopoly, e.g. Figure 6.8 of Chapter 6).

- Policies to 'correct' these market failures and improve resource allocation can be reviewed, including:
    - (a) the use of market-based policy instruments (taxes and subsidies) to correct externalities (Figure 9.1)
    - (b) the use of non-market-based policy instruments, such as regulations and standards (Figure 9.5)
    - (c) the use of 'mixed' policy instruments, which embody both market-based and non-market-based policy instruments, such as tradeable permits (Figure 9.3).

Make your answer stand out

Clearly drawn and fully labelled diagrams can be presented and used to explain both the adverse effects of market failures and how government intervention can improve the resource allocation by 'correcting' for these market failures. Examples such as climate change and congestion charging can be used to show how these corrective policies work in practice.

Read to impress

Books

Griffiths, A. and Wall, S. (2011) *Economics for Business and Management*, 3rd edition, Chapter 8, Pearson Education.

Parkin, M., Powell, M. and Matthews, K. (2012) *Economics*, 8th edition, Chapters 6 and 15, Addison Wesley.

Sloman, J., Wride, A. and Garratt, D. (2012) *Economics*, 8th edition, Chapter 11, Pearson Education.

Journals and periodicals

The following are useful sources of articles and data on many aspects relevant to this and other topics:

Business Review, Philip Allan (quarterly)
Economic Review, Philip Allan (quarterly)
Economics Today, Anforme (quarterly)
Harvard Business Review (monthly)
The Economist (weekly)

Newspapers

Newspapers are important sources of up-to-date information, examples and data. Below are some of the main UK newspaper sources, many of which have websites with search facilities to identify specific topics and articles:

The Guardian
The Times
The Financial Times
The Independent
The Telegraph

Companion website

Go to the companion website at **www.pearsoned.co.uk/econexpress** to find revision support online for this topic area.

Notes

Notes

And finally, before the assessment . . .

You should by now have developed your skills and knowledge in ways that can help you perform to the best of your ability, whatever the form of assessment used on your course.

At this stage you should be aware that your assessment involves one or more of the following.

- **Assignment** where one or more essay type question(s) must be answered in your own time and to a specific word limit (e.g. 1,500 words)
- **Examination** where a timed test is set in a specified location with a range of possible questions, such as:
  - *Essay-type questions*
  - *Data response questions*
  - *Multiple choice questions*

Whatever the form of your assessment, the examiners will be looking to award marks for particular skills that you have displayed in your answers.

- **Application** The ability to apply knowledge of economic principles, theories or concepts to data or issues raised in the question. For example, you may be able to use demand, supply and elasticity concepts to explain why the price of gold is so volatile.
- **Analysis** The ability to identify the assumptions on which a particular line of reasoning depends. For example, you may be able to demonstrate that the benefits of a flexible exchange rate in achieving balance of payments equilibrium depend on there being sufficient price elasticity of demand for a country's exports and imports.
- **Evaluation** The ability to make reasoned judgements about the validity of different arguments. For example, you may be able to explain why some argue that austerity measures involving sharp reductions in budget deficits are needed for sustainable economic growth, whilst others argue that austerity measures must be abandoned if sustainable economic growth is to be achieved.

- *Synthesis* The ability to link ideas together in order to form a coherent and logical argument that is not immediately obvious. For example, you may be able to explain why the characteristics of the market in which the firm operates and the objectives the firm is pursuing must be identified if you are to understand the pricing behaviour of a particular firm.

How to approach and present assignments

Assignments will challenge you to write for different types of task, but the following steps will help you plan, structure and deliver your assignment whatever the task.

- **Realistic time planning:** Check the assignment submission date, work out how long you have from now to that date and allocate a specific amount of time each week to work on your assignment
- **Identify what you need to do:** Make sure you are clear on the word length, on the type of task (e.g. essay/report), on the topic (e.g. firm objective/ economic growth) and on the instructions in the questions (e.g. assess/ evaluate)

Here are some widely encountered instructions or 'command words' for assignments.

Instruction word	What you are expected to do
Analyse	Give an organised answer reviewing all aspects
Assess	Decide on relative value/importance of issues
Discuss	Give own thoughts and support your opinions or conclusions
Evaluate	Decide on merit of situation/argument and give a balanced judgement
Explain	Give reasons for
Review	Present facts and arguments

- **Find and use relevant materials:** Read and make notes on any readings/ sources provided on the assignment brief. The 'Read to impress' section at the end of each topic based chapter in this book will help here.
- **Structure your assignment:** Make sure the following elements are present:
  - **Introduction:** brief explanation of how you intend to approach the question, key definitions etc.

- **Main body of the answer**: a clearly organised set of themes/issues relevant to the question (often using sub-headings)
- **Conclusions**: referring back to the original question, provide a review of the key points raised, perhaps with a balanced judgement
- **Reference accurately**: accurate and full referencing is a key part of any assignment and will help avoid any issue of plagiarism (i.e. taking credit for the work of others)
  - Identify and use a consistent referencing approach, e.g. Harvard style
  - Reference from the text wherever appropriate (e.g. Sloman, J. 2013) and provide full details of the source in your bibliography
  - Identify where you use exact words or sentences from a source using quotation marks or italics, followed by the source reference
- **Re-draft your material**: Try to give yourself time in your plan for re-drafting your first attempt. The second or third draft will invariably be better than the first!

How to approach your examination

- *Plan your revision:* use a calendar to put dates on to your planner and write in the dates of your exams. Fill in your targets for each day. Be realistic when setting the targets, and try your best to stick to them. If you miss a revision period, remember to re-schedule it for another time.
- *Check what will be examined and in what ways:* identify the topics on your syllabus. Get to know the format of the papers – time, number of questions, types of questions.
- *Make a summary* of the key definitions, theories, empirical evidence, case study examples and diagrams relevant for each topic you are revising.
- Read again the chapters in this book for each topic you are revising. Make sure you have worked through all the questions and activities and can tick the 'confident' box for each element in the revision checklist at the end of each chapter.
- Work out the 'minutes per mark' available for each question in your exam. For example, if you have a 2-hour exam, then you can allocate 1.2 minutes for each mark; so you should allocate 12 minutes for a 10-mark question, 24 minutes for a 20-mark question and so on.

How to tackle your examination

What you do in the exam room depends, in part, on the type of question you are answering.

Essay questions

- Read every question on the examination paper carefully before deciding which questions to answer.
- Answer your 'best' question first, to help gain confidence.
- Make a brief plan for your answer before you begin to write.
- Structure your answer, with an introduction, main body, and conclusion (see earlier) and check that you are answering the question actually set – not the one you wish had been set.
- Throughout your answer bring in relevant economic theory, refer to relevant empirical evidence, draw, label and use relevant diagrams.
- Manage your time effectively. Try not to go over the time allocation for each question. If you have not finished in that time, write a few extra sentences to conclude and leave space to return to the question if you have time later.

Data response questions

There are different types of stimulus-based or data response questions, but all require the same basic approach. Much of what has been written earlier with respect to essay questions also applies here, though you must remember that the purpose of providing data is to test your understanding of the principles contained in the data.

- Base your answer on the data (numerical or textual) you are provided with. Failure to do this will seriously reduce the mark you are awarded.
- Use economic principles to illustrate your points. Search hard for them. They are not always apparent, especially in real-world data.
- Look for trends and relationships in numerical and statistical data. Manipulate any 'raw' or untreated numerical or statistical data to give it meaning, e.g. find measures of central location or dispersion, trend line etc.
- Try to recognise the limitations of any statistical data you are given and to recognise the assumptions on which any conclusions of some extract you are given are based.

Multiple choice questions

- Work out the minutes per question; e.g. 50 multiple choice questions in a one and a half hour exam is 1.8 minutes per question.
- Check there is no penalty for wrong answers. If there is no penalty, make sure you attempt all questions.
- Don't spend too much time on any one question – leave it and return later. The following questions may be easier.
- Towards the end of the exam, if you still have some remaining questions unanswered, have an intelligent guess rather than miss them out.

Final revision checklist

❑ Have you revised everything in the 'Revision Checklist' at the start of each chapter and topic?
❑ Have you read and made notes on the additional materials in the 'Read to impress' section at the end of each chapter and topic?
❑ Can you see how to structure your answer after working through the 'Answer guidelines' for the question at the end of each chapter and topic?
❑ Have you tried all the questions and activities for each topic in this book and on the companion website?

Notes

And finally, before the assessment . . .

Notes

Glossary

Advertising elasticity of demand (AED) Advertising elasticity of demand (AED) is a measure of the responsiveness of demand for product X to a change in advertising expenditure on the product. The intention of most forms of advertising is to reinforce the attachment of existing consumers to the product and to attract new consumers. In this latter case the advertising is seeking to change consumer tastes in favour of the product, i.e. shift the demand curve to the right with more of X bought at any given price.

$$AED = \frac{\% \text{ change in quantity demanded of X}}{\% \text{ change in advertising expenditure on X}}$$

Allocative efficiency Allocative efficiency means allocating outputs so no one can be made better off without someone else being made worse off. This is sometimes referred to as a 'Pareto optimum' resource allocation, named after the Italian economist Vilfredo Pareto.

Average product (AP) Average product is usually measured in relation to a particular factor of production, such as labour or capital.

$$\text{Average product of labour} = \frac{\text{Total product}}{\text{Total labour input}}$$

Average profit Average profit is average revenue minus average total cost (AP = AR − ATC).

$$\text{Average total cost} \quad \text{Average total cost (ATC)} = \frac{\text{Total cost}}{\text{Total output}} = \frac{TC}{Q}$$

i.e. $$ATC = \frac{TFC + TVC}{Q} = \frac{TFC}{Q} + \frac{TVC}{Q}$$

$$ATC = AFC + AVC$$

Cardinal utility Cardinal utility can be measured, e.g. in 'utiles' of utility.

Compensated budget line This is the budget line which reflects reducing the consumer's real income, but retaining the new price ratio after the fall in P_x so that the consumer is only able to achieve the same level of utility as before the price fall.

Complements in consumption Complements in consumption are two (or more) products seen by consumers as fitting together, in the sense that purchasing one product will usually involve purchasing the other(s). Personal computers and printers are obvious examples of complements in consumption, as are tennis rackets and tennis balls.

Complements in production Complements in production are when the process of one or more production for X yields by-products. These complements in production are also known as *jointly supplied products*.

Conditions of demand Conditions of demand are the variables that will cause the demand curve for product X to shift, either to the right or to the left. These include the price of other products (P_o), the real income of households (Y), the tastes of households (T) and so on.

Consumer surplus Consumer surplus is the benefit to consumers of paying a price for a product which is less than the amount they are willing to pay.

Contestable market This is a market in which the threat of new firm entry causes incumbents to act as though such potential competition actually existed.

Cross-elasticity of demand (CED) Cross-elasticity of demand (CED) is the responsiveness of demand for a product to changes in the price of some other product.

$$CED = \frac{\% \text{ change in quantity demanded of X}}{\% \text{ change in price of Y}}$$

The CED for *substitutes in consumption* is positive ($-/-$). The CED for *complements in consumption* is negative ($+/-$). CED involves shifts in demand.

Deadweight loss This is the loss of economic welfare (consumer surplus + producer surplus) as a result of a market imperfection.

Economic rent Economic rent is any extra (surplus) payment to the factor over and above its transfer earnings.

External economies of scale These are the cost advantages to a business from a growth in the *size of the sector of economic activity* of which the business is a part. In other words, the sources of the cost reductions are external to the business itself.

Externalities Externalities occur when economic decisions create costs or benefits for people other than the decision taker; these are called the *external costs* or *external benefits* of that decision.

Game theory This term refers to various theories which analyse oligopoly situations as though they were 'games' in which 'players' can adopt various strategies and counter-strategies in order to improve their position.

Giffen product A Giffen product (or Giffen good) is an inferior product which has a positive substitution effect but a negative income effect such that the total price effect is negative.

Income effect The rise in real income (purchasing power) now that the price of one product is lower within the bundle of products purchased by the consumer is called the income effect.

Income elasticity of demand (IED) Income elasticity of demand (IED) is the responsiveness of demand for a product to changes in consumer (national) income. Here, as for CED, we are considering shifts in the demand curve of the product.

$$IED = \frac{\% \text{ change in quantity demanded of X}}{\% \text{ change in real income}}$$

Inferior products Inferior products are goods or services that are cheaper but poorer-quality substitutes for other goods or services. As real incomes rise the more expensive but better-quality substitutes may eventually come within the purchasing power of the consumer, so that demand for the inferior product decreases (shifts to the left).

Internal economies of scale These are the cost advantages from a growth in the *size of the business* itself over the long-run time period.

Long run The long run is that period of time in which all factors of production can be varied. New firms can enter an industry only in the long-run time period in which they can bring together *all* the resources (land, labour, capital, etc.) needed for production to begin.

Marginal cost This is the addition to total cost from producing one extra unit of output. Marginal cost is entirely variable cost.

$$\text{Marginal cost (MC)} = \frac{\text{Change in total cost}}{\text{Change in total output}} = \frac{\Delta TC}{\Delta Q} \text{ where } \Delta Q = 1$$

Marginal physical product of labour (MPP$_L$) This is the additional (physical) output contributed by the last person employed.

Marginal product (MP) Marginal product is the change in total product when one more unit of the factor is used.

Marginal profit Marginal profit is marginal revenue minus marginal cost (MP = MR − MC).

Marginal revenue product of labour (MRP$_L$) This is the addition to total revenue contributed by the last person employed. In a perfectly competitive product market, MRP$_L$ is found by multiplying MPP$_L$ by the price of the product:

$$MRP_L = MPP_L \times \text{product price}$$

Marginal utility Marginal utility is the change in satisfaction from consuming an extra unit of the product.

Monopoly Monopoly in product markets refers to situations where a firm is responsible for at least one third of the output of a product or group of linked products. Monopoly in labour markets refers to situations where sellers of labour have market power, e.g. trade unions.

Monopsony Monopsony in labour markets refers to situations where buyers of labour have market power, e.g. employer associations.

Non-organic growth Non-organic growth occurs when firms seek to grow in size by merger, acquisition or joint venture.

Normal profit This is the level of profit that is just enough to persuade the firm to stay in the industry in the long run, but not high enough to attract new firms. It can, therefore, be considered as a 'cost' to the firm in that this minimum acceptable rate of profit must be met if the firm is to stay in the industry in the long run.

Ordinal utility Ordinal utility cannot be measured, though different combinations of products can be ranked in order as regards the utility they provide for an individual.

Organic growth Organic growth occurs when firms use their own resources to grow in size, such as by ploughing back profits.

Perfectly contestable market This is a market where there is free and costless entry and exit.

Pigouvian tax Pigouvian tax is a tax on each unit of output which is exactly equal to the marginal external cost.

Price elasticity of demand (PED) Price elasticity of demand (PED) is a measure of the responsiveness of demand for a product to changes in its own price. PED indicates the extent of movement along the demand curve for X in response to a change in price of X:

$$PED = \frac{\% \text{ change in quantity demanded of X}}{\% \text{ change in price of X}}$$

Price elasticity of supply (PES) This measures the responsiveness of the supply of product X to a change in its own price.

Producer surplus This is the excess payment to producers over and above the amount required for them to supply the product.

Productive efficiency Productive efficiency means producing the output for which average total cost is a minimum.

Quasi rent Quasi rent applies where factors of production earn economic rent in the *short run* which is eliminated in the *long run*.

Relative unit labour cost (RULC) The calculation of RULC is as follows:

$$RULC = \frac{\text{Relative labour costs}}{\text{Relative labour productivity}} \times \text{Relative exchange rate}$$

Revealed preference If a consumer chooses some bundle of goods A, in preference to other bundles B, C and D which were also available, then if none of the latter bundles is more expensive than A, we can say that A has been revealed preferred to the other bundles.

Short run The short run is that period of time in which at least one factor of production is fixed.

Substitutes in consumption Substitutes in consumption are two (or more) products seen by consumers as alternatives, possessing broadly similar characteristics, e.g. gaming consoles such as Nintendo Wii, Microsoft X-boxes and Sony PlayStations.

Substitutes in production Substitutes are used when another product (O) could have been produced with the *same resources* (land, labour, capital, raw materials, etc.) as those used for product X.

Substitution effect The extra purchase of a product X now that it is, after the price fall, relatively cheaper than other substitutes in consumption is called the substitution effect.

Sunk costs These are costs that cannot be reversed when exiting the industry.

Total cost

Total cost = Total fixed cost + Total variable cost

i.e. $TC = TFC + TVC$

Total price effect The total price effect is the sum of the substitution effect and the income effect.

Total product (TP) Total product is the total output a firm produces within a given period of time.

Total profit Total profit is total revenue minus total cost ($TP = TR - TC$).

Total utility Total utility is the overall satisfaction from consuming a given amount of a product.

Transfer earnings Transfer earnings are defined as the payments that are absolutely necessary to keep a factor of production in its present use.

'Veblen effect' The psychological association of price with quality by consumers, with a fall in price taken to imply a reduction in quality and therefore greater reluctance to purchase.

Zero sum In a zero sum game, any gain by one player must be matched by an equivalent loss by one or more other players. A market share game is zero sum, since only 100% is available to all players.

Notes

Index